THE FUTURE OF
AMERICAN DEMOCRACY

A Former Congressman's Unconventional Analysis

Glen Browder

University Press of America,® Inc.
Lanham · New York · Oxford

Copyright © 2002 by
University Press of America,® Inc.
4720 Boston Way
Lanham, Maryland 20706
UPA Acquisitions Department (301) 459-3366

12 Hid's Copse Rd.
Cumnor Hill, Oxford OX2 9JJ

Library of Congress Cataloging-in-Publication Data

Browder, Glen
The future of American democracy : a former congressman's
unconventional analysis of America's great experiment in the
twenty-first century / Glen Browder.
p.   cm
Includes bibliographical references and index.
1. Democracy—United States. 2. United States—Politics and
government—2001- I. Title.

JK1726 .B76 2002
320.973—dc21   2002020281 CIP

ISBN 0-7618-2307-7 (paperback : alk. ppr.)

⊖™ The paper used in this publication meets the minimum
requirements of American National Standard for Information
Sciences—Permanence of Paper for Printed Library Materials,
ANSI Z39.48—1984

To Becky and Jenny with complete love and gratitude.

Contents

Preface

The message of this book is simple: America is changing in ways that are important and unsettling for American democracy. We are undergoing a democratic metamorphosis that, for better or worse, is transforming our nation and the world; therefore, we owe it to coming generations to deal constructively with these challenges.

When I left Congress five years ago, I decided to pursue an idea—the rhetorical "dying" of America—that has intrigued me for many years and that I consider critical as we journey into the Twenty-First Century. Consequently, I'm spending most of my time lecturing and teaching and trying to encourage a national discussion about the future of American democracy. This unconventional, provocative essay is my contribution to our national dialogue; and I hope that it will help readers in their appreciation of the strengths—as well as the fragilities and limitations—of the "Great Experiment" of American history.

Glen Browder

Acknowledgements

I want to acknowledge Jacksonville State University and Naval Postgraduate School for their generous support of this project. This book would not have been possible without my appointments as Eminent Scholar in American Democracy (JSU) and Distinguished Visiting Professor of National Security Affairs (NPS). I also want to acknowledge the assistance of Donna Trombly and Jamie Todd, who provided varied and gracious help with this manuscript. Finally, I want to thank America for its many challenging opportunities and inexpressible inspirations. Obviously, this essay represents my intrepretation of American democracy (and any misstatements and errors clearly are the fault of my computer).

INTRODUCTION

****

BROWDER'S THESIS OF AMERICAN DEMOCRACY

The original existence of an open natural environment and the subsequent popular expansion of national public authority, working together, have been central to the history and progress of American democracy. The open frontier of the New World established an indelible character of freedom, individualism, and independence; and the popular growth of national public authority created a supportive political environment for equality, security, and justice in our young republic. These central forces have shaped America's "Great Experiment" (our progressive pursuit of democratic ideals through limited, representative governance) for two centuries. Combined, they provided a favorable systemic setting for American democracy (our magical mix of people, politics, and government) to pursue progressive ideals (such as freedom and equality) while balancing the somewhat contradictory strains of those ideals for a diverse society.

However, America is changing in ways that are important and unsettling for the future of American democracy. Inevitable limitations of the aforementioned natural environment and national authority—and growing philosophical tensions over democratic ideals, cultural values, and principles of governance—are transforming the American democratic system. With the two central forces of American democracy—a favorable natural environment and expanding national government—gone awry, our civic mix of people, politics, and government no longer works the way it has in the past; and, despite economic strength and international power, we seem to be tiring of the Great Experiment itself.

In short, arguably, America may be dying! Thus it is time for a serious national dialogue about America—including some alternative scenarios and the possibility of a transformational "New America"—in the Twenty-First Century

****

SECTION ONE

IS AMERICA DYING?

Despite America's obvious economic strength and military power as we enter the Twenty-First Century, these are anxious times for American democracy

Democratic Distemper. Clearly, the United States remains the standard, by most accounts, of progressive democracy and "the good life" at this point in world history. But—as I will argue in this unconventional analysis—tell-tale signs of democratic distemper belie our contemporary well-being. The systemic environment of American democracy is seriously constrained. The American people are losing their civic virtue. The political machinery of American democracy is broken. American government is functioning in unacceptable manner. Consequently, we seem to be tiring of our historic national democratic experiment.

Centrifugal Dynamics. Just as importantly, along with these tell-tale signs of political distemper, fundamental patterns of American history appear to have erupted into contradictory, confounding turmoil. Two centuries of irresistible democratic nationalization now clash head-on with the equally powerful dynamics of centrifugal democracy. Increasingly, as a result, our diverging populace is reassessing the nature of America's "Great Experiment".

An Uncertain Future. In many ways, the opening election of the new century reflected the present turbulence and uncertain future of transforming American democracy. Election 2000 revealed an American nation bifurcating into two distinct philosophical personalities and cultural societies—simultaneously competitive, commingled, and interdependent—each with legitimate but starkly different visions of our national destiny. On one hand is "Traditional America"—an historically-dominant white society, rooted in rural, small town, middle regions, which subscribes to religious convictions, community values, and relatively conservative government. On the other hand is "Emerging America"—a growing, eclectic society of relatively liberal and historically disadvantaged citizens in urban and coastal areas who are inclined toward social diversity, moral tolerance, and activist government. "Traditional America" asserts its right of national control as the historic majoritarian democratic culture and, in the recent case of selecting our presidential leadership, by constitutional virtue of the Electoral College. Just as vehemently, "Emerging America" boldly defines itself as the future of our nation, not only in demographic terms but also as the demonstrated electoral majority of American democracy.

Interestingly, at this point in our national consciousness and public debate, neither "Traditional America" nor "Emerging America"—nor the first President of the Twenty-First Century—evidences sufficient comprehension of the transformational ramifications of their differing electoral mandates and our raging philosophical civil war.

This cultural bifurcation—combined with the aforementioned clash between historic democratic nationalization and contemporary centrifugal democracy—greatly exacerbates the distemperate course of American government and democracy. An America that so proudly proclaims itself "one nation . . . indivisible, with liberty and justice for all" increasingly seems wayward, irrelevant, and ungovernable.

The Fundamental Question. In this unconventional manuscript, I will ask some tough questions about troubled, transforming America. For example, how do we make sense of our basic democratic distemper during good times? Can we deal with the political realities of our changing world? Could we survive a serious streak of economic-military-civil disorder in the next few decades? Will we address the philosophical challenges of the Twenty-First Century? Or—rhetorically but most fundamentally— "Is America dying?"

_____
_____
_____

CHAPTER 1

IS AMERICA DYING?

AN UNCONVENTIONAL ANALYSIS
OF TRANSFORMING AMERICAN DEMOCRACY

The possible demise of America is an unpleasant thought; but that is my compelling "what if" question after three decades in public life—as a political scientist and public official—including most of the past decade as a Member of the United States Congress. My rhetorical inquiry does not represent projection of national death; in fact, I have almost mystical confidence in America and American democracy. But I believe that analyzing America's democratic destiny—thoroughly, critically, and perhaps terminally—is the central public debate of our time.

Dangerous Disarray. I have come to the disturbing suspicion, amid the hype and hysteria of a New Millennium, that we may be drifting perilously away from the Great Experiment of American history. Anger, cynicism, extremism—and a pernicious irrelevancy—are taking their toll on our national democratic experiment. Our grand and glorious America seems to be experiencing dangerous disarray—sometimes noisily, sometimes unconsciously, and often by popular decree—as we enter the Twenty-First Century!

There is no doubt about the survival of America—the real mystery is "What kind of America will survive our contemporary disarray?" Therefore, it is time to ask some serious questions, despite the pain of their articulation, about the democratic health of the American system.

America is experiencing systemic change of unclear nature and uncertain destiny; so I ask the rhetorical question— "Is America dying?" —as an heuristic exercise to encourage constructive discussion about the future of American democracy. While Socratic inquiry is a time honored way to confront, head on, the elusive and disconcerting possibilities of our transformational experience, I anticipate that some will reject reflexively such pejorative terminology. However I hope that this provocative analysis will help focus needed attention on some of the enduring principles and contemporary challenges of American democracy.

Unconventional Debate. **Clearly, it is time for unconventional public debate about the worrisome disarray of American democracy; without serious discussion now, our condition will only worsen in the coming years.**

Our national challenges will not be solved through mystical civic revival; and it is unlikely that our problems will be addressed effectively by conventional instruments of political reform such as ideological debate, journalistic outrage, campaign finance legislation, criminal prosecution, a third party movement, or spiritual resurgence in public life. Such actions are incrementally insufficient, lacking both analytical strength and political power for comprehensive change.

Most certainly, we will not address the needs of American democracy with another conventional textbook on American government. Instead, we must initiate a broad, public, systemic discussion about the future of our national democratic experiment, with hard-hitting analysis that incorporates theoretical understanding, political insight, and practical recommendations.

We desperately need, as part of that unconventional discussion, the perspective of competent reform analysts who have academic expertise and practical experience in the real world of American democracy. To put it self-servingly, we could use the services of someone with theoretic background who also has struggled—as a responsible, accountable, conscientious public official—with the conflict between democratic ideals and democratic reality. Someone who has juggled the national interest with local needs, representational judgment with popular will, partisan allegiance with individual preference, and personal conscience with the demands of electoral politics. Someone who has stood between powerful Presidents, Governors, Speakers, Majority Leaders (all wanting support for their agendas) and opposing constituents who hold the electoral strings. Someone who has endured the consuming, contentious life of governmental responsibility, party warfare, media scrutiny, and campaign hell. Someone who has championed campaign finance reform while "dialing for dollars" from the special interests. Someone who has regularly put his name on the ballot for collective judgment, affirmation, or rejection "by, of, and for" the American people.

Obviously, I figure I'm "someone" as described in the preceding paragraph. In this unconventional manuscript, then, I will pursue the outrageous rhetorical question— "Is America Dying?" —to help encourage dialogue about the transformational challenges and uncertain future of

American democracy. **Accordingly, I will begin with my assessment of our current democratic distemper.**

....

THE AMERICAN NATIONAL DREAM
IS TURNING INTO NATIONAL DEMOCRATIC DISTEMPER

Americans historically have subscribed to an American dream, the notion that life will always get better . . . that somewhere, over the rainbow . . . tomorrow, tomorrow, just a day away . . . anybody can get a better job, live in a better home, enjoy a better life, and maybe become President of the United States. Waves of immigrants and settlers began new lives here, despite hardship and possible death, with dreams of personal opportunity.

THE AMERICAN NATIONAL DREAM

Along with their unbridled individual aspirations, furthermore, the American people nurtured and cherished a collective national dream of freedom, equality, and justice. Thus, for over two centuries, they have pursued, not only their individual aspirations, but, more importantly, an American national dream of unlimited democratic destiny.

Staid **George Washington** was inspired to poetic articulation of America's divine democratic destiny in his first day on the job as President of the United States, with fanciful references to "propitious smiles of Heaven," "the sacred fire of liberty," and "humble anticipation of the future blessings which the past seem to presage" ("First Inaugural Address", 1789). Equally plain-spoken **Abraham Lincoln** consecrated America's democratic destiny on a bloody battlefield almost a century later by resolving "that this nation under God shall have a new birth of freedom, and that government of the people, by the people, for the people shall not perish from the earth" ("Gettysburg Address", 1863). Historian **James Truslow Adams** re-stated the democratic promise of America, ironically during our Great Depression, as "a land in which life should be better and richer and fuller for every man, with opportunity for each according to his ability or achievement" (*The Epic of America*, 1931, 374). For modern society, civil rights martyr **Dr. Martin Luther King** pricked our democratic conscience with his passionate declaration of the American national dream on the steps of the Lincoln Memorial in 1963: "I have a dream that one day this nation will rise up and live out the true meaning of its creed . . . that all men are created equal" ("I Have A Dream", 1963). Finally, our forty-third President, **George W. Bush**, most recently affirmed this national dream of "America" for the Twenty-First Century in his inaugural address:

> America has never been united by blood or birth or soil. We are bound by
> ideals that move us beyond our backgrounds, lift us above our interests and

teach us what it means to be citizens. Every child must be taught these principles. Every citizen must uphold them. And every immigrant, by embracing these ideals, makes our country more, not less, American. Today, we affirm a new commitment to live out our nation's promise through civility, courage, compassion, and character. ("Inaugural Address", 2001)

In this essay, I define America analytically as an inspired but uncertain civic exercise—that is, "a national experiment in democratic ideals"—and I hitch our national dream inextricably to the political process of American democracy. Despite its fuzzy and varying articulation, America has enjoyed unprecedented greatness by most standards; and the American national dream, ably assisted by the seemingly endless capacities of American democracy, has sustained generation after generation over the years.

NATIONAL DEMOCRATIC DISTEMPER

During the past few years, however, there has been much commentary about America's deteriorating condition at the close of the Twentieth Century. Academicians and journalists have been articulating bluntly what many politicians suspect but can not say publicly—that America is developing national democratic distemper. We seem afflicted with a fundamental illness of body and spirit, coughing and wheezing and limping through the motions of disoriented democracy. Our historic national experiment—which has made America great for two centuries—no longer works the way it used to work, procedurally or substantively; and we seem to be losing our commitment to that experiment.

✶✶

EDITORIAL NOTE: The dictionary defines "distemper" in several ways, one of which is "disorder or disturbance, particularly of a political nature;" another is "a deranged condition of mind or body." I think that the term also appropriately conveys the state of American democracy when considered as an infectious, sometimes fatal disease of four-legged animals. Among dogs, the condition is characterized by "lethargy, fever, loss of appetite, vomiting, and a dry, hot nose;" and it is accompanied by "a short, dry cough and loss of strength." The problem with cats is "fever, refusal of food, vomiting, and diarrhea." And horses suffer from "catarrh of the upper air passages and the formation of pus by the submaxillary and other lymphatic glands." Whether it's an affliction of dogs, cats, horses, or American democracy, "distemper" is not a pretty or healthy condition.

✶✶

It is tempting to cite the rash of terrorist activity and the militia movement and other violent incidents that have jolted our country over the

past decade as evidence of troubled America. Such traumatic developments—and societal over-reaction—certainly disrupt traditional American life.

Most of us appropriately dismiss international terrorist threats about "the destruction of America" (BBC News interview, November 15, 2001, accessed at http://news.bbc.co.uk). However, the terror of September 11, 2001—multiple airplane crashes into New York City's World Trade Center and The Pentagon in Washington, DC—rattled and rallied the American psyche just as did Pearl Harbor in the 1940s. America's President spoke to the nation with emotion that resonated painfully in my small Alabama town:

> "Today, our fellow citizens, our way of life, our very freedom came under attack in a series of deliberate and deadly terrorist acts."

> The words of President George W. Bush had barely registered upon the hearts of the American people when the news, borne of tragedy, came ringing home to Jacksonville. Images of death and destruction clouded the airwaves of every television network, and Americans everywhere were being shocked into the realism that we are not exempt from the evils of this world . . .

> Over the course of the first day, it became apparent that Jacksonville would not be spared the brunt of this tragedy. It was discovered that one of our native sons was among those missing in the attack on the Pentagon, and our hearts grew a little heavier, our sighs a little deeper. ("Williams Still Listed Among Pentagon Missing," *The Jacksonville News*, September 20, 2001)

According to David McCullough, one of our leading historians, the "Attack on America"—with horrific destruction and thousands of deaths—constituted a major turning point in American history. "Things will never be the same for America, that's for certain," he said the day of the incidents; "They'll be for the worse." Noting that Laura Bush recently had eaten lunch outdoors with 25,000 attendees of the National Book Festival, he added, "Who knows if we'll ever have anything like that again" ("Terrorist Attacks 'Worse Than Pearl Harbor,' Says Nation's Premier Historian," *The Hill*, September 12, 2001).

Virtually everyone has agonized, too, over Oklahoma City, the previously worst terrorist attack on U.S. soil. An anti-government Gulf War veteran loaded common fertilizer and fuel oil unto a commercial rental truck and destroyed the Murrah Federal Building, killing 169 persons (including children attending a daycare center in the building). President Clinton warned about "forces that threaten our common peace, our freedom, and our way of life," and Timothy McVeigh's defense attorney hinted at deep, dark, cultural troubles— 'If we close our eyes to the social and political reality in which this crime occurred, we are fools" ("The worst terrorist attack on U.S. Soil," CNN, December 30, 1995).

There also was Waco, with 75 people dead, including 25 children, in a tragedy involving the government and a religious sect. And there was Ruby Ridge, an incident in which the government shot the wife and son of a right-to-bear-arms advocate . . . and sporadic abortion attacks . . . and hate crimes . . . and anti-social venom flourishing publicly on the internet . . . and on and on and on.

It's also tempting to talk about killings in the schools of normal sounding places like Paducah, Edinboro, Jonesboro, Springfield, and Littleton as convenient evidence of our exhausting distemper. At Columbine High School in Colorado, for example, a couple of bright, shy, misfit teenagers apparently hated blacks, hispanics, religious people, jocks, and who knows what else. So they killed twelve classmates, a teacher, and themselves. Across the land there was grief—and the horror of something terribly wrong in America. In a floral shop thousands of miles away, a woman lamented that "The things we assumed are evidently no longer true"; and in Washington, an angry parent of a seven-year-old exclaimed "I am so sick of this world being so screwed up!" ("Across America, Grief and Horror," *The Washington Post,* April 22, 1999)

We could even point to the "Clinton Wars" of the past decade as the illustrative example of distempered American democracy. In some ways, William Jefferson Clinton aptly symbolizes America's wearied condition. Despite having presided over a powerful country during a period of unprecedented excitement and vibrancy, he starred in a jaded political drama that is now dragging into the new century. Ironically, the President from Hope generated an industry of discord; and there developed around "Bill and Hillary" a demeaning environment of destructive public discourse. The bitterness of the Clinton era (illustrated most clearly in the impeachment process) still corrodes historic relationships among the White House, the Congress, the Judiciary, our political parties, our media, and our people. It has been a debilitative experience of public angst, and America has suffered dearly in the process.

However, I will bypass diatribes about terrorist attacks, school shootings, and the Clinton Wars because there are other, more telling, more systemic indicators of distempered American democracy. Throughout our country— in our national capital, big cities, and rural areas, in centers of money and influence and obscure, rundown neighborhoods, among powerful leaders and powerless nobodies, on major public policies and inconsequential private issues—seemingly unrelated, unruly, disruptive developments now challenge our national experiment in democratic ideals.

THE HISTORIC ESSENCE OF AMERICA

How can I say such things when the average American is doing relatively well, the American economy is still the envy of the world, and the United States stands alone as the reigning global super power?

The answer is that America means more than personal gain, economic prosperity, and international dominance. History abounds with regimes and empires possessing material riches and military might, but America is special because of ever-expanding freedom and equality. We have indeed been a wealthy and strong nation, and those qualities have facilitated the workings of our civil society, politics, and government. But the essential, definitive character of America has been its national experiment in democratic ideals—this is a place where, first and foremost, we as a national people have enjoyed the progressive blessings of democracy for many generations.

All of us—rich and not-so-rich—cherish our opportunities and blessings; however, it would be a major mistake for America to postpone serious debate about basic political weaknesses in American democracy—the cumulating impact of our deteriorated systemic environment, the divisive debate about values and governance, and evolving conflict between freedom and equality.

By my reckoning, the first decade of this new century is our window of opportunity. For the near future, the United States probably will continue to enjoy economic comfort, and there are no rising "evil empires" on the immediate international horizon. However, the contemporary dynamics of American society (particularly problems associated with an aging, diverse, distended populace) dictate that we must prepare, in relatively good times, for perhaps the greatest demographic challenges of our country's history; and the obvious dynamics of international society (transnational ethnic, religious, and economic tensions) spell certain turmoil for American hegemony. Clearly economic or international crisis would severely strain our national democratic character, personality, and capabilities (as began to happen in the early 1990s).

But, even if we enjoy extended economic expansion and military prowess, ongoing systemic developments are transforming America and its national democratic experiment in fundamental ways. Sooner or later in this new century, we will have to deal with mounting challenges to historic American democracy; conflicted issues of liberty, equality, and justice will assume more than rhetorical interest; and questions of culture and governance may prove systemically disruptive. We would do a disservice to future generations if we fail to address, now, the essential challenges of American democracy.

The central truth, then, is that the historic essence of America is democratic ideals—not personal gain or economic prosperity or military power. A correlative truth, as revealed in the next few pages, is that fundamental faults underlie the surface calm of American democracy; and these faults will only worsen without corrective treatment.

SOME SOBER PUBLIC REFLECTIONS

As the 1990s unfolded, a series of reputable academicians, journalists, and distinguished "public citizens"—whose lifelong service to America qualified them for special status in any discussion of American democracy—began expressing their own questions about the distempered state of our nation. These diverse Americans, in written reflections on public life, articulated sober, surprising concerns about our civic health at century's end. Their individual assessments and perspectives varied, but their commentary conveyed similarly ominous overtones about the future of American democracy.

- **John Chancellor**—a respected television anchorman whose comfortable style touched and informed Middle America throughout most of the past half-century—opened the 1990s democracy discussion with commentary about an America that seemed to be running out of steam at century's end. Chancellor's message of political despair was communicated clearly in his prologue to *Peril and Promise: A Commentary on America* (1990):

> This book was written in anger and frustration in the autumn of 1989 and the winter of 1990, as the United States continued to demonstrate an inability to manage its affairs.
>
> My anger is caused by our borrowing from foreigners to maintain what seems to me a sham prosperity; by the failure of the federal government to address America's indebtedness in an honest way; by the loss of our competitive position in the world; by the scandalous performance of the country's education system; by the decay of our inner cities; by the beggaring of America's children; and perhaps, most of all, by the infuriating custom of our political leaders to avoid difficult decisions.
>
> My frustration is caused by the realization that millions of Americans underestimate the enormous strength of the United States, by the fact that many appear to have given up the fight, and by the sad spectacle of an America that seems to be running out of steam. (11)

Chancellor refused to predict the inevitable decline of America, but he said that "If these problems can't be solved, I believe the country will slide downhill and perhaps never regain its primacy in world affairs . . . I am an optimist, not a declinist, but I am a frightened optimist." (12)

• Shortly thereafter, America heard dour rumblings from economic icon **John Kenneth Galbraith** in *The Culture of Contentment* (1992). Galbraith's progressive positivism had been established during his long career as a celebrated academician, writer, and advisor to numerous administrations; but in this book he claimed that a bipartisan majority of the wealthy and complacent had taken over our country at the expense of the economic underclass:

> We now have democracy—a democracy of the contented and the comfortable. The comfortable monopolize or largely monopolize the political franchise; the uncomfortable and the distressed of the poor urban and rural slums and those who identify with their bad fortune do not have candidates who represent their needs and so they do not vote. As has been emphasized, the democracy of contentment is the policy of the untroubled short run, of the accommodating economic and political thought and of a separate and dominating military power. Its foreign policy, devoid of the financial support that was decisive in the past, is heavily dependent on the military and, in keeping with a well-established tradition, is recreational rather than real. (154-155)

Uncharacteristically, Galbraith offered no optimistic solution for what he perceived as wayward democracy. He closed with pessimism and sadness:

> In the past, writers, on taking pen, have assumed that from the power of their talented prose must proceed the remedial action. No one would be more delighted than I were there similar hope from the present offering. Alas, however, there is not. Perhaps a slight, not wholly inconsequential service, it can be said that we have here had the chance to see and in some small measure to understand the present discontent and dissonance and the not inconsiderable likelihood of an eventual shock to the contentment that is the cause. (182-183)

• At about the same time, acclaimed historian **Arthur Schlesinger, Jr.**— a longtime supporter of FDR's New Deal and once an assistant to John F. Kennedy—announced the cultural "disuniting" of America. In a provocative essay, *The Disuniting of America: Reflections on Multiculturalism* (1992), Schlesinger marked the end of the Cold War by counseling America to avoid the disturbing, destabilizing pattern of ethnic discord then racking the world community. More pointedly, he assailed extreme ethnicity for straining the bonds—common ideals, common institutions, common language, common culture, common fate—of American national cohesion.

> Other countries break up because they fail to give ethnically diverse peoples compelling reasons to see themselves as part of the same nation. The United States has worked thus far, because it has offered such reasons . . . The vision of America as melted into one people prevailed through most of the two centuries of the history of the United States. But the twentieth century has brought forth a new and opposing vision . . . The new ethnic gospel rejects the unifying vision of individuals from all nations melted into a new race. Its underlying philosophy is that America is not a nation of individuals at all but a nation of groups, that ethnicity is the defining experience for most Americans, that ethnic ties are permanent and indelible, and that division into ethnic communities establishes the basic structure of American society and the basic meaning of American history. (10-16)

The ethnic interpretation, Schlesinger said, "reverses the historic theory of America as one people—the theory that has thus far managed to keep American society whole," and he warned, "The historic idea of a unifying American identity is now in peril in many arenas—in our politics, our voluntary organizations, our churches, our language" (16-17).

• Political theorist **Robert A. Dahl**, one of the modern era's leading analysts of American democracy, provided a normatively different but equally troubling systemic assessment in *The New American Political (Dis)Order* (1994). Dahl noted that America had changed so radically since mid-century as to make the new political order almost inoperable.

To be specific, Dahl identified two major changes in the new order. First, the power to make authoritative decisions for society had become much more fragmented than ever before because of the increasing number and power of special interest groups and declining concern for the public interest. He also cited the mass media's depiction of politics as individual conflicts and the decline of integrating institutions such as the presidency and the political parties. Secondly, Dahl declared, communication between citizens and leaders had become much more direct without the development of institutions necessary for democratic mediation. "The plebiscitary aspect of American political life has grown, one might say, without a corresponding improvement in its representative and deliberative aspects" (2). The new order, Dahl said, thereby presents several problematic consequences:

> One of the most striking consequences is its sheer incomprehensibility. Americans must now cope with a political system that works in opaque and mysterious ways that probably no one adequately understands . . . The new order also makes it even more difficult than before for the president and Congress to adopt a reasonably consistent set of policies . . . The new order also makes it more difficult than ever for voters to hold political leaders accountable for public policies. (13- 14)

Dahl suggested that these developments could prove systemically disruptive:

> Because the way the government works is largely incomprehensible to ordinary citizens, when they look for remedies for what they see as the defects of government their diagnoses and prescriptions are likely to be inappropriate . . . If in due time citizens discover that their cure for the ills of government is an ineffective nostrum, they may turn to other possible solutions, including fundamental changes in the structures of governance. (15-16)

• Diplomatic stalwart **George F. Kennan**— architect, statesman, and analyst of "The American Century"—questioned, more fundamentally, the adequacy of our nation and its national institutions for dealing with America's future.

In *Around the Cragged Hill: A Personal and Political Philosophy* (1994), Kennan expressed particular concern about the increasingly deleterious impact of America's "bigness" on traditional American democracy; and he speculated, half-heartedly, about decentralizing America into constituent republics:

> I have often diverted myself, and puzzled my friends, by wondering how it would be if our country, while retaining certain of the rudiments of a federal government, were to be decentralized into something like a dozen constituent republics, absorbing not only the powers of the existing states but a considerable part of those of the present federal establishment . . . Perhaps the interaction among different values, different outlooks and different goals, which here as elsewhere has served in the past as one of the greatest sources

of intellectual and aesthetic fertility, could be allowed once more to fulfill that function. (149-151)

Kennan offered this fanciful suggestion to emphasize his "considerable uneasiness" about America's antiquated system of democratic governance:

There are grave problems of the American future that are not going to be and probably cannot be, as things stand today, adequately anticipated or confronted at the national political level . . . This conclusion, if well founded, is an extremely serious one. It says something about the enduring viability of American democracy, as we now know it. (155-156)

Kennan's critique was more pointed in *At a Century's Ending: Reflections 1982-1995* (1996):

But the fact remains that our present federal system is simply not working well—not well enough, in any case—in a number of areas of decision where the entire future of the country may be at stake. These are, in the main, the areas that require the long view: environmental protection, immigration, drug control, public finance, and above all nuclear arms control. In all of these areas, the failures are evident; in some of them, the Congress even confesses its helplessness. It is idle to shrug these failures off with the comforting reflection that our institutions have worked well enough in the past. So great have been the changes in the physical and technological environment of our lives in this present century that there can be no assurance that what was adequate to the past will continue to be adequate in the future. (216-217)

• Similarly, **Samuel P. Huntington**—another of the just-concluded century's most influential leaders in national policy and scholarly discourse—produced a sweeping assessment of Western civilization, with particular warning for America (*The Clash of Civilizations and the Remaking of World Order*, 1996).

Huntington (former Carter Administration official, American Political Science Association President, and founder of *Foreign Policy*) concluded that all civilizations go through similar stages of emergence, rise, and decline. He drew a picture of the West (including the United States) that included two different, perhaps simultaneous, scenarios: dominance and decline:

The West is overwhelmingly dominant now and will remain number one in terms of power and influence well into the twenty-first century. Gradual, inexorable, and fundamental changes, however, are also occurring in the balances of power among civilizations, and the power of the West relative to that of other civilizations will continue to decline. As the West's primacy erodes, much of its power will simply evaporate and the rest will be diffused on a regional basis among the several major civilizations and their core states. The most significant increases in power are accruing and will accrue to Asian civilizations, with China gradually emerging as the society most likely to challenge the West for global influence. (82-83)

Huntington observed that the West differs from other civilizations mainly in the character of its values and institutions; and he cautioned Westerners about moral decline, cultural suicide, and political disunity. He particularly warned Americans against simplistic visions of national immortality:

> A more immediate and dangerous challenge exists in the United States. Historically American national identity has been defined culturally by the heritage of Western civilization and politically by the principles of the American Creed on which Americans overwhelmingly agree: liberty, democracy, individualism, equality before the law, constitutionalism, private property . . . Rejection of the Creed and of Western civilization means the end of the United States of America as we have known it. (305-307)

THE TROUBLING PUBLIC RECORD

America's public discourse—especially the written word—of the past decade provided ample documentation of these sober reflections.

Unpleasant Headlines. Consider, for prime example, some commonly unpleasant newspaper stories about various dysfunctions of American democracy: "The Moral Crisis of Democracy", "The Can't Do Government"; "The End of Government"; "Divided We Brawl"; "Public Grows More Receptive to Anti-Government Message"; "Americans Losing Trust in Each Other and Institutions"; "Is Democracy Losing its Romance?"; "Loss of Faith: As Cynicism Becomes an Industry, Distrust of Washington Grows"; "The Death of Civility"; "The Politics of Belligerent Banality"; "The Politics of Ugliness"; "A Nation Divided"; "Citizens' Anger at Leaders Mounting"; "Sound and Fury Over Values, Signifying A Cultural Divide"; "America: What Went Wrong?"; and "America: Who Stole the Dream?"

Gloomy Bestsellers. Many best-selling books of the 1990s were equally dismal about America's raging democratic discontent as the century wound down: *The Paradox of American Democracy: Elites, Special Interests, and the Betrayal of Public Trust; Democracy Derailed; Is America Breaking Apart?; Government's End: Why Washington Stopped Working; Freedom in Chains; The Corruption of American Politics; American Democracy In Peril; The Disuniting of America; Disunited States; The Decline of Representative Democracy; The End of Democracy?; The Age of Extremism; Why People Don't Trust Government; The Triumph of Meanness: America's War Against Its Better Self; Poison Politics: Are Negative Campaigns Destroying Democracy?; The Death of Common Sense: How Law Is Suffocating America; The Angry American: How Voter Rage I Changing the Nation; Americans No More: The Death of Citizenship; The System: The American Way of Politics at the Breaking Point; The Coming Race War in America; The Frozen Republic: How the Constitution Is Paralyzing Democracy; Breaking the News: How the Media Undermine American Democracy; The Twilight of Democracy;*

Democracy On Trial; Revolt of the Elites: And the Betrayal of Democracy; Lost Rights: The Destruction of American Liberty; Demosclerosis: The Silent Killer of American Government; and *Why Americans Hate Politics.*

Negative Commentary. **Also, at some time within the recent past, most of our national journals and periodicals of political commentary focused special attention on America's democratic and governmental debility.** A *Time Magazine* (October 23, 1989) cover story—"Is Government Dead?"—opened the discussion with typically cynical references to "special-interest politics," "government by symbolism," "a costly irrelevancy," "neurosis of accepted limits," and "a frightening inability to define and debate America's emerging problems." *National Journal* (June 18, 1994) ran a special anniversary issue entitled "America: A Harder Place To Govern." *U.S. News* (July 10, 1995) issued a special report on "Divided We Stand: America's New Cultural Landscape." *New Republic* (March 27, 1995) showcased "For a New Nationalism: A Manifesto for America's Future." *Foreign Affairs* (July/August 1994) focused on "The Moral Crisis of Democracy" as one of its featured items. A *New York Times Book Review* (January 22, 1995) cover essay bluntly asked "Does Democracy Have a Future?" *Brookings Review* (Winter 2000) closed the century with a special edition on "The State of Governance in America 2000," aptly describing the poisonous environment of American Democracy:

> American politics, at least as it is practiced in Washington, is not a pretty sight these days. In contrast to the vibrancy of the U.S. economy and society, the political arena abounds in personal animosity, bitter partisanship, pettiness, negativity, and transparent disingenuousness. (4)

The state of American governance, as depicted in the Brookings report, is one of nonstop presidential campaigning, gridlocked congress, criminalized politics, muddled federalism, irrelevant governmental service, media abdication of its responsibilities, declined leadership on foreign policy, and deficient debate about the future of America. Unfortunately, according to **Thomas Mann** in his introductory essay, these tendencies likely will continue into the Twenty-First Century ("Governance in America 2000").

Of course, anybody can say or write anything—and will. Political prognosticators throughout time have warned that the sky is falling. Particularly during the past several decades, we have seen a glut of shrill, moralistic, panicky pronouncements about the ills of American and American democracy. But, obviously, something is happening here at the dawn of a new century that is different and troubling.

ADDRESSING OUR DISTEMPERANCE

The pertinent concern is whether and how we will address our democratic distemperance during comfortable times in a fundamentally changing world. More specifically, can we deal realistically and constructively with the inherent tensions of transformational "America"? Do we sufficiently understand the nature of "E Pluribus Unum" in our increasingly diverse society? Are we willing to acknowledge the volatile possibilities and limitations of American democracy in the Twenty-First Century?

A great part of our problem, of course, lies in our historically vague conception and contemporary obsession with the idea of "America". After two centuries of patriotic but unsophisticated acceptance, the American people now distemperately debate what America means. David G. Lawrence, California political scientist and former practicing politician, states the troubling democratic dilemma in *America: The Politics of Diversity* (1998):

> The dilemma . . . lies in the tension between two views of what America was, is and ought to be. Is the essence of the United States that of one nation, one people, and one destiny? Or is it a nation of nations, many peoples, and different (even competing) destinies? At the heart of the dilemma is an undeniably diverse political culture consisting of many races, ethnic groups, subnational economies, regional contrasts, and ideological differences. (2)

Thus the challenge for the American people is dealing temperately with competing visions in a changing America. However, as the Twentieth Century expired, many professional analysts wondered whether democratic distemper would dim the historic destiny of our Great Experiment.

• Veteran journalists **Haynes Johnson and David Broder**, for example, after watching the 1990s healthcare debacle, worried about the American system's ability to withstand the cumulative, destructive forces of cynicism (*The System: The American Way of Politics at the Breaking Point*, 1996):

> Americans have always distrusted government, often for good historical reasons. They have also distrusted all 'isms,' including at times capitalism. So they divide power, create joint authorities—private/public, city/county, state/federal,   House/Senate,   courts/press—and   display   continuing ambivalence about the role of government in their lives . . . And, always, they are reluctant to place too much faith in any one leader, or any one institution. Therefore, they seek ways to check power and the inevitable abuses from those who wield it.   These conflicting attitudes produce an exceedingly complicated system. But at no point, we believe, has the cumulative assault on the idea of responsible government been so destructive of the very faith in the democratic system as now.   A thoroughly cynical society, deeply distrustful of its institutions, leaders and the reliability of information it receives, is a society in peril of breaking apart. (639)

• At about the same time, **Jean Bethke Elstain**, University of Chicago ethics professor, revealed increasing nervousness among academicians about whether America can rise to the challenge. In *Democracy On Trial* (1995), she writes:

In America today, fearful people rush to arm themselves, believing safety to be a matter of aggressive self-help. Angry people want all the politicians to be kicked out of office, but they believe new ones will be no better. Anxious people fear that their neighbors' children may get some unfair advantage over their own. Despairing people destroy their own lives and lives of those around them. Careless people ignore their children and then blast the teachers and social workers who must tend to the mess they have made, screaming all the while that folks ought to "mind their own business." Many human ills cannot be cured of course. All human lives are lived on the edge of quiet desperation. We must all be rescued from time to time from fear and sorrow. But I read the palpable despair and cynicism and violence as dark signs of the times, as warnings that democracy may not be up to the task of satisfying the yearnings it unleashes for freedom and fairness and equality. (20-21)

- Political Scientist **William E. Hudson** worried, too, that America may not recognize the nature of its condition or the seriousness of its debility (*American Democracy in Peril: Seven Challenges to America's Future* (1998):

I believe that democracy is in peril in the United States today; the challenges it faces, in uncorrected, may substantially reverse, in the next few decades, the degree of democracy we have attained (xi) . . . To say American democracy is in peril, however, does not mean that it will perish tomorrow. Military coups or dictatorial takeovers are not a feature, thankfully, of our political history and tradition. An abrupt end to democratic practices is not the sort of peril we face. As the discussion in this book should have made clear, the challenges American democracy faces are much more subtle than coups or takeovers by avowed authoritarians. Each challenge produces a gradual erosion of democracy that most Americans are not likely to notice. The very subtlety of the challenge constitutes its danger and justifies the need for words like peril, alarm, challenge, and danger to describe their collective effects. (315)

These sober public reflections, media observations, and academic concerns are not the irrelevant rants of shrill, moralistic, panicky opportunists. While some of these comments reflect the political tone of the times (and the 1990s certainly were partisan, vitriolic, anti-government times), these reflections, observations, and concerns represent thoughtful analysis that "something is wrong" in our country. Surely, the notion that something is wrong helps explain why the American people, despite acknowledging a Clinton-Gore legacy of peace and prosperity, charted a different, unpredictable course under George W. Bush and Dick Cheney in their first electoral decision of the Twenty-First Century.

The important issue raised in these public ruminations—and our immediate concern as a nation—is whether our current discontent represents a natural, acceptable process of adjustment during an era of fundamental transformation or a serious threat to America. Are we simply

experiencing the necessary molting of democratic regeneration? Are we entering middle-aged democratic malaise? Or is America dying?

....

IT IS TIME FOR A TOCQUEVILLIAN ASSESSMENT OF THE "GREAT EXPERIMENT" OF AMERICAN DEMOCRACY

Thus, it is time, as we begin the New Millennium, for a serious national dialogue about America—and it is time for a full assessment of the changing health of America's "Great Experiment". We must now pay attention not only to the enduring promise of democracy but also to the dark, subtle signs of our times. We must assess the nature, the essence, the cause, and the cure for our civic troubles in an era of economic and military strength. In sum, we must attempt to address our democratic distemper while we feel good.

Our examination of transformational America must be guided by more than academic curiosity, by more than pride, and by more than cynicism. We would be wise to follow the lead of **Alexis de Tocqueville**, a young Frenchman who came to America early in our country's history—during the 1830s—in search of the future of democracy *(Democracy in America,* 1835):

> *I confess that . . . I sought there the image of democracy itself, with its inclinations, its character, its prejudices, and its passions, in order to learn what we have to fear or to hope from its progress. (Vol. I, p. 14)*

****

EDITORIAL NOTES:

*(A) Citing Alexis de Tocqueville and De la Democratie en Amerique (1835) presents literary problems because there are so many translations from the original French text; and these translations vary considerably in their actual interpretation and arrangement of the original version. In this essay, I will use the **Henry Reeve** text of Democracy in America as revised by **Francis Bowen** and further edited by **Phillips Bradley** (1951) except in a couple of instances when practicality and stylistic preference incline me toward **George Wilson Pierson**'s account of Tocqueville in America (1938). The reader may also be interested in consulting the recent translation of Democracy in America by **Harvey C. Mansfield** and **Delba Withrop** (2000).*

(B) On a more personal note, when I first envisioned this project, I pledged to myself that I would not, under any circumstances, invoke Alexis de Tocqueville and Democracy in America. The plain truth is that Tocqueville and Democracy have become trite. The Frenchman's work has been quoted and cited to numbing excess, and it has come to mean anything and everything. Democracy is exhaustive, vague, and inconsistent in general (for example its discussions of equality and democracy), and wrong in some

*particulars (for example, its prediction of the declining future of centralized government). Furthermore, the story of America's democratic origins has been told very well by other foreign visitors, such as **Hector St. John de Crevecoeur** during the American Revolutionary period (Letters from an American Farmer, 1782) and **James Bryce** in the 1880s (The American Commonwealth, 1888). However, over the course of time and in dealing with the travails of America, I came to the realization that Tocqueville and Democracy are essential. The reality is that Democracy is the benchmark discussion of American democracy. Its historic timing (capturing the character of upstart America, a half-century into its development, for a waiting and watching world) and methodology (a comprehensive, empirical, and geographical tour of the young nation) established it as the basic source for all following commentary. But most important is the power of Tocqueville's message. For all its weaknesses, Democracy in America is a strong and original explanation of the nature and future of America's Great Experiment.*

****

Assessing contemporary America through Tocquevillian perspective seems appropriate not only because of the original analytic strengths of *Democracy in America* but also because of Tocqueville's concerns about the uncertain prospects for the future of political equality in majoritarian democracy. As **Robert Dahl** reasons in an essay on "Political Equality in the Coming Century" (*Challenges to Democracy: Ideas, Involvement, and Institutions,* 2001):

> Whatever we may think of the accuracy of his observations in his own time, it is altogether possible that during the coming century citizens in existing democratic countries may become more unequal in their capacities to influence the conduct of their government—or governments. This outcome may result, at least in part, from the increased adoption of alternative processes at the expense of democracy and political equality . . . One can readily imagine ways in which the expansion of one or more of these alternatives might erode support for political equality as a desirable and feasible goal during this new century . . . those of us who believe that political equality is a desirable goal need to search for ways of meeting the challenges I have suggested, if only to prevent a regression toward greater inequality. (11-14)

So our Twenty-First Century Tocquevillian analysis means more than simply complaining about our problems. We have had enough whining from disgruntled citizens, politicians, and the media. I am reminded of a conversation with an older gentleman a few years ago when I visited Ross Perot's national convention in Dallas. As a long-time reform analyst and politician, I wanted to find out what "United We Stand" stood for. "Why are you here?" I queried "Perotistas" at the convention center and in the hotels and streets. My favorite conventioneer laughed and said, "I'm here to participate in our great American national past-time, and it's not baseball, sex, or even politics. It's bitching!"

Rather than just fussing about America, we need to develop a coherent "big picture" of what's troubling us; and we need to frame that big picture within theoretical and practical analysis. We need to incorporate classic interpretations of American history into a broad thesis of American democracy. We need to sort out the clatter and clutter of contemporary public discourse about the problems of American democracy. More importantly, we should offer some constructive projections about where we are heading and suggest how we might strengthen our Great Experiment in the Twenty-First Century.

....

THE OBJECTIVE:
"TO LEARN WHAT WE HAVE TO FEAR OR TO HOPE FROM ITS PROGRESS"

My objective is ambitiously similar to Tocqueville's inquiry of almost two centuries ago—exploring our national democratic experiment boldly and comprehensively, with a combination of approaches and methodologies, and with broad literary license, "in order to learn what we have to fear or to hope from its progress." My idea is to subject America to a Tocquevillian assessment—a normative and empirical examination of America's democratic condition during these critical, volatile, transformational times.

A PROVOCATIVE QUESTION

"The Future of American Democracy" is an unconventional, unsettling, but constructive examination of our historic national experiment in democratic ideals. My examination—reflecting many of the substantive issues and concerns raised by Tocqueville—will pose a provocative question to the American people as we enter the New Millennium:

> **"Can our nation—a people of growing cultural diversity, with increasingly divergent ideals, values, and principles of governance, in a constrained systemic environment—continue our collective pursuit of freedom, equality, and justice through the traditional framework of limited, representative government?"**

MY THESIS AND APPROACH

My simple thesis is that America is changing—transforming—in important and unsettling ways for the future of American democracy. This

thesis (stated succinctly and comprehensively in my Preface as "Browder's Thesis of American Democracy") is that the original existence of an open natural environment and the subsequent popular expansion of national public authority have been central to the history of American democracy— but times have changed. These twin forces fostered freedom, equality, and justice for our American nation for over two centuries. However, inevitable limitations of that natural environment and national authority—combined with growing tensions over democratic ideals, cultural values, and principles of governance—now challenge our democratic march. Our civic mix of people, politics, and government no longer work the way it used to; and we seem to be tiring of our Great Experiment in democratic ideals. Thus, it is time for a serious national dialogue about our transformational distemper and the future of American democracy.

The following discussion will proceed as a semi-Socratic series of questions, propositions, and observations about American democracy. The general objective of my Tocquevillian checkup is to determine the present and future health of our national experiment in democratic ideals. How healthy—or how sick—is America? Is American democracy working for America? Does American democracy still produce—as it has in the past—civic blessings and benefits of sufficient nature to sustain public support for our collective experiment? Can American democracy continue its historic "magical mix" indefinitely into the future? Is there anything that can be done to strengthen America and American democracy in the New Millennium?

I do not plan to retrace Tocqueville's geographic journey, but I have lived, worked, and taught American democracy for several decades on the East Coast, West Coast, and Gulf Coast. I also have served my country extensively in local, state, national, and international politics. Furthermore, for the past few years I have vigorously probed the future of American democracy through public lectures and seminars in varied forums throughout our country; and I have examined our Great Experiment from abroad in structured sessions with academicians, public officials, and other leaders throughout Europe, Asia, Africa, and South America. All in all, I have experienced first hand— academically, politically, and personally—America's inclinations, its character, its prejudices, and its passions. The test of my provocative inquiry, of course, will be the validity of my transformational analysis and its contribution to our national dialogue.

SOME CLARIFICATIONS

Before proceeding with my examination, it is important to make very clear several points about this endeavor:

• **First, I want to reiterate that this is a very unconventional analysis of**

American democracy. I am attempting, in serious theoretical manner, to analyze America's contemporary democratic distemper as a fundamental, perhaps fatal, civic illness— "Is America Dying?"

Perhaps it would be equally useful here at the outset to say what my inquiry is not. Most importantly, my thesis is not that America is dead. I am confident that America is very much alive; and I do not really believe that America is going to die. Let me repeat that last statement—I do not really believe that America is going to die!

Nor does my definition of America as "a national experiment in democratic ideals" represent any agenda other than my commitment to our Great Experiment as an ingenuous accommodation of progressive dream with political reality. There's enough unconventional speculation in this manuscript to antagonize Democrats and Republicans, liberals and conservatives, communitarians and multiculturalists, optimists and pessimists.

I also want to emphasize that my "dying" terminology is not based on the soap opera political drama—partisan bickering, institutional gridlock, budgetary fights, public scandal, personal failings, morality debates, political incivility, or other such media preoccupations—of contemporary American politics. I plan to sprinkle policy, political, and personal commentary throughout the following pages, but our national dialogue must focus primarily on more basic, fundamental, structural developments—troubling systemic changes—in American democracy

- Secondly, I will try to pull together in this essay the confusing variety of theoretical analysis, scholarly research, political commentary, and daily news reports regarding our current distemper. While the citations in this manuscript are not exhaustive or conclusive, they represent and illustrate the broad nature and enduring problems of American democracy.

- Normatively and simply, as I point out repetitively in this manuscript, my dying analogy is not a prediction of doom but a positive attempt to strengthen America's Great Experiment in democratic ideals. Actually, as I mentioned earlier, I have almost mystical confidence in America and American democracy.

- Methodologically, I claim neither the rigor, nor the neutrality, nor the data of scientific research; I will not try to prove that America is alive or dead or dying. We have no scientific basis to justify any clean bill of health or certificate of death for our Great Experiment.

- Stylistically, since this is an unconventional, provocative analysis, I will exercise full, self-declared literary license in order to convey the pertinent points of my essay as effectively and as graphically as possible. For example, I will employ personal reference and rhetoric often; I'll even create some new terminology. In brief, my literary style will accommodate the unconventional nature of this essay.

Very simply, my approach is a provocative "big picture" essay based on my own political-theoretical-personal experience and a review of academic scholarship, political commentary, and newsmedia reports. I will begin by asking, rhetorically, "Is America Dying?" Then I will present a logical theory with propositional observations; and I will conclude by suggesting how we might chart our course to a healthier future.

TIMELY AND IMPORTANT INQUIRY

My rhetorical inquiry is especially timely and important because the entire world is now experiencing revolutionary transformation—the massive, irresistible force of democratization—similar in its historic implications to the sweeping egalitarianism of Tocqueville's time. We are witnessing an unprecedented level of global democratic fervor, in some cases with mixed and scary results. Virtually no one anticipated the changes wrought during the 1990s; and it would be ridiculous to think that these transformations are over or that the United States is immune to such forces.

Thus, the contemporary democracy movement is a development of unpredictable nature that represents volatile possibilities for our American republic. There's no clearer statement of the monumental issue facing the American people—and the central question posed in this manuscript—than the eerily contemporaneous and final words of *Democracy in America*:

> The nations of our time cannot prevent the conditions of men from becoming equal; but it depends upon themselves whether the principle of equality is to lead them to servitude or freedom, to knowledge or barbarism, to prosperity or wretchedness. (Vol. II, p.334)

Journalist **Robert D. Kaplan**, in a recent essay on "The Return of Ancient Times" (*The Atlantic Monthly*, June 2000), translates Tocqueville's eerie warning about the dark potential of democracy into our contemporary dilemma:

> The outlines of the post-Cold War world have now emerged. The evils of the twentieth century—Nazism, fascism, communism—were caused by populist mass movements in Europe whose powers were magnified by industrialization; likewise, the terrors of the next century will be caused by populist movements (themselves an aspect of worldwide democratization), this time empowered by post-industrialization. Because industrialization depended on scale, it concentrated power in the hands of state rulers; the evils of Hitler and Stalin were consequently enormous. Post–industrialization, with its miniaturization, puts power in the hands of anyone with a laptop and a pocketful of plastic explosives. So we will have new evils and chronic instability. The world will truly be ancient. (18)

We clearly are undergoing a democratic metamorphosis that, for better or worse, is reshaping our nation and world history. It is time to address the transformational future of America and American democracy.

....

IN THE FOLLOWING CHAPTERS . . .

I plan to assess the democratic health of America in this manuscript as an ailing organic system subject to diagnostic analysis and treatment.

In Chapter #2, I will introduce myself—politically, academically, and personally—as qualifying background for my outrageous question about the future of American democracy.

In Chapter #3, I will define America as "a national experiment in democratic ideals" and question the health of that experiment. I will explain that American democracy—"a magical mix of people, politics, and government that allows us to pursue democratic ideals"—is not working the way that it is supposed to work (or the way that it has worked for the past two centuries); and, as a result, we seem to be giving up on the Great Experiment itself. Systems theory will provide the general framework for a more structured examination of troubled American democracy, thereby laying a clear analytic foundation for the rest of this book.

Chapters #4, 5, 6, and 7 will present several transformational propositions— the possible "whys" and "hows"—of struggling America as follow-up to the preceding systems theory. These hypothetical observations—drawing from my own experience and expertise and the scholarship of many others—deal with our deteriorated systemic environment, our philosophical civil war, our dysfunctioning people, politics, and government, and our declining commitment to the Great Experiment.

Chapter #8 will raise the question of whether America is really going to die and speculate about some of the wild things—such as the nazification of our nation ("the United State of Amerika"), the triumph of left-wing extremists ("the Union of Socialist States of America"), or even disintegration and "death" of America—that might occur if we continue to push our Great Experiment beyond its limits.

In Chapter #9, I will project where America may be heading—"The American Federation"— by mid-century.

Finally, in a Conclusion, I will speculate about the transformational future of American democracy and challenge America to a national democratic renaissance.

_____

_____

_____

CHAPTER 2

HOW DARE I ASK
SUCH AN OUTRAGEOUS QUESTION
ABOUT AMERICA?

THE DISCOMFORTING VENTURE
OF A VETERAN POLITICIAN, POLITICAL SCIENTIST,
AND "AMERICAN DREAMER"

Of course, speculating about the "dying" of America is an outrageous venture. It seems almost unpatriotic to raise such a chilling idea amid the comfortable warmth of our post-cold war world. But I dare to ask "Is America Dying?" because (a) my interconnected lives as a U.S. Congressman, political science professor, and concerned citizen have convinced me that America is changing in important and challenging ways, and consequently (b) we, as a nation, must now address the transformational future of American democracy.

Uncomfortable Acknowledgement. It is always somewhat awkward breaking the ice in public meetings and private conversations with the proclamation that "America may be dying!"—even when I quickly qualify my statement as a rhetorical inquiry. My associates in the political world and academic community often react with incredulity and indignation when I first bring up my hypothetical notion of national democratic mortality (and younger Americans often seem oblivious to any questions about the future of democratic society).

I can appreciate adverse reaction to my disconcerting proclamation. The fact is that legions of loonies, morality mongers, and partisan hacks regularly mourn our national decline and predict national doom. Such off-base proclamations constrain productive discussion; they keep us from sorting out basic problems from what is symptomatic, trivial, or just objectionable.

Furthermore, it is difficult for many of my friends—particularly women, blacks, and other historically disadvantaged citizens—to accept any seeming reverence for America of yesteryear. As one young female from North Carolina angrily complained to me, "I certainly don't want to go back to the white male society of my childhood, much less to the oppressive system of earlier history."

But historical reverence is clearly not my message. I have lived and studied long enough to fully appreciate progressive democratic improvements in American life. My contention is more subtle and fundamental. I believe that historic America demonstrated dynamic capability for continuous democratic progress—because of favorable systemic and philosophical conditions—and I am concerned that we may be experiencing decreased capability and inclination toward comparable democratic progress in the future.

Once I explain what I mean by the terms "America", "American democracy", and "dying"—then my colleagues and friends (and even some younger citizens) eagerly enter into lengthy philosophical discussions. Many disagree strongly with my rhetorical pronouncement about America's possible demise; but many more acknowledge similar discomforts about various apects of contemporary American democracy. And most acknowledge the need for a national discussion about the uncertain future of our national democratic experiment.

A Unique and Pertinent Perspective. Admittedly, other political scientists of greater academic standing provide sound theoretical analysis of the American system; and other politicians with greater prominence have shared interesting real-world reflections. However, I bring to this discussion a unique and especially pertinent combination of theoretical, political, and personal experience. I bring the passionate perspective of a veteran political scientist, experienced politician, and "American Dreamer".

While my background as a U.S. Congressman and political science professor may not qualify me to dictate national policy or to update *Democracy in America*, it certainly has broadened my perspective, enriched my insight, and spurred my interest in American democracy. Just as importantly, I am living the American dream—and I have strong emotional commitment to American democracy. This inquiry, then, is a personal as well as professional endeavor.

In this chapter, I want to introduce myself politically, academically, and personally, and to discus the nature of my outrageous inquiry.

....

A POLITICAL-ACADEMIC-PERSONAL INTRODUCTION

"The Future of American Democracy" is my purposefully entwined political, academic, and personal analysis of changing America; therefore, I want to introduce myself—public official, political scientist, and "American Dreamer"—as prelude to that analysis.

First, I should clarify my present situation. Since leaving Congress in 1997, I've been living a semi-public life while reflecting on American democracy of the past few decades. My family has contributed significantly to my career (and sacrificed more so because of my aspirations) over the years, and now we're trying to enjoy a more normal lifestyle.

Professionally, I am enjoying an interesting assignment as Eminent Scholar in American Democracy at Jacksonville State University (1999-present). This Eminent Scholar appointment is a unique opportunity to combine teaching, research, and public service in the area where I lived and worked as a political scientist before entering Congress in 1989. My specific assignment is translating my academic and political experience into public lectures, seminars, and writings about "The Future of American Democracy." (For a special feature on this self-assumed mission, see **Chloe Albanesius**, "A Lesson in Democracy," *Roll Call*, October 11, 2001).

Also, since leaving Congress, I have served as Distinguished Visiting Professor of National Security Affairs at the Naval Postgraduate School (1997-present) in California, teaching democratic civil-military relations to young officers of all branches of the U.S. defense team and military students from foreign countries. In this capacity, I have the privilege and honor of participating, through our Center for Civil-Military Relations, in the worldwide democratization movement. In the recent past, I have helped conduct seminars and other programs on democratic civil-military relations on five continents. I also have participated in similar programs for parliamentarians from Russia, the new republics of the old Soviet Union, Eastern Europe, and other aspiring democracies around the globe. Obviously, too, my work assignments to such interesting locales as Mongolia, Colombia, South Africa, and the Balkans should have sharpened my conception of American democracy.

These appointments have given me an opportunity to review my experience in public office and pull together the notes that I've been compiling about our political system over the past decade. Furthermore, jogging in North Alabama's Appalachian foothills and along the scenic Central California coast certainly should have cleared my mind for this assignment.

Now back—in chronological order—to my personal, academic, and political background.

MY "AMERICAN DREAM"

My academic background and political career, combined, have given me a unique perspective for analyzing American democracy. However, perhaps

the most important contribution I bring to our national dialogue is personal. It will sound overly dramatic, but I am living the American dream—I have risen from childhood tragedy and poverty to enjoy the full blessings of American life. Along the way I've learned some things—as a human being—about America and American democracy.

Rest assured, I do not plan to make my personal life the maudlin framework of this essay. "The Future of American Democracy" is primarily a theoretical and political analysis—based on my perspectives as a political scientist and public official. But my life story inevitably colors that analysis in such a way that I think I should explain, briefly, my version of the American dream.

<u>**Dismal Origins.**</u> **My dream began dismally and tragically, over a half-century ago on the wrong side of the tracks in South Carolina.** My birth certificate shows that Johnnie Glenn Browder was born on January 15, 1943, in Sumter, South Carolina, the third child of Archie Calvin Browder, a 29-year-old house painter, and his 21-year-old wife Ila; and an official South Carolina death report shows that Archie Browder died a year later of smoke asphyxiation in a jailhouse fire, leaving a widow and three young boys (five-year-old Billy, three-year-old A.C., and one-year-old Glen). As with most public documents, those official accounts cannot begin to tell the drama of our struggling family.

****

*EDITORIAL NOTE: For insights into my life on the wrong side of the tracks and some interesting perspectives about the world of poor white southerners in general, consult **W.J. Cash**'s Mind of the South (1941), **J. Wayne Flynt**'s Dixie's Forgotten People (1979), and **Jim Goad**'s The Redneck Manifesto (1998); or check out **Angel Price**'s intriguing website on "Working Class Whites" (accessed online at http.//xroads.virginia.edu).*

****

<u>**Growing Up Poor in a Small Southern Town.**</u> **Sumter was like many southern towns of the 1940s, 1950s, and 1960s, projecting gentility and progress despite burgeoning problems of poverty and segregation. Our family was poor by all standards, so we never experienced Southern gentility and progress.** After World War II, my mother married Charlton McLeod—just returned home from combat in Europe—and three more children (Janice, Larry, and Stanley) swelled the family to eight people living in cramped quarters on the poor side of town. Neither Charlton nor Ila had much education (they had dropped out of elementary school to work on the farm); Charlton worked as a sander in the furniture mill, while Ila worked as a sewing-machine operator for various businesses (including the coffin factory). The McLeod/Browder family lived simply and honestly. We went to church off-and-on; we paid our bills; and we took care of ourselves with a hardscrabble dignity that I could only appreciate as I matured into adulthood.

For most of my childhood, I felt the continuous sting of social deprivation and self-conscious stigma. Overall, however, my childhood memories, while stark, are wrapped in a positive, retrospective fuzz, partly because of nostalgia and partly because those experiences made all of us stronger and better. Our family survived; we all made it; and we now realize that "we had to go there to get here".

Acquiescence to Deep South Culture. Perhaps the most interesting and puzzling aspect of my young life is the fact that I grew up in a time and place and environment of intense national significance—the civil rights revolution—without any apparent passion, or personal involvement in that revolution. I sometimes even ask myself—"Why?" How could any decent, intelligent person grow up in the south of that time without active engagement or without any life-altering experiences from the civil rights movement?

Part of the explanation is simply that I was a working class white kid; and my part of society was particularly isolated from such movements. Poor whites weren't asked and did not participate in public affairs (except when the issue exploded into rowdy gatherings and/or Ku Klux Klan actions). Besides, on a more personal level, I had enough problems of my own. I was too engaged in my struggle against adversity to worry about racial segregation (or what was happening in far-off places like Vietnam). Of course, I recognized the tragic history of black-white relations in the south; I felt sorry for black people, individually and collectively; and I treated them kindly in our limited relationships. But I never challenged the system.

The truth, then, is that I was an acquiescent product of the Deep South culture of class and caste. I proceeded, as did many otherwise decent working class whites, through the civil rights revolution with awkward, conflicted accommodation to the southern way of life. That's certainly nothing to brag about, nor do I overly agonize over it—it's just what happened, and it is part of my story growing up poor in a small southern town.

Developing Ambition, Drive, and Mystical Confidence. Growing up in such an environment made me sensitive to social, economic, racial, and other tensions in American life; but it also gave me ambition and drive. Interestingly, my struggle did not make me very bitter or cynical; nor did I become overly emotional or ideological. Instead, I adopted an optimistic, methodical approach to things; and, over time, I developed almost mystical confidence in the American system. I knew that I had a tough road to travel; but I also figured that, with perseverance and patience, I might climb out of my hole to the top of the hill where I could enjoy the blessings of American life.

Climbing the Hill. Eventually, I climbed that hill. To make a long story short, I got a good education in South Carolina and Georgia, became a college professor in Alabama, and set course for the United States Congress. Just as importantly, I married the love of my life (Sara Rebecca

Moore), we were blessed with a beautiful daughter (Jenny Rebecca Browder), and our family (including dogs, cats, snakes, and insects) settled on a rural mountainside in Alabama. Life was good atop the hill.

Assuming Civic Responsibility. **I had been interested in the news media and public affairs in high school and college; and, I worked briefly as a sportswriter for the Atlanta Journal (1966) and as an investigator for the U.S. Civil Service Commission (1967-68). In this latter work, I served brief stints as a federal voter registrar and poll watcher in southern elections under purview of the Voting Rights Act. But I did not engage seriously in civic endeavors until becoming a professional political scientist (1971); and eventually I assumed full-time responsibility—as an elected public official (1982)—for making American democracy work for the American people.**

Thus, I achieved my version of the American dream; and that dream would serve me well in my academic and political endeavors.

MY ACADEMIC BACKGROUND

Other than politics, I have lived, studied, and taught in the world of academe for most of my adult life. Since earning my B.A. degree in History from Presbyterian College in South Carolina (1965) and Ph.D. in Political Science from Emory University in Atlanta (1971), I have taught as Professor of Political Science at Jacksonville State University in Alabama (1971-86), as Distinguished Visiting Professor of National Security Affairs at the Naval Postgraduate School in California (1997-present), and as Eminent Scholar in American Democracy at JSU (1999-present).

Over the years I have benefited not only from my own research and analysis but also from the keen minds and critical observations of my colleagues and predecessors in political science, history and other scholarly disciplines. I also am indebted to countless public officials and political candidates who allowed me to work with them in the real world of politics and government. Obviously, too, it has been a tremendous experience interacting over the past few years with accomplished leaders throughout our country and around the globe. Clearly, though, my political education has been enhanced most significantly in my relationship with first generation college students in Alabama.

Making a Difference. **My students in Alabama always reminded me in many ways of myself**—working class kids who didn't have any idea what they were going to do in life but who knew that they didn't want to relive their parents' lives in the mills and fields and coal mines. Many of our students had to work their way through school; and many struggled academically. About a fifth of them were black—adding another obstacle to their struggle. Too often they had to drop out after an unsuccessful semester or two. But many of them also had dreams and grit—something that can't be taught anywhere, not even at our most prestigious universities. I remember the part-time undertaker who overcame a terrible upbringing in Alabama-Georgia moonshine country and today is one of the most successful businessmen (a mortician) in the area. I remember the young deaf lady from Dothan who danced her way to "Miss America" stardom. I remember the struggling boy from Fort Payne who organized and became lead singer of the super-successful band "Alabama". I remember the rough-edged kid from nearby Possum Trot Road who dropped out after a few classes to chase his writing dreams and who, within the past three or four years, has won a reporting Pulitzer with the New York Times and written a No. 1 national best-selling account of his Alabama upbringing.

I enjoyed teaching at Jacksonville State University during the 1970s and 1980s and 1990s; and I can pick up the phone and call countless of my former students who went on to state and national prominence. I've run into them in Alabama, in Washington, among corporate, legal, medical, academic, creative, and entertainment elites; I also see them on the playing fields of major league sports. Our paths have even crossed unexpectedly in foreign lands.

But I'm just as proud of those everyday people who walk up and re-introduce themselves to me—business people, teachers, law enforcement personnel, homemakers, all kinds and all colors—whose lives are better due to their schooling at this relatively uncelebrated but special institution. I like to think that I made a difference, that I had something to do with helping them live better lives.

Teaching and Research. My substantive teaching interests throughout my political science career have focused on American government, political behavior, and the nature of democracy.

Fortunately, I also was able to conduct relatively unsophisticated but empirically instructive research on the workings of the American political system. For example, one of my best learning experiences was a small survey research project and case study of the public, influential leaders, and city council members in Anniston, Alabama; I discovered that political policy linkage between the people and their representatives is just as likely to occur through shared community culture—almost by accident—as by the purposeful design of the players in the local political system. My research also has convinced me that race is still the strongest dynamic in Alabama politics, and such is probably the case in the rest of the south and perhaps throughout the nation. I have concluded, furthermore, that public officials have much more discretion for bold, positive leadership than they think they have or are willing to exercise.

Consulting Experience. I also began applying my political science theory and methodological training (particularly survey research) to real-world problems during those early years in academia. I worked as a professional consultant with countless officials and agencies at the local, state, and federal levels; and I tested my ideas about American democracy through polling, media, and strategy development on their behalf. I'm biased, but I always felt that my advice was pretty close to reality; as a matter of fact, my success as a consultant helped convince me eventually to put my own name on the electoral ballot.

My consulting experience was both intellectually and politically rewarding. It also was fun—especially the political campaigns. Very few things in academia and life are as challenging as electoral politics; and there's always a clear, timely, and consequential outcome. Just as in sports, when the time clock runs out, you look at the scoreboard—and you win or lose.

I worked for some very good candidates (and some of the other kind too); and my best consulting work was sometimes in losing campaigns. Among the most memorable experiences (other than my own electoral wins) was the first campaign I worked on; my polling hit the bulls-eye and helped a good man enter the state senate. Another was an unprecedented write-in campaign that got a friend back into the senate after he had been dumped by his party and wasn't even on the ballot (we really didn't know what we were doing but it worked). The worst experiences (besides losing) were having to choose between friends running against each other and having to tell candidates very candid things, based on my polling, about their personal reputations and political standing.

"Lessons Learned". Are the lessons of academia applicable to the real world of politics? Did I learn anything from political science and consulting that helped me in my political career? It is fashionable to disparage "book learning" and "ivory tower" academicians; and my political colleagues seem to enjoy poking me in the ribs with the barb that "I bet you didn't learn that from your civics book." However, the fact is that the principles and concepts of political science have proven very useful to me in the political arena.

I have found, from the beginning of my academic career, that certain themes and ideas recurringly shaped my conception of American democracy—such as Alexis de Tocqueville's fascination with "equality" and Frederick J. Turner's "frontier thesis." Of course I've been influenced greatly by twentieth century writers such as David Easton ("systems theory"), Robert Dahl ("democratic pluralism"), and Gabriel Almond and Sidney Verba ("civic culture"). Three thinkers in particular—Thomas Jefferson, V.O. Key, Jr., and John Naisbitt— have shaped both my academic and political careers. Jefferson convinced me that real leadership quite often consists of educating the people so that they can make good decisions democratically; V. O. Key, Jr., helped me comprehend the historic twin problems (race and poverty) of southern politics; and John Naisbitt impressed me with his statement of the dominating systemic changes, or "megatrends," of contemporary American life.

In general, the insights gained from my academic experiences have been invaluable in my understanding of the noble possibilities of American democracy; and my work as a professional consultant has made me aware of the realities—the good, the bad, and the ugly—in the rough and tumble world of political life. In particular, political science gave me advance understanding of such things as pluralism, leadership, and practical politics which I otherwise would have had to develop through experience—rough experience and mistakes that unfortunately entail significant battle scars and lost opportunities. I carried many of these academic insights and lessons into public life.

MY POLITICAL CAREER

For much of the past two decades, I have served in elective public office, most recently as a Member of the United States House of Representatives. I like to think of myself as a practical, public-spirited, reform-oriented, "Big-D" Democrat and "little-r" republican—working for congressional, budgetary, and political reform in Washington (1989-96); for election reform as Alabama's Secretary of State (1987-89); and on education reform as an Alabama State Legislator (1982-86). I have struggled—with Bill Clinton, George Bush, Newt Gingrich, Dick Gephardt, Tom Foley, Jim Wright, George Wallace, numerous other big-name and no-name politicians, the news media, lobbyists, everyday citizens, and my own conscience—to make American democracy work.

I'll not dwell here on the personalities and issues of my career in politics since that is not what this book is about (and we'll venture into some of those areas in the more analytical chapters of this manuscript). But I will try to sketch an explanation of "how" and "why" I got into (and out of) the public arena.

Getting In. I entered public service originally, as did many others, with an ambitious, arrogant, burning urge to help make American democracy work better than it was working in the 1970s and 1980s. I was never really moved by ideological issues; nor did I develop any powerful support constituencies. I was pretty much self-driven by civic love of the game of American democracy.

But my flame of ambition and arrogance—fueled by a combination of philosophical motives, political savvy, and textbook knowledge—probably burned stronger and hotter and more self-reflectively than most. I wanted, from the beginning, to be different from run-of-the-mill public officials. I wanted to do something special. I had no delusions about being America's "Philosopher-King"—but I did aspire to be a "philosopher-politician," a visionary leader with the practical ability to achieve as much civic progress as is politically possible. In short, I wanted to do it right—and to make it work!

It had become obvious to me, during my academic days, that civic vision—the inclination to think in "Big Ideas" about America and American democracy—is a very powerful and positive force in politics. Civic vision is critically important because it endows political leadership with the personal drive, public aura, and popular support for achievements of enduring significance.

So, I embarked on a journey of civic vision—from Jacksonville State University, to the state capitol in Montgomery, and then on to the United States Congress in Washington—trying to implement the ideals of American democracy while conducting myself in such a way that the people of Alabama—particularly young people—might regain trust in their leaders and government.

A Revelational Experience. **Early in that journey—while campaigning for the state legislature—I experienced a personal revelation about my future in politics. I realized that, with guts and luck, I just might become Alabama's "philosopher-politician"—because nobody else wanted the job. Furthermore, and later on, I encountered similar problems—remember "the vision thing"—at the national level.**

Throughout my political career I have been struck by the lack of interest in civic issues among both aspiring candidates and established public officials. Other than in their campaign propaganda, very few professional politicians seem really interested in such things as clean elections, political ethics, and constitutional reform.   I found that I could indeed exercise leadership on important matters of public policy in Alabama and Washington—in great part because normal politicians generally do not care for the civic responsibilities and heavy lifting of American democracy.

Much of the explanation is that a Peter Principle of civic vision applies in politics just as in other endeavors. Most politicians enter the political arena with some vision, but their capabilities and inclinations toward visionary leadership seem to stagnate as they get elected and climb the political ladder. Over time, they tend to focus their attention toward more practical concerns—waging partisan and special interest warfare, dividing the goodies of public largess, and securing their re-election. Upon reaching their maximum level of power, many public officials tend to function with the limited perspectives and concerns of their previous political and personal lives. Too often, for example, state and federal officials still think in terms of petty politics, paving roads, and school board appointments. They sit in our chambers of power and are happy just to be there, performing mundane functions, somewhat like the furniture and potted plants. They do not think about our historic experiment in democratic ideals; and they are not about to bite into anything tough, hot, or dangerous to their political health. Therein, in an environment of vision deficiency, lies continuous opportunity for sharp, ambitious, civic-minded young leaders.

Revelations II. **Over time, it became clear to me—a second revelational experience—that, in addition to the lack of civic vision among run-of-the-mill politicians, there was a major "vacuum of leadership" on critical civic issues at the top of state and federal government.** Even esteemed national leaders—who quite often embraced and articulated the nobler ideals of American democracy—seemed disinterested, inattentive and inept at critical points in the political process. I kept muttering to myself that "this is a heck of a way to run a railroad;" and my railroad metaphor would prove repetitively appropriate.

It did not take long for me to realize the full interconnectivity of vision, leadership, and the political railroad. The fact was that despite all of our visionary hoopla, no powerful political leaders or any powerful interest groups—within the system—were willing to flex their muscles for a reform agenda. The absence of vision and leadership on reform issues was no accident—that's how those in control keep things from happening that they do not want to happen. That is how they run the railroad.

"Philosopher-Politician". **I said earlier that I got into politics with ambitions toward being a philosopher-politician, that I wanted to do it right. My "do it right" statement may strike some as overly self-indulgent rationalization; but my sense of responsibility was genuine—I sincerely wanted to do everything within my power to strengthen our national experiment in democratic ideals within its historic framework of limited, representative government.**

From the beginning, I took my job in public service seriously. I enjoyed doing it. Every day in Montgomery and Washington was a seminar in American democracy, and I would have paid for those privileges and experiences.

I was good at it because I took on the burdens of public office conscientiously—maybe too conscientiously. I engaged virtually every aspect of public service as a personal civic responsibility. I agonized over most issues and even constituent cases. I felt that I should reach the "right" decision among public policy options where there were no clearly right or easy options. For example, I truly believed that restoring control of our fiscal destiny (meaning balancing the budget) was a critical national objective for our children and posterity. But I also pushed for economic help for our local business community, medical treatment for our sick veterans, and social security benefits for our elderly citizens.

I considered it my obligation to show up for work wherever, whenever, and however my constituents asked. Weekends, nights, holidays, even special personal and family occasions. I found it impossible to say "no" if anybody or anything in my district wanted or needed me there.

All in all, however, I had an idea from the beginning that I couldn't last forever in politics because my public life was built primarily on my civic commitment rather than real political terra firma. The viability of my career as a philosopher-politician depended, to a great extent, on my own personal civic drive; and it couldn't last forever.

Philosophy, Politics, and Democracy. **In addition to pursuing progressive democratic philosophy and practical politics, I had strong academic interest in understanding the nexus of philosophy, politics, and democracy. I tried constantly to sort out the working mix of these important parts of our national democratic experiment—and I'll share here a few of my conclusions.**

In the first place, it became apparent to me early on that philosophy—defined broadly in ideological terms such as liberal-conservative, left-right, big government-little government—is important, but American democracy is much more complex and practical than such theoretical conceptualization. Philosophical ideology seldom comes into play, and ideologues comprise few of the players in the political game. Besides, most participants are pretty inconsistent in their political issues and demands. While philosophical liberals and conservatives differ generally in their ideas about the size and scope of government, in day-do-day life both sides seem to want more government—wherever, whenever, and however it suits their predilections. Of course, people such as George W. Bush (and Bill Clinton and others before him) must articulate our national dreams in context of philosophical principles; but at the risk of sounding naive, I found that the practical mix of personalities, parties, issues, interests, and regions most often proceeded, quite successfully, without serious philosophical concern or consideration.

I also have come to appreciate the interplay between economics and democracy. Despite my statement about America being more than financial prosperity, the fact is that a healthy economy contributes immensely to our national democratic experiment. In strong economic times, the private sector is flush with jobs, profits, new houses, and other amenities of the good life; and tax revenue flows into public coffers for progressive policies and expanding initiatives. In weak economies, the private sector anxiously turns toward or against government, which under those conditions is less prepared to respond to such demands. Needless to say, in the good times (as in the late 1990s), American democracy hums along beautifully; and in the bad times (as in the early 1990s), we're not very democratically inspired.

I learned, furthermore, that raw politics and political pork quite often go hand-in-hand with American democracy. I'll cite, for example, the work of two of my former colleagues in key political positions in Washington and Alabama. I served with both Dan Rostenkowski (D), chairman of the all-powerful House Ways and Means Committee during several administrations, and Tom Coburn (D), chairman of the equally important Alabama House Ways and Means Committee during the Wallace Administration. These men exercised tremendous skill in relative obscurity rounding up votes in their committees and on the floor to pass public policy initiatives considered essential for their administrations. Sometimes they preached the message of good government ("This is right for the American people"); or they pled that "Our President needs this legislation"; or more desperately, they argued that "This is critical for our party!" Often they had to fight and threaten and politically extort support from members; at times they had to outright "buy" votes from various individuals and groups. Their special talent, and in my opinion their special contributions to our democratic destiny, lay in their ability, sometimes, to assess the personalities and peculiarities of diverse politicians and to turn pork barrel and raw politics into generally progressive policy for Alabama and our nation.

I've concluded too that money (as in special interest influence in electoral politics and on public policy) is an enduring political dilemma of American democracy. We require politicians to raise huge sums (to pay for the advertising that is necessary in today's political campaigns); we don't want to give them our money (so they go to the special interests who have the will and the way to invest in politics); they then run advertisements against the "special interests" (so that we will vote for them), which we do; and we're shocked when the special interests get special attention from government. We all get very demeaned, disgusted, and ugly in the process; but that's the way it is when we run a public electoral operation as a private, capitalistic enterprise. Public campaign financing sounds like a possible solution, but it is politically unacceptable and in a way simply subsidizes the special interests. I don't really know of any alternatives (because there's no "one size fits all" solution) other than full disclosure, better politicians, and more enlightened voters.

Finally, I learned that leadership is the key ingredient in American democracy. The American public is made up of basically decent people, incorporating both positive and negative inclinations. Those of us in public office quite often complain about the constraints of constituency and politics, and we sometimes act as though the most important thing is election (and re-election). But we generally have greater freedom as public policy-makers and societal leaders than we like to acknowledge. Even during tough times, the American people will respond to leaders who combine straight talk with hope and vision for a better future. Despite whatever flaws we see in our voters, in our political opponents, and in the demands of politics, the performance of American democracy rests largely within our discretion and leadership.

Political Burnout. **My years in elective office were intensely exhilarating. But over the course of my career I simply enjoyed about as much as I could stand—and I burned out!** It was not a case of idealism-turned-into-cynicism (my background had prepared me well for the realities of a public career). I was not physically fatigued (although it was a grinding schedule, especially during the 1994 Republican "Contract with America" session). I wasn't moved by personal economics (money has never been that important to me). By all accounts, I was secure in my district and could have held my seat indefinitely.

I think that I just experienced too much of a good thing—and I lost the "fire in my belly." The best way to describe my change-of-life experience is to say that, over time, I became less willing to do things that did not fit my notion of public service. I had always understood that policy and politics inevitably go hand in hand; and I was pretty successful at both, pursuing as much "good" policy as was politically possible. In the beginning, I actually enjoyed the game of politics as much or more than governing. But I probably reached the point where I tried to separate policy—to an unrealistic and unreasonable extent—from politics.

The most important change was my idea of representation. As my years in political life wore on, I moved away from defining my representational responsibility as a "delegate" (doing what the constituents direct you to do) toward being a "trustee" (relying upon your judgment about what should be done). I still emphasized hard work, constituency service, and trying to do what the 600,000 citizens in east Alabama elected me to do. But increasingly I found myself thinking and acting more independently, becoming more concerned with what I thought was right for America and less attentive to immediate electoral and special interest demands.

To put it another way, I became pickier about what I was willing to do for my political career. When you're young and burning with political ambition, you are more likely to do certain things—such as couching your thoughts in acceptable terminology, courting special interest groups for their endorsement, taking campaign contributions from anybody, putting political activities ahead of family time.   These actions do not necessarily mean compromising or corrupting your integrity; but they do require you to be very personally solicitous. Toward the end of my years in Congress, I became less inclined to be so solicitous.

I have to admit too that those years in politics affected my "love of the game". One of the guiding principles of my leadership style as a philosopher-politician had been a conscious, inspired attempt to apply my professional background as an educator to my work as a politician. As much as possible, I tried to engage my constituents in "seminars" about local and national issues. I announced to town meetings that I could not solve their problems for them but that I would work with them to address our national interests. I conducted programs ("Citizen Congress") whereby groups of Alabamians would deliberate the national situation and attempt to pass their own budget. I visited civic groups, classrooms, and editorial boards to talk in deliberative manner about the future of our country.

Of course, the key to success as a political educator is how to keep these "seminars" from turning into "lectures."   Throughout my career, I have challenged constituents to accept collective responsibility for America. As a neophyte politico eager to make the democratic system work, I would listen deferentially to constituents—even when I thought they were politically wrong, or irresponsible, or rude. I would explain to them the other side of the issue and to try to work them through their own needs and interests to an appreciation for the common good. Over the years, I got to the point where, if someone were persistently unreasonable or confrontational, I might politely tell that person that we were not going to agree and that we would just have to let the voters of Alabama decide whose vision of leadership they preferred. Obviously, not everybody shared my political style or vision of America; and these interactions sometimes became less than educational.

In particular, I became increasingly turned off by constant partisan politics. Being a member of Congress (or virtually any high public office) puts you in a war zone, forcing you to engage in never-ending combat if you want to maintain your voice and influence in serious discussion.   The Washington environment (driven in great part by the parties, media, and money) encourages you to attack or defend an entire partisan agenda of issues, institutions, and people far beyond the substantive reality and reasonableness of the situation. It doesn't take long for new public officials to learn that they—just as athletes and other celebrities—enhance their stature and power most effectively and efficiently through emotional posturing, outrageous antics, and shameless personalization; and the most ready, common, and rewarding forum for this enhancement is partisan politics. I guess there's an argument for such partisanship. But I never had a partisan mentality, and I got my fill of partisan warfare.

Getting Out. **Ultimately, I had too much pride in myself—and too much respect for American democracy—to hang around too long.** I had seen too many friends go out politically frustrated and personally bitter. I saw life-long public servants consumed by politics and power and perks. Some even went to jail. Others had to be carried out feet first.

I also recall the personally pivotal comment of a relatively young, successful, untainted Congressman during the intense national ugliness of the early 1990s. He had decided not to run for re-election, and in a private moment he explained that "I woke up one day and realized that I no longer liked the people I worked for".

In all honesty, I too realized that, after fourteen years in public office, I was tired of doing what I was doing. It was time for me to consider something different—either move up to the Senate (where service as a philosopher-politician is more appropriate and rewarding) or get out of politics (where perhaps I could address more effectively some of my concerns about the future of American democracy).

So I ran for the Senate and I lost and I'm out of politics. There are many excuses that politicians can give for leaving public service, but the simple fact is that I got out of politics because I lost my last election (a race for an open seat in the U.S. Senate in 1996).

Just as candidly, I can say that I am happy to be a former Congressman. Serving in public office has been a treasured highlight of my life. But it was very difficult balancing philosophical inclinations with the grinding, consuming, partisan demands of political office while struggling to maintain some semblance of personal life. Now I am directing my attention to other, equally meaningful concerns—such as "the future of American democracy." I can participate in the democratic process in Alabama and Washington and internationally without having to bear all the awesome (as well as trivial) burdens and trappings of public service. Furthermore, I can spend family occasions and national holidays—such as birthdays and anniversaries and the Fourth of July—wherever and however I want, with my wife and daughter, rather than going to "must attend" political events with large crowds, influential power-brokers, financial contributors, and total strangers who for some reason want to spend their time with a politician.

In Retrospect. **It is not easy acknowledging some of these things about myself and my public career; and in no way should my remarks be taken as a negative judgment of politics (or as a cynical basis for my rhetorical speculation about dying America). I make these candid and personalized observations simply to introduce myself to the reader and to convey something of the dynamics of American democracy as I experienced them. In retrospect, I have to say that my public career has been fun and**

worthwhile. In fact, I feel very positive about public service and my work as a "philosopher-politician."

I guess I am most pleased and proud of my work on national fiscal policy. I ran for Congress in great part because I felt that the budget deficit at that time was the greatest threat to American democracy; and I lobbied hard for my position on the House Budget Committee. The federal budget had been in a deficit sinkhole for several decades, in my opinion depriving our people of the opportunity to address important public needs and jeopardizing our control of our own national destiny. When I first went to Washington, the federal budget was about three hundred billion dollars in the hole, the largest annual deficit in modern history; when I left Congress, the foundation for a balanced budget was in place; and, as a result, our country enjoyed budget surpluses for several years.

I also feel pretty good about my earlier work in Alabama on election reform ("The Alabama Fair Campaign Practices Act") and on education reform ("The Browder Education Reform Act").

To generalize broadly, my political career—including work as a party activist, campaign consultant, and elected official (in local, state, national, and international politics)—gave me a full appreciation of the positives and negatives of public service, a realization of my own civic strengths and weaknesses, and a better understanding of the interplay of philosophy, politics, and American democracy. I enjoyed public life; and I would still be in politics, happily serving in the United States Senate, if I had won my last election.

....

THE DISCOMFORTING NATURE
OF MY RHETORICAL INQUIRY

I have long been fascinated and optimistic about America. But fascination and optimism shifted toward concern early in my political career; and that concern has now evolved into discomforting questions about the future of American democracy.

Early Concerns in Alabama. I first began wondering whether America might be "dying" in the early 1980s, while serving in the Alabama Legislature (and while continuing to teach a full load of American government classes at Jacksonville State University). Although I enjoyed public service, I began to question whether the conventional mantra of "political reform" that we chanted so fervently and repeatedly in our classrooms would be enough to breathe life into dysfunctional government programs, processes, and institutions. Furthermore, after moderate (but limited) reform success as a state legislator and secretary of state, I concluded that the problem was bigger than Alabama. I determined that our democratic ills extended beyond the symptomatic politics of Montgomery to the fundamental core of our nation.

Rancor in Washington. **Burning with ambition and arrogance, I set out for Washington as a rookie Congressman in 1989; and I arrived on the national scene at a time—the 1990s—of intense political rancor.** The collapse of the Soviet Union had unleashed hellish domestic demons of intractable budget deficits and partisan warfare; and the American people were in a foul, revolting, rebellious, mood—unreasonably demanding and dangerously impatient with the American democratic system. My biggest shock was that political leaders in our nation's capital really had no clues about how to deal with such public distemper. Their most often response to a cynical, dispirited electorate was equally cynical political gamesmanship.

Post-Politics Reflection. **Since leaving Congress, I increasingly have found myself wondering whether something is fundamentally wrong in America.** Despite unprecedented economic and international prosperity, the American democratic process has not worked very well for some time now; and the American people evidence increasing detachment from the historic "Great Experiment" of American history. Thus, I now articulate—often and publicly— my rhetorical thesis of potentially "dying" America.

Still an "American Dreamer". **I am still an "American Dreamer". But after decades of experience as a political scientist and public official, I am concerned about whether America is working for today's young people— and future Americans—the way that it worked for me.** The reader therefore should be forewarned of the lingering normative question, somewhere in the back of my mind, throughout this analysis: "How does this systemic development or that particular proposal—or even my own paradigm for 'New America'—affect the ability of today's little Johnnie Glenn Browders to cross those tracks to the American dream?"

I do not pretend that my "poor boy" story entitles me to impose my own personalized interpretation of "America" on our nation. Nor do I think that the essence of the American dream is a massive public or governmental program to cater to the needs and interests of the "National Association of Poor Boys of America." My work as a public official and political scientist taught me long ago the realities and limitations of American government and politics. In short, I do not subscribe to the knee-jerk, bleeding-heart, big-government political philosophy.

However, my experience has kept me sensitive to "America" as a national experiment in democratic ideals; and it has attuned me to "American democracy" as the process that allows all of us to pursue those ideals. My personal background has added a special perspective—from the heart—to go along with my political and theoretical thinking about the nature and workings of the American system. In other words, I see historic America and American democracy as synonymously integral to an "equal opportunity American dream."

But Is America Still Alive? **Now I wonder: Is America still alive and well?** Does American democracy still allow poor little boys—and poor little girls, and old people, and sick people, and blacks, browns, yellows, reds, and all other colors and creeds and ideas—to pursue those ideals? Do the American people still accept sufficient individual and collective responsibility for helping everybody and anybody chase the American dream? Is America still a national experiment in democratic ideals?

Or is America just a giant pyramid scheme? Is America nothing more than a successful political game that has worked very well for two centuries—because of its favorable environment and good management—but which now is playing itself out? Is America just an attractive racket whose winners are the many generations of Americans who got in-and-out (with disproportionate blessings and benefits of American democracy) in timely fashion? Has America become a winning proposition just for privileged people who are positioned to take advantage of the game? Is America now a failing political operation for too many citizens? What about the growing number of Americans, especially younger citizens, who simply have lost interest in the old political order? Why are so many Americans talking about investing in new and different political schemes?

In short, has my American dream turned into an irrelevancy, or even a nightmare, for today's generation?

....

SUMMARY COMMENT

I will try to resist excessive psycho-babbling in this manuscript. My essay is, essentially, about American democracy—not my American dream; and my rhetorical proclamation about "dying" America is more than nostalgic pining for the good old days.

My central purpose is a theoretical and political proposition—based on my dual careers as a political scientist and public official—that serious socio-economic, technological, and political developments have changed and will continue to change American democracy in important and unhealthy ways unless we address these challenges.

CHAPTER 3

WHAT DO I MEAN BY "AMERICA", "AMERICAN DEMOCRACY", AND "DYING"?

A SYSTEMS THEORY OF TRANSFORMATIONAL AMERICA

The outrageous assertion that America may be dying carries an obligation to conduct a thorough examination, with sound theoretical analysis, of our national health. In this chapter, I want to explain first what I mean by the terms "America", "American democracy", and "dying". Then, I will develop a conceptual framework—systems theory and an accompanying diagrammatic model—incorporating the dynamics of transforming America.

....

"AMERICA"

A NATIONAL EXPERIMENT IN DEMOCRATIC IDEALS

My conception of "America" does not fit any simple geographic, legalistic, or jurisdictional definition. It does not mean "the government." Nor is it a shorthand reference to the United States of America. I use the term "America", as did Tocqueville, connotatively, to express the subjective character as well as the objective parameters of the system within which "we, the people of the United States" conduct our public affairs. I define America as a national experiment in democratic ideals.

A CONNOTATIONAL IDEA

My connotational definition is based on the notion that America has always been an idea more than a thing. Too often we tend to talk about America within a formal context focusing on distinctly national and powerful leaders (such as the President and the Secretary of State), on prominent governmental institutions (such as the Congress and the Supreme Court), and on centers of governance (such as Washington DC). But America is not just powerful officials or big buildings or important places. These are only obvious, representative parts of our corporeal body. I am talking also about something different, something bigger, something special—an almost spiritual America where close to three hundred million people in far-flung territory live their lives in great diversity but with a surprising mixture and level of common national purpose.

Of course, in this manuscript I quite often speak about America with references to powerful leaders and big governmental institutions in Washington, DC. But a better understanding comes from considering America, in sports analogy (since I once was a sportswriter), as much broader than and different from Washington officialdom, as a never-ending game of agony and ecstasy among countless players and teams competing loosely in diverse leagues and arenas for the trophies and rewards of American political life. We can think of America as the national past-time for entities and activities such as Minnesota, Guam, the Alabama Democratic Conference, the Independent Women's Forum, Dade County, the VFW, Portland, the Dallas Chamber of Commerce, Close-Up, the AFL-CIO, the Sierra Club, and the Salvation Army.

COLLECTIVE PUBLIC PURPOSE

My broader conception of America (which is critically important to my rhetorical "dying" inquiry) applies anywhere, anytime, any way in which Americans come together—in some democratic manner—and work toward collective public purpose in the spirit of our national experiment in democratic ideals. Thus in my mind, America extends to virtually any public endeavor by "we the people"—whether governmental or nongovernmental, national or local, big or little—including political parties, charitable organizations, rural electric cooperatives, community theaters, schools, churches, libraries, town meetings, radio talk shows, little league baseball games, and other such societal undertakings. I also consider such endeavors to be integral parts of our national democratic experiment even when there's personal motivation, partisan political activity, or a buck to be made in the process.

As a matter of fact, I've always thought that if Alexis de Tocqueville were to return and ask me to show him the best example of American democracy in the modern world, then I would take him to a meeting of my local voluntary fire department and introduce him to a splendid bunch of Twenty-First Century American democrats.

"THE GREAT EXPERIMENT"

To be more specific, my America is what Tocqueville billed as "the great experiment . . . a spectacle for which the world has not been prepared by the history of the past" (*Democracy in America*, 1835; Vol. I, p. 25). My America is the unprecedented pursuit of freedom, equality, and justice through a precarious framework of popular self-government. My America is a national experiment in democratic ideals. At the risk of being boringly repetitive (and because very few analysts actually define what they mean by "the American experiment"), I want to emphasize the essential concepts of our Great Experiment.

- **First, and perhaps of most historic importance, America represents a unique case of inspired nationalism.** A hodge-podge of New World people rejected the Old World and voluntarily came together as a nation. Not a single-minded, homogeneous, unitary state, but a confederation of peoples and regions joined together by common spirit and destiny—sufficiently alike to be a nation and distinctly different from other nations of the world. Historically meaningful, for example, is our original, collective national commitment as expressed in the Preamble to the Constitution:

> "We the people of the United States, in order to form a more perfect union, establish justice, insure domestic tranquility, provide for the common defence, promote the general welfare, and secure the blessings of liberty to ourselves and our posterity, do ordain and establish this Constitution for the United States of America."

- **Second, this new American nation attempted a strange experiment—a federal republic—whereby national public sovereignty would be exercised through limited, representative governance.** Although the Founders borrowed from numerous sources, they essentially created a new system of government reflecting both elitist reality and the possibilities of popular self-rule. My appreciation of their bold, ingenious experiment triggers anew whenever I articulate that dangling homage to "the republic" midway through our Pledge of Allegiance:

> "I pledge allegiance to the flag of the United States of America and to the republic for which it stands, one nation under God, indivisible, with liberty and justice for all."

- **Third, the American experiment was founded primarily on enlightened theoretical principles—democratic ideals—rather than monarchical, religious, or class considerations.** Many of these democratic ideals found specific enumeration in the Bill of Rights; however no better, simpler, nobler, generalized expression exists than the opening, universal principle of our Declaration of Independence:

> "We hold these truths to be self-evident, that all men are created equal,
> that they are endowed by their Creator with certain unalienable rights,
> that among these are life, liberty, and the pursuit of happiness."

Thus the Great Experiment—the spectacle for which the world had not been prepared by the history of the past—was an effort to let a nation of theoretically free and equal people pursue fuzzy, imperfect, imperfectible democratic ideals such as freedom, equality, and justice through a restrained government of elected representatives. These essential concepts— inspired nationalism, republican governance, and the pursuit of democratic ideals—of our Great Experiment have withstood challenging tests of war and peace and time; and they have found repeated refinement through the documents and struggles of American history. I could rhapsodize forever—Lincoln's Gettysburg Address, Franklin D. Roosevelt's fireside chats, John F. Kennedy's "Ask not what your country can do for you", Martin Luther King's "I have a dream". Our ongoing experiment certainly sparkles with familiar words of inspirational national purpose.

....

"AMERICAN DEMOCRACY"

THE MAGICAL MIX OF PEOPLE, POLITICS, AND GOVERNMENT WHEREBY WE PURSUE DEMOCRATIC IDEALS

If, as I have proposed, America is a "national experiment in democratic ideals," then "American democracy" is the practical chemistry and civic laboratory for translating our community of ideals into progressive public policy.

Of course, the familiar words of our definitive national documents such as the Declaration of Independence are fuzzy philosophical inspirations; in practice they present complexities and contradictions. Inevitably, "freedom" and "equality" defy easy conceptualization and operationalization; quite often they clash; and most of the time they simply do not matter in our real lives. For example, is our self-evident truth one of opportunity or one of fairness? Is our society one of freedom, individualism, and independence or one of egalitarian security? How do we balance our democratic ideals when freedom of speech conflicts with freedom of religion? What do we do when the news media insist upon disseminating information that damages an accused citizen's ability to get a fair trial? Is it possible to resolve these legitimate democratic contradictions without endangering our treasured ideals and principles of governance? How do we deal with the fact that implementing these democratic ideals and principles sometimes leads us toward undemocratic and anti-democratic outcomes? Can we really pursue democratic ideals when many people just don't care? Can we make the Great Experiment work despite our own self-destructive inclinations?

I use the term "American democracy" to refer to the practical process through which we address such fuzzy philosophical inspirations and political problems; or more normatively, American democracy is the magical mix of people, politics, and government whereby we have pursued democratic ideals, fairly effectively, for the past two centuries.

FUNCTIONAL ELEMENTS AND CENTRAL QUESTIONS

The functional elements—our people, politics, and government—have provided critical contributions to the democratic process; and collectively, they have represented extraordinary civic chemistry. For most of our history, that civic chemistry has encouraged democratic ideals, even when those ideals represented abstractions, uncertainties, contradictions, and dangerous tensions within our polity.

Indeed, our people, politics, and government have fashioned a remarkable record in dealing with the key sequential questions of our Great Experiment:

(a) "Can we pursue democratic ideals through limited, representative government without succumbing to the inherent, destructive tendencies of democracy?"

(b) "How can we pursue democratic ideals through limited, representative government without succumbing to the inherent, destructive tendencies of democracy?"

(c) "And, finally, how far can we pursue democratic ideals through limited, representative government without succumbing to the inherent, destructive tendencies of democracy?"

American democracy is acknowledged universally for its historic success in dealing with these sequential questions and its progressive realization of substantive democratic ideals. In truth, our Great Experiment has been a spectacular national march, for more than two centuries, by a diverse people, toward universally positive principles of democratic society—such as liberty, equality, and justice. In the process, our experiment also has secured the material benefits of democracy for generation after generation of American citizens. This unprecedented, often circuitous march has led us through war, constitutional crisis, executive-legislative-judicial struggle, economic depression, social unrest, and much public soul-searching. It has been, and always will be, a fitful journey of competing visions and real political danger.

America's Great Experiment, then, as I see it, is a philosophical and practical exercise in national democratic self-government, a procedural and substantive exercise designed to answer the important sequential question: (a) Can . . . , (b) How can . . . , and (c) How far can we pursue democratic ideals through limited, representative government without succumbing to the inherent, destructive tendencies of democracy? How far can an increasingly diverse, divergent, and demanding people push a restrained-but-popular process of governance toward fuzzy and contradictory democratic ideals without damaging that process or those ideals. In other words, how far can we carry our national democratic experiment without going too far? This simple question conveys the noble quest and potential danger of America's historic spectacle.

ELABORATIONS, QUALIFICATIONS, AND DISCLAIMERS

I should acknowledge here several important elaborative points pertinent to this discussion about "American democracy".

No Official Democratic Ideology. To begin, there is no formal, official American democratic ideology; and it is impossible to define any consensual set of democratic ideals and values. Furthermore, it is critical to acknowledge the historic realities of public consciousness—an unstructured, detached, softness—in any discussion of "the American belief system." As a generalization, the American people do not think or act ideologically. While their political passions can be aroused at times of political drama, sometimes with lasting consequence, they focus for the most part on non-public events and ideas. In fact, this quality—this informal, soft democratic acquiescence—has proven very functional for American democracy. It has allowed a non-ideological society to move in surprisingly progressive ways at critical junctures of American history.

Nevertheless, we can acknowledge a broad, national, democratic identity throughout our history. **Samuel Huntington**, for example, has noted in *American Politics* (1981) that:

> For most peoples national identity is the product of a long process of historical evolution involving common ancestors, common experiences, common ethnic background, common language, common culture, and usually common religion. National identity is thus organic in character. Such, however, is not the case in the United States. American nationalism has been defined in political rather than organic terms. The political ideas of the American Creed have been the basis of national identity. (23)

Clinton Rossiter places that national political creed in consonance with a liberal tradition, in *Conservatism in America* (1962):

> There has been in a doctrinal sense, only one America. We have debated
> fiercely, but as men who agreed on fundamentals . . . The American political
> tradition is basically a liberal tradition . . . its articles of faith, a sort of
> American Holy Writ, are perfectability, progress, liberty, equality,
> democracy, and individualism. (67, 71)

Herbert McClosky and **John Zaller** define the historical but dynamic continuities of this powerful democratic belief system in their conclusion of *The American Ethos* (1984):

> In the course of this book we have seen that the ideals to which the nation's
> Founders appealed—values such as freedom, equality, individualism, and
> private property—are, for the most part, still prized by Americans and their
> opinion leaders. Yet, despite this continuity, dramatic changes have occurred
> in the norms through which these general values have been translated into
> everyday practice. Suffrage, for example, once largely limited to white males
> who owned property, has been extended to include all adults, of both genders
> and of every race and religion . . . Over time, they are bound to rise even
> further in response to the play of democratic forces and the competition
> among elites for public favor. As the size of the attentive, educated, and
> democratically oriented public expands and becomes increasingly articulate
> in its demands, a freely elected government cannot help but respond. (29,
> 302)

Robert L. Erikson and **Kent L. Tedin** put these ideas into a useful, practical description of "political consensus" (*American Public Opinion: Its Origins, Content, and Impact*, Fifth Edition, 1995):

> America has perhaps been most fortunate in that there have been few intense
> group or issue cleavages dividing the population. As long as some modest
> consensus exists, and most of the population has a minimal degree of
> economic security, the system seems able to tolerate a wide variety of
> personality types, a relatively low level of trust in government, and
> considerable lack of enthusiasm (although perhaps not outright hostility) for
> procedural democratic norms. (173-175)

Elite-Mass Interactions. The foregoing practical description brings me to a second important observation about "American democratic consensus." Any discussion of popular commitment to our national democratic experiment must consider elite-mass interactions in American society. You don't have to be an elitist politician or political theorist to recognize the critical, positive contribution of political leaders and influentials to American history. As McClosky and Zaller explain:

> While most members of the general public are preoccupied with the problems
> of daily life—earning a living, raising a family, recreation, and so forth—the
> political elite are characterized by a more intense and continuing concern
> with the affairs of the larger community . . . By reason of their greater

involvement in the public life of the nation, the elites also have a better grasp
of how the system works and exhibit higher overall levels of support for its
values than do members of the mass public . . . Thus opinion leaders (or
elites) become for most purposes the principal carriers and expositors of the
nation's political creed. (9)

Or, as **V.O. Key, Jr.**, puts it more succinctly and normatively, " . . . perhaps a
healthy democracy must contain within itself a suitable strain of political
aristocracy" ("Public Opinion and the Decay of Democracy," *Virginia Quarterly
Review*, 1961, 490).

**Multiple Personalities. Third, I recognize the difficulty of writing or
talking about American democracy as though there were a singular
national democratic personality or community at play in this discussion.**
Analysts commonly attempt to explain our national history and politics with the
implication that we speak in one voice with clearly identifiable meaning, when
in fact there is a diversity of speakers, conversations, and messages underlying
our actions.

For example, too much significance is attached to so-called "national mood
changes" from one election to another, such as in 1992 when Bill Clinton was
elected president, ending the reign of Ronald Reagan and George Bush, or when
the Republicans took over congress in 1994 after decades of Democratic
dominance (or whatever happens at our millennial turn in 2000). The reality is
that the American electorates of various years are more similar than different
from previous or following years. America usually splits into two roughly equal
electoral camps, with only very small margins changing control of government
from time to time. While it is possible to talk about very consequential policy
differences in "swing" elections, it is inaccurate to characterize them as
expressions of a singular mindset or a massive mood change. The idea of
important but unclear mandates (such as in 1996, 1998, and 2000) more
accurately conveys the multiplicity of our national community and its political
personality.

**Partisan Politics. Fourth, our experiment generally has been conducted
within an ambience of partisan politics; but it also transcends partisanship.**
Democrats preach "fairness" (equality) and Republicans push "opportunity"
(freedom), but what we're all talking about is the endless pursuit of small-d
democratic ideals (interestingly, within a small-r republican framework). I have
served with Presidents Bill Clinton (D) and George Bush (R), House Speakers
Newt Gingrich (R) and Tom Foley (D), and Senate Leaders Trent Lott (R) and
George Mitchell (D); I've worked with Al Gore (D), Dan Quayle (R), Dick
Cheney (R), Dennis Hastert (R), Dick Armey (R), Tom DeLay (R), Dick
Gephardt (D), David Bonior (D), Bill Grey (D), John McCain (R); I was a
sometime floor leader for Governor George Wallace (D) in the Alabama
legislature; I've worked with Democrats, Republicans, Independents, Socialists,
and Libertarians—and I can attest to the politicization and partisanship of their

American visions; but I also can attest to their support of the progressive democratic march.

Somewhat Mythical. **Fifth, I should acknowledge that, despite my sentiments, American democracy, as I have defined it, has always been something of a myth.** Our Founders were, after all, persons of privilege and men of their times, subject to the same human faults and prejudices of most of us. Among their primary concerns—in addition to liberty, equality, and justice—were the practical issues of personality conflicts, political order and private property (including ownership of other human beings). Furthermore, our national experiment in democratic ideals has never worked very smoothly or as sublimely as we like to pretend. Slavery, injustice, violence, even civil war—these are only a few of the many unpleasant elements of the American experience.

Our Defining Character. **Finally, however, despite its mythical nature, our progressive democratic experiment has proven sufficiently real and powerful throughout our country's history to serve as the defining and distinguishing character of American democracy.** The interesting thing is that Americans historically have subscribed to this positive notion of America regardless of whether that notion fit their own personal experiences and lives. The vast majority of Americans—including most women, minorities, the poor, and the powerless—have stood erect, placed their right hands across their hearts, and loyally pledged their allegiance with a closing litany of "with liberty and justice for all." This phenomenal allegiance was a positive aspect of their individual civic development, our collective civil society, and a great service to the American experiment.

....

"DYING"

AMERICAN DEMOCRACY NO LONGER WORKS THE WAY IT HAS IN THE PAST; AND WE SEEM TO BE TIRING OF THE GREAT EXPERIMENT ITSELF

The central idea of this transformational analysis (as stated in my introductory remarks) is a complex and disturbing question for Twenty-First Century America:

> **"Can our nation — a people of growing cultural diversity with increasingly divergent ideals, values, and governance principles, in a constrained systemic environment—continue to sustain our collective pursuit of freedom, equality, and justice through the traditional framework of limited, representative government?"**

To put this idea into more urgent terms, "How far can America pursue the Great Experiment without succumbing to the inherent, destructive tendencies of democracy?" My rhetorical contention, of course, is that America may be dying—that American democracy no longer works the way it used to work and that we seem to be tiring of the Great Experiment itself. It is not my contention that America has died. Nor are we comatose. We are very much alive. But America is evidencing democratic distemper that, without treatment, jeopardizes the future of our national experiment in democratic ideals.

A TRICKY ENDEAVOR

Our Great Experiment is a tricky endeavor, and its course can never be easy or straight. It requires sustained national commitment—by a multiplicity of citizens, political subcultures, and geographical entities—to democratic ideals and the balancing of inevitable strains among those ideals, such as freedom-versus-equality, individualism-versus-security, and majority rule-versus-minority rights.

Tricky too is the notion of controlled, popular governance, which has within it, not only the potential for what philosophers call the "good life." but also the democratic seeds of tyranny and anarchy and perhaps dissolution. Interminable conflict is built into a system which gives authority to the people (through their elected representatives) to resolve their conflicts by adopting undemocratic policies and practices. The people even have within their authority (through constitutional revision) the power to alter or to terminate the Great Experiment itself.

ULTIMATE, UNHEALTHY AUTHORITY

That ultimate, unhealthy authority—the vast power of a democracy to pursue undemocratic "ideals"—is what I mean in my warning about "the inherent, destructive tendencies of democracy". Our constitutional founders hoped, of course, that America would—forevermore—pursue democratic ideals within a limited, representative framework. But they realized that, with the passage of time, Americans might divide into opposing camps—partisanly contesting democratic ideals for some faction over another, or pitting democratic ideal (such as freedom) against democratic ideal (such as equality)—in a win-lose game to be determined by a weak, fragmented governmental apparatus. An angry, divided America—perhaps exhausted in its pursuit of democratic ideals—might decide to expand (or constrain) our system of ideals and governance beyond (or to a lesser extent than) its intent. Future Americans might ask the American experiment to produce something that it is incapable of producing—perfect blessings and benefits—or we might inhibit the experiment from doing what it was designed to do—assisting, in a practical way, the perpetual pursuit of imperfect, imperfectible democratic ideals.

DANGER OF IRRELEVANCY

Perhaps the most pernicious danger is that the American people might begin to view the Founders' experiment as no longer relevant to their lives. Middle-Class Americans—comfortable, cynical, or apathetic—could simply ignore the essential concepts of civic life, perhaps adopting the "whatever" attitude and "nothingness" ethos of the popular "Seinfeld" television show. Like Jerry, Elaine, George, and Kramer, we could just walk away from the civic arena, thereby abandoning our national system of ideals and governance to more radical activists and interests. (This sitcom foursome, by the way, ended their long-running series by going to jail because of their civic irresponsibility.)

I'm reminded here also of a less comedic message in an obscure movie that runs occasionally on late-night television. Two laid-off, desperate, overalled workers hijack a train and head for Chicago to confront the president of the big corporation that has just closed the packaging plant in their rural Arkansas hometown. In the course of their rambling conversation, while busting through railblocks, destroying police cars, and generally creating havoc for Middle America, one complains about what's happening in our country. And he says something to the effect that "I was takin' a shower the other night and I tried to say the pledge . . . you know . . . the American one . . . and I couldn't remember how it goes." That scene communicates, Hollywood-style, what I mean by the danger of irrelevancy.

The real-life danger of civic irrelevancy concerns no less an authority on American democracy than Supreme Court Justice Stephen Breyer. The Constitution established a general theoretical framework for making decisions, according to Breyer, leaving specific political decision-making to the democracy that it created. But American democracy requires a certain level of responsible participation by its citizens; and the Supreme Court Justice worries about civic indifference. In a 1999 Law Day public speech Breyer said:

> It does not bother me when I read that the public is less aware of the names of Supreme Court justices than of the Three Stooges. But it does bother me when I read that more teen-agers can name the Three Stooges than can name the three branches of the federal government; or that three times as many know that "90210" stands for Beverly Hills than that the birthplace of the Constitution stands for Philadelphia . . . The Constitution not only foresees participation by the public, it demands that participation . . . For without trust and participation, the Constitution cannot work. ("Breyer: America Cynical About Government," Associated Press, May 4, 1999)

Irrelevancy, then, could prove just as dangerous to the future of America as extreme expansion or extreme constriction of American democracy. Any of these three options could democratically disrupt the course of America's historic mission. Dangerous inclinations toward democratic excess, democratic incapacitation, and democratic irrelevancy, then, are potential pathways to the demise of our Great Experiment.

Thus our Founders structured an invitation to constant political assault on the delicate balance of the American system. They struggled vigorously with this fundamental dilemma; and it has challenged our political leaders and fascinated a worldwide audience ever since. Nevertheless, from the beginning, our American experiment has progressed toward the broad, general ideal of democracy. Now, after two centuries of the continuing dilemma, our delicate experiment may be in trouble.

THE LOGIC OF "DYING"

We will conduct an empirical examination of our ailing American system in the next section ("Why and How, Arguably, Is America Dying?"); but for now I want to establish the logic of my "dying" terminology.

Organic Analogy. Speaking in physiological terms, "dying" can be defined as the process of terminal degeneration—the increasing inability of an organism to perform normal, sustaining, critical functions of life. Most healthy organisms experience spurts of growth, perform vital functions, and regenerate themselves periodically over the course of their lives. All organisms also represent an inevitably changing mixture and balance of growing, functioning, regenerating . . . and eventual degeneration. This mixing, balancing, transforming process can be altered, disrupted—and terminated—by unhealthy developments within the organism and/or its environment. Organic degeneration can take the form of a specific, sudden, dramatic development—such as a heart attack, a brain aneurysm, or drowning; however, more often than not, it represents the general onset of something like immune deficiency, metastatic cancer, or just old age. Quite often, furthermore, this degeneration is gradual, subtle, and not easily perceived. Regardless of the form or perceptibility, without environmental correction (to fit organic needs) and/or organic adjustment (to accommodate changed environmental conditions), the organism will experience increasing degeneration and eventual shutdown.

Terminal Degeneration. In this manuscript, accordingly, I approach America's contemporary problem rhetorically as terminal degeneration—"dying". It would be irresponsible to invoke such pathological terminology to refer to imagined discomforts, minor pains, routine ailments, or malfunctioning body parts. However, the term "dying" may be rhetorically appropriate if the suspect malady is of such widespread, critical nature as to jeopardize the continued functioning of American democracy.

PROPOSITIONAL OBSERVATIONS

I will implement my "dying" inquiry by suggesting four propositional observations about troubled American democracy: (a) "The favorable systemic environment of American democracy has disappeared;" (b) "We have entrapped American democracy within a philosophical civil war;" (c) "American democracy no longer works the way it used to work;" and (d) "America seems to be tiring of its historic Great Experiment." According to my rhetorical analysis, if contemporary America conforms to these four hypothetical propositions, our national democratic experiment is in serious danger.

In short, as stated in the terminology of my unconventional analysis, "Is America experiencing fundamental change to a degree that threatens the future of our Great Experiment?" This discussion will continue in the following chapters; before beginning my theoretical propositions, however, I want to suggest a diagrammatic model of rhetorically dying America.

....

A SYSTEMS THEORY
OF TRANSFORMATIONAL AMERICA

A quick reference to a field of analysis known as systems theory will help clarify my transformational thesis; it also will provide the conceptual framework for the remainder of this manuscript.

Systems theory has proven useful in explaining how various entities (such as large organizations and living organisms) work procedurally and substantively. Technically speaking, a system is a regularly interacting or interdependent group of elements forming a unified whole.   Physiologically (the applicable perspective for my "dying" analysis), a system is a group of body organs that together perform the vital function of "life".

More pertinent to our discussion, systems theory, as presented by **David Easton** in *A Systems Analysis of Political Life* (1965), helps us understand how nations succeed or fail in the face of significant challenges. According to Easton, "a political system can be designated as those interactions through which values are authoritatively allocated for a society"; and "in a given society, the systems other than the political system constitute a source of many influences that create and shape the conditions under which the political system itself most operate" (21-22).

Thus a political regime's stability is dependent upon proper functioning and interaction among the organic elements of that regime and upon a healthy relationship between that regime and the broader system within which it operates.   Most importantly, there must be a positive relationship between systemic inputs (such as public opinion) and outputs (such as public policy). Another principle of systemic stability is the necessity of balance between two kinds of inputs—demands (that place pressure on authorities and processes) and supports (that sustain the system).   This latter category includes diffuse supports (deriving from the belief that the systemic regime is the proper and legitimate way to make decisions for society) and specific supports (for particular authorities, processes, and policies).   The trick for the system, and any democratic regime, is whether its political institutions and processes can translate a variety of positive and negative inputs into acceptable outputs within a generally unfocused and unruly systemic environment.

Furthermore, fundamental environmental transformations seriously imperil the political system. As Easton elaborates:

> In a world of newly emerging political systems, we do not need to pause to illustrate the impact that a changing economy, culture, or social structure may have upon political life . . . One of the important reasons for identifying these essential variables is that they give us a way of establishing when and how the disturbances acting upon a system threaten to stress it. Stress will be said to occur when there is a danger that the essential variables will be pushed beyond what we may designate as their critical range. What this means is that something may be happening in the environment—the system suffers total defeat at the hands of an enemy, or widespread disorganization in and disaffection from the system is aroused by a severe economic crisis. Let us say that as a result, the authorities are consistently unable to make decisions or if they strive to do so, the decisions are no longer regularly accepted as binding. Under these conditions, authoritative allocations of values are no longer possible and the society would collapse for want of a system of behavior to fulfill one of its vital functions. (22-24)

This brief review of demand/support balance, the input/output relationship, and changing systemic environment provides insight into why so many regimes worldwide are falling apart or have collapsed. More to the point, systems theory provides the basis for understanding what's happening in contemporary America. Systems analysis helps us sort out basic, causal, transformational factors (independent variables) from effect (dependent variables); it also helps identify factors that, while not basic, causal functions, are related and contribute to the problem (intervening variables). Such analysis further aids in recognizing factors that simply occur or appear to occur simultaneously (co-incidental or spurious variables).

A SYSTEMIC MODEL

Take a look at my "Systemic Model of 'Dying America'", which depicts pertinent elements, variables, and relationships of the American system— and our trending condition—through a diagrammatic illustration of Historical America (as our nation has functioned for the past two centuries) and hypothetically "Dying America".

My systemic model is an admittedly simple presentation, since it is designed to emphasize the broad outlines of our developing democratic predicament without the clutter of exacerbating or irrelevant problems. The value of this model is that it demonstrates graphically and concisely the theoretic foundation of my general inquiry; and it provides the conceptual framework for specific propositional observations in the next few chapters.

The rationale of America's Great Experiment—and the basis of my model—is the idea that democratic ideals (even competing, contradictory ideals) can best be pursued by a diverse people through a loose framework of mediating political mechanisms and popular but restrained governance.   Furthermore, that experiment works only under certain conditions. In other words, American democracy (our mix of people, politics, and government) was designed and has evolved within an environment of increasing openness and opportunity and support—relatively free from any rigid, stagnant, stifling orthodoxy of unworkable ideals, values, and governance.

Unhealthy changes in that supportive systemic environment obviously would create tremendous negative pressures on American democracy; and any changes among the organic elements (our people, politics, and government) of American democracy would further complicate our experiment. Eventually, these changes might begin to impact, negatively, our system of governance—and our pursuit of democratic ideals.

Historical America. The Historical Diagram shows American democracy pursuing democratic ideals within a favorable systemic environment (shaped originally by open natural conditions and sustained by the popular expansion of national public authority). This favorable environment provides positive inputs (both demands and supports) to allow and encourage American democracy (a civic people, functional political machinery, and effective government) to magically mix and implement national democratic ideals. These positive outputs then feed back into the environment for systemic regeneration.

"Dying America". The transformational model also projects struggling American democracy at the center of a troubled system. According to my hypothetical depiction of "Dying America", our closing natural conditions and declining support for national authority have produced an unfavorable systemic environment for American democracy; furthermore, a philosophical civil war has entrapped, or "boxed" American democracy in a destructive fight over ideals, values, and governance. Within this altered setting, an uncivic people and broken political machinery press ominously on beleaguered government, crippling day-to-day governance and more generalized aspects of American public life.   American democracy functions very poorly under such circumstances, and our national democratic march slows to a contentious crawl. The resulting democratic distemper then feeds back into the system as recycling negative environment.   Over time, without correction, this pattern could translate into systemic degeneration and, hypothetically, the death of America.

Transforming America? Since I don't really believe that America is going to die, then where do we go from here? The answer, as will unfold throughout this manuscript, is that American democracy must adjust in accord with systemic developments; and my transformational thesis is that our Great Experiment will change fundamentally to meet the needs of a different America in the Twenty-First Century.

SYSTEMIC MODEL OF "DYING AMERICA"

HISTORICAL AMERICA

Favorable Systemic Environment

Open Natural Conditions

Popular Expansion of National Authority

American Democracy

People

Politics

Government

National Democratic Ideals

"DYING AMERICA"

Unfavorable Systemic Environment

Philosophical Civil War

Closing Natural Conditions

Decreasing Support for National Authority

American Democracy

People

Politics

Government

Democratic Distemper

Causal Factors. **According to my model, the causal factors in the systemic transformation of America are the historic decline of our systemic environment and a growing philosophical civil war over democratic ideals, cultural values, and governance principles.** These two inter-related factors are the primary independent variables impacting American democracy, whose organic elements are experiencing significant changes and problems of their own. Together these developments are straining and changing our Great Experiment.

Unconventional Wisdom. **In this latter respect, my theoretic perspective differs markedly from conventional wisdom. Most commentators blame our government, politicians, and political institutions (and a few criticize the public) for America's civic problems. While I hold these participants accountable for their actions, I also see them all as struggling players in a "fixed" game of stud poker democracy in which the trump cards—an unfavorable systemic environment and a philosophical civil war—are stacked against our people, politics, and government.**

My model also differs from much of today's punditry in identifying what is not "the" problem—terrorism, political scandals, declining morals, liberalism, conservatism, abortion, pornography, homosexuality, prayer in the schools, affirmative action, breakup of the family, crime, drugs, racism, incivility, talk radio, television, Hollywood, crooked politicians, campaign money, negative campaigning, the special interests, party politics, budgetary squabbling, media scrutiny, or any of a variety of hot-button issues and villains. These issues and villains are important; some are corrosively controversial (but others are simply objectionable nuisances or trivial diversion). Many of them derive, in part, from the fundamental dysfunctions of the American system; in turn, they infect our national environment with political toxins and seriously exacerbate our civic ills. Expectedly, our public debate and media tend to focus disproportionately on them. But they are, from an analytic perspective, merely coincidental or spurious elements of our unhealthy situation, problems that the American system is expected to address (and has addressed historically in times of duress).

....

SUMMARY COMMENT

My unconventional thesis is that the basic causal, fundamental problems of contemporary America are transformational developments: (a) our declining systemic environment and (b) our philosophical civil war. Together, these historic developments are stressing our people, politics, and government; and their cumulative effect is democratic distemper and systemic democratic degeneration.

The important question is whether American democracy can continue to mix its magic for the long run. In the past, an irrepressible "spirit of America" seemed to immunize us against threats to our national health—we made it through the depression, two world wars, and even a civil war. But today's threat is different and more pathogenic, challenging our national commitment to democratic ideals (and the continued functioning of limited, representative governance). In the next four chapters, we will address this threat through specific propositions about the functional vitality and future of America's Great Experiment.

SECTION TWO

WHY AND HOW, ARGUABLY, IS AMERICA DYING?

PROPOSITIONAL OBSERVATIONS OF TRANSFORMING AMERICAN DEMOCRACY

In preceding discussions, I laid the theoretic foundation— systems analysis—for my "dying" analogy. Beginning in this chapter, I will present propositional observations (based on my own direct examination and assessments by others) about the possible "whys" and "hows" of ailing America. I also plan to elaborate on some other important and personally interesting developments—such as the revolutionary rise, nature, and impact of "electronic democracy"—in contemporary America.

Basic Proposal. **My basic rhetorical proposal, of course, is that America is experiencing transformational trauma; and our national democratic experiment may be dying.** Despite economic and international prosperity, the historic advance of substantive democratic ideals has stalled, and the democratic process is not producing acceptably effective governance; most importantly, we seem, as a nation, to be tiring of the experiment itself.

The essence of my analytic theory (presented in the previous chapter) is that the basic, causal forces driving the contemporary American system are our unfavorable systemic environment and philosophical civil war; and the result is degenerating American democracy—and, of course, our faltering Great Experiment.

Propositional Observations. **In the next few chapters, I will explore the condition of American democracy through a series of propositional observations:** (a) "The favorable systemic environment of American democracy has disappeared;" (b) "We have entrapped American democracy within a philosophical civil war;" (c) "American democracy no longer works the way it has in the past;" and (d) "America seems to be tiring of its historic Great Experiment."

Cumulative Distemper. **In a sense, I might speculate that America is dying because we're giving up on our national democratic experiment because American democracy no longer works because of a philosophical civil war and because of a deteriorated systemic environment.** Of course, it is impossible to prove empirically any cause-and-effect pattern or to sort out precisely our sickness from our symptoms. I simply will proceed on the hypothetical premise that our adverse environment, philosophical civil war, dysfunctioning American democracy, and dispirited democratic culture are interrelated and that, cumulatively, they are hurting our national democratic experiment.

CHAPTER 4

PROPOSITION NUMBER ONE:

"THE FAVORABLE SYSTEMIC ENVIRONMENT OF AMERICAN DEMOCRACY HAS DISAPPEARED."

My thesis of American democracy begins with the truism that a political regime reflects, to a great extent, the environment within which it operates. More pertinent to our discussion, American democracy—as we have known it throughout our national history—has reflected the favorable systemic conditions under which our country was founded and developed; and the erosion of those conditions in recent decades may help explain our democratic distemper.

The theoretical foundation for this first proposition, of course, is **David Easton**'s systems analysis discussed at length in the previous chapter. To reiterate, according to Easton, the political regime operates within a broader environment; and, of particular pertinence to our proposition, social, cultural, and economic dynamics within the environment have important ramifications for the nature and function of that system's political order (*A Systems Analysis of Political Life*, 1965).

Pulitzer Prize winning Physiologist **Jared Diamond** provides interesting support for my systemic proposition in *Guns, Germs, and Steel* (1997), wherein he proffers causative, exogenous explanations for the development and shape of varying political systems in the modern world. After surveying human societal development over thousands of years, he asserts that "the striking differences between the long-term histories of peoples of the different continents have been due not to innate differences in the people themselves but to differences in their environments" (405).

Jeffry Sachs, Harvard Professor and Director of the Center for International Development, buttresses the environmental perspective in his discussion of important elements of growth and development in the western world ("Notes on a New Sociology of Economic Development," 2000). "Three broad explanations may help explain the growth puzzle," Sachs says: Geography ("Certain parts of the world are geographically favored"), Social Systems ("Certain social systems have supported modern economic growth"), and Positive Feedback ("A chain reaction in which current innovations provide the fuel for future breakthroughs"). While Sachs is concerned specifically with economic growth differences between western nations and the third world, his general analysis suggests why, in some ways, our New World environment was so favorable for the development and refinement of American democracy (30).

Accordingly, in this manuscript I contend that American democracy was established and prospered in a setting of propitiousness unknown to any previous society. Despite its adversities, the New World was a fairly open environment teeming with economic, social, and political opportunity; and these conditions provided a favorable laboratory for American nation building. The Founders' awkward experiment of jumbled theoretical principles and political practices probably would never have worked in any other setting; but the loose, unstructured, advantaged environment of the New World encouraged a collective chemistry for pursuing the progressive ideals of our national purpose.

However, as the following discussion will demonstrate, this historically propitious setting is not one of guaranteed permanency.

....

OUR ORIGINAL, OPEN, NATURAL ENVIRONMENT ENCOURAGED FREEDOM, INDIVIDUALISM, AND INDEPENDENCE (BUT IT CLOSED LONG AGO)

Their course was tough, but early Americans encountered a world of unlimited resources; most importantly, they had room to breathe, to grow, to experiment, to exercise freedom, individualism, and independence.

TOCQUEVILLE'S "BOUNDLESS CONTINENT"

As Alexis de Tocqueville wrote in *Democracy in America* (1835), the practical attraction of this rich New World was the key motivation for early

settlers and would-be Americans to leave their Old World homelands and cross the ocean:

> Thus the European leaves his cottage for the transatlantic shores, and the American, who is born on that very coast, plunges in his turn into the wilds of central America. This double emigration is incessant; it begins in the middle of Europe, it crosses the Atlantic Ocean, and it advances over the solitudes of the New World. Millions of men are marching at once towards the same horizon; their language, their religion, their manners differ; their object is the same. Fortune has been promised to them somewhere in the West, and to the West they go to find it. (Vol. 1, p. 292-293)

Tocqueville specifically cited these motives and blessings not only because of their importance to settlers but also as central to the foundation of democracy in America:

> The chief circumstance which has favored the establishment and the maintenance of a democratic republic in the United States is the nature of the territory that the Americans inhabit. Their ancestors gave them the love of equality and of freedom; but God himself gave them the means of remaining equal and free, by placing them upon a boundless continent. General prosperity is favorable to the stability of all governments, but more particularly of a democratic one, which depends upon the will of the majority, and especially upon the will of that portion of the community which is most exposed to want. When the people rule, they must be rendered happy or they will overturn the state; and misery stimulates them to those excesses to which ambition rouses kings. The physical causes, independent of the laws, which promote general prosperity are more numerous in America than they ever have been in any other country in the world, at any other period of history. In the United States not only is legislation democratic, but Nature herself favors the cause of the people. (Vol. I, p. 290-291)

These circumstances produced American democrats who were optimistic, confident, and adventurous; and created in such setting was a society of new dimension and mentality:

> There is not a country in the world where man more confidently seizes the future, where he so proudly feels that his intelligence makes him master of the universe, that he can fashion it to his liking. It's an intellectual movement which can only be compared to that which led to the discovery of the new world three centuries ago; and one can really say that America has been discovered a second time. (Pierson, *Tocqueville in America*, 1938, 119)

TURNER'S FRONTIER HYPOTHESIS

A half-century later, in a little noticed speech at the Chicago meeting of the American Historical Association, another unknown young scholar named Frederick Jackson Turner expanded this idea into, perhaps, the

most significant essay in American historiography. In the opening paragraph of his paper, Turner stated that "the existence of an area of free land, its continuous recession, and the advance of American settlement westward, explain American development" (*The Significance of the Frontier in American History*, 1893, 1).

****

EDITORIAL NOTE: Reliance on Frederick Jackson Turner evokes concerns similar to my earlier note regarding Tocqueville. Turner's frontier thesis has been questioned, criticized, and dismissed by hordes of historians as monocausal, deterministic, inconsistent, exaggerated, culturally biased, and scientifically suspect. But the reality is that Turner, like Tocqueville, provided a benchmark analysis through his timing (explaining America's democratic character at a critical transitional period in our national development), his method (examination of census data purporting the end of the frontier), and the power of his message (the positive impact of New World challenges and opportunities on American development). Turner's analysis has tremendous value because it helps us understand how we got where we are and it forces us to consider our future in a changed world. Although professional historians will protest my use of Turner's simplistic and dated version of western democracy, I think that it is worthwhile—both substantively and as background to my own analysis—to revisit the frontier thesis of American history.

****

Turner's thesis (generally known as the frontier hypothesis of American history) emphasized the challenge as well as the riches of the New World:

The peculiarity of American institutions is the fact that they have been compelled to adapt themselves to the changes of an expanding people—to the changes involved in crossing a continent, in winning a wilderness, and in developing at each area of this progress out of the primitive economy and political conditions of the frontier into the complexity of city life. (1)

All nations undergo developmental experiences, Turner said, but in most cases this development has occurred in fixed environs with limited consequences or real growth for the polity. The case of the United States was different, with initial developments on the Atlantic coast recurring endlessly in a process of progressive evolution as Americans expanded westward:

Thus American development has exhibited not merely advance along a single line but a return to primitive conditions on a continually advancing frontier line, and a new development from that area. (1)

> This perennial rebirth, this fluidity of American life, this expansion westward with its new opportunities, its continuous touch with the simplicity of primitive society, furnish the forces dominating American character. (2-3)

In imagery reminiscent of Hollywood, Turner traced the transformational experience from Old World to New America:

> The wilderness masters the colonist . . . It strips off the garments of civilization . . . Before long he has gone to planting Indian corn and plowing with a sharp stick; he shouts the war cry and takes the scalp in orthodox Indian fashion . . . Little by little he transforms the wilderness, but the outcome is not the Old Europe . . . The fact is, that here is a new product that is American. (4)

American democracy derived not from some theorist's dream, Turner declared:

> It came out of the American forest; and it gained new strength each time it touched a new frontier. Not the constitution, but free land and an abundance of natural resources open to a fit people, made the democratic type of society in America for three centuries while it occupied its empire. (293)

WEBB'S THEORY OF "GLOBAL BOOM"

Walter Prescott Webb, one of the Twentieth Century's foremost historians, placed the development of American democracy within a broader theory of world history. Webb acknowledged the importance of the American frontier, but he proposed that the American experience was but a small part of the "Great Frontier" of western civilization.

****

EDITORIAL NOTE: Once again I have selected for my rhetorical thesis a prominent scholar whose ideas have proven somewhat controversial over the years. But Walter Prescott Webb is acknowledged as one of America's most influential historians (he served as president of the American Historical Association); and his global interpretation in The Great Frontier (1952) and his interesting ideas in "Ended: 400 Year Boom" (1951) have merit. Besides, my entire analysis is purposefully provocative.

****

Webb maintained that the American democratic drama could best be understood as "but a detail in a much greater phenomenon, the interaction between European civilization and the vast raw lands into which it moved . . . three new continents, a large part of a fourth, and thousands of islands in oceans hitherto hardly known" ("Ended: 400 Year Boom," *Harper's Magazine,* October, 1951). He depicted the "Great Frontier" (beginning with the unlocking of the New World by Columbus) as "a gigantic operation extending over more than four centuries, a process that may appear to be the drama of modern civilization" (27).

Webb also articulated an interesting "boom" hypothesis regarding the "Great Frontier" and Western civilization:

> The frontier was basically a vast body of wealth without proprietors. It was an empty land more than five times the size of western Europe, a land whose resources had not been exploited . . . The boom began when Columbus returned from his first voyage, and it continued at an ever-accelerating pace until the frontier that fed it was no more . . . It is conceivable that this boom has given the peculiar character to modern history, to what we call Western civilization. (29)

Furthermore, he attributed magnificent democratic emanations from the "Great Frontier," asserting that "Before nature all men are free and equal." He also added:

> The important point is that the abstract man we have been following did not have to win his freedom. It was imposed upon him and he could not escape it. Being caught in the trap of freedom, his task was to adjust himself to it and to devise procedures which would be more convenient for living in such a state. His first task was to govern himself, for self-government is what freedom imposes. (32)

Speaking more specifically of the American experience, Webb wrote:

> It was the magnitude and the unbroken continuity of the experience that gave the frontier major importance in American life. It made no difference what other tasks the Americans had on their hands at a given time, there was the additional, ever-present one of moving into and settling new country. They did it while they fought for independence, before and after; they did it while they hammered out the principles of a democratic government shaped to the needs of frontiersmen; and they did not cease doing it in the period of civil strife. They never reached the limits of the vacancy they owned before they acquired another vacancy, by purchase, by treaty, by conquest, and in every case the frontiersmen infiltrated the country before the nation acquired it. Like locusts they swarmed, always to the west, and only the Pacific Ocean stopped them. Here in this movement beat the deep overtone of a nation's destiny, and to it all kept step unconsciously. (26)

Tocqueville, Turner, and Webb stressed that such an environment not only transformed people but also facilitated the development of a rowdy, uniquely American brand of democratic society. As Webb said, "The effects were everywhere, in democratic government, in boisterous politics, in exploitative agriculture, in mobility of population, in disregard for conventions, in rude manners and in unbridled optimism" (27).

In sum, the openness and richness of the expanding frontier fostered freedom for America's settlers, and they proceeded with their own individualistic endeavors. Government was relatively unimportant, and most people went about their lives without resorting to political institutions for help or redress of their grievances. As long as the frontier worked, people left government alone; and a select, elite leadership ran government with impunity so long as it did not antagonize the public egregiously. The result was a functioning partnership, within an environment of freedom and opportunity, among the people, their government, and the simple political machinery linking them together.

"ANXIETY", "SHOCK", AND "UNPLEASANT LOGIC"

But, as these astute observers of American democracy recognized, the frontier represented a passing phase of the American experiment. Each understood that, eventually, the frontier environment—which fostered freedom, individualism, and independence—was destined to lose some of its vitality and impact.
Tocqueville cryptically expressed his own anxiety about the future of American democracy after a pioneer encounter in the frontier wilderness. The Frenchman referred to his pioneer host as "a representative of a race to which belongs the future of the new world"; but he also added, without explanation, a strange comment on the inevitable problems and national discontent that would accompany the exhaustion of the frontier:

> It's this nomad people which the rivers and lakes do not stop, before which the forests fall and the prairies are covered with shade, and which, after having reached the Pacific Ocean, will reverse its steps to trouble and destroy the societies which it will have formed behind it. (Pierson, 244)

Turner saw the beginnings of this discontent in his lifetime. In a 1914 commencement address at the University of Washington, he said:

> To-day we are looking with a shock upon a changed world . . . We have so far won our national home, wrested from it its first rich treasures, and drawn to it the unfortunate of other lands, that we are already obliged to compare ourselves with settled states of the Old World . . . The disappearance of the frontier, the closing of the era which was marked by the influence of the West as a form of society, brings with it new problems of social adjustment, new demands for considering our past ideals and our present needs. (Turner, 293-307)

Webb raised the pertinent, provocative question by articulating the "unpleasant logic" of transiency inherent in the frontier thesis. While his comments referred to the global "Great Frontier", his point is equally applicable to America's western experience:

There is an unpleasant logic inherent in the frontier boom hypothesis of modern history . . . If we grant the boom, we must concede that the institutions we have, such as democracy and capitalism, were boom-born; we must also admit that the individual, this cherished darling of modern history, attained his glory in an abnormal period when there was enough room to give him freedom and enough wealth to give him independence. The future of the individual, of democracy and capitalism, and of many other modern institutions are deeply involved in this logic, and the lights are burning late in the capitals of the Western world where grave men are trying to determine what that future will be. (Webb, 33)

Eventually Tocqueville's nomadic people reached the Pacific Ocean; Turner's open frontier closed, at least by census count, at the end of the Nineteenth Century; and Webb's global "Great Frontier" disappeared by the middle of the Twentieth Century. But, contrary to their anxious, shocked, and unpleasant warnings, America has continued to experience the progressive blessings of American democracy.

How do we account for the durability of our Great Experiment despite systematic change and adversity? My conjectural explanation is that our original, open, natural frontier—rather than closing suddenly, completely, and traumatically—matured along with the developing American nation. The early West helped build American democracy (particularly individual freedom); and, frontier sentiments nurtured expansive democratic sentiments as America moved into the Twentieth Century.

Perhaps the Great Experiment endured, then, despite a burgeoning population and the absence of free land, because the American people nurtured and expanded their connotative endeavor beyond its origins. Most importantly, according to my thesis, a new frontier—a political frontier—arose to help deal with the needs, ideals, and demands of changing America.

....

THE POPULAR EXPANSION OF NATIONAL PUBLIC AUTHORITY FOSTERED EQUALITY, SECURITY, AND JUSTICE (BUT IT APPEARS TO HAVE REACHED ITS LIMITS)

My thesis of American democracy holds that, as the original, open, natural frontier faded into history, America gradually turned toward a political frontier—national public authority—to continue the benefits of its progressive experiment.

A NEW FRONTIER OF POLITICAL AUTHORITY

Inevitably, the wild frontier had to yield to the political frontier of an emerging nation. The depleted, crowded, unruly wilderness gave way to a more propitious public forum and a governmental cornucopia of progressive democratic development. A society of rugged individualists exchanged their constricting state of nature for the equality, security, and justice of national public authority.

****

EDITORIAL NOTE: My "political frontier" proposition lacks the drama, precision, and documentation that normally accompany the announcement of another "new frontier." But the popular expansion of national public authority was a "new frontier" in the sense of an historical, societal, transforming experience in which our nation encountered an environment of challenge and adversity and—freshly infused with population, capital, and energy—expanded social, economic, and political opportunity. My "political frontier" thus performs an essential basic service (in the same way as did the original frontier hypothesis) of explaining history in a way that helps us simplify the past, understand the present, and speculate about the future.

****

The popular expansion of national public authority exerted a clear and important impact on America for a century after the closing of the original frontier. It enabled our young country to deal with serious national challenges; and it enhanced our democratic opportunities in much the same way and to a comparable extent as did the open natural environment. Expanding public authority also provided a nurturing and protective governmental environment for the continuing series of national experiences, or "mini-frontiers" (immigration, urbanization, industrialization, education, globalization, science, space, civil rights) that have shaped America and American democracy.

TWO TIMELY FRONTIERS
FOR AMERICAN DEMOCRACY

In fact, Americans discovered that national public authority functioned, in some ways, just as well as or better than the wild frontier. Whereas New World conditions fostered freedom, individualism, and independence, the subsequent popular growth of public authority secured the more elusive blessings of equality, security, and justice for the people of our republic. The government actually could create, distribute, and re-distribute values and benefits more progressively than did the state of nature.

We might say, then, that we have experienced two timely, overlapping "frontiers," or challenging developments, that have proven historically central to our Great Experiment—the original challenge of an open, natural environment and the subsequent challenge of political nationalization. These natural and political frontiers—working together as a continuous, favorable systemic environment—began and sustained America's pursuit of democratic ideals throughout our national history. Thus American democracy continued to work well within a favorable national environment—encouraging democratic ideals such as equality, security, and justice.

However, just as with our original natural frontier, there is no reason to assume that national public authority can last forever; and Webb's "unpleasant logic" hangs hauntingly over distempered America.

....

AMERICA'S NEXT DEMOCRATIC FRONTIER?

Now, therefore, grave men and grave women are still searching for the next great frontier of American democracy, trying to define and achieve the proper systemic environment, philosophical foundation, and political formula for sustaining our historic Great Experiment.

"THE NEW ECONOMY"

Furthermore, with communism now moribund, future democracy is being defined almost exclusively within a capitalist frame of reference. Interestingly, too, some now consider the "New Economy" (rapid business growth and high employment through modern technology, limited government, and globalism) the next best thing to a new frontier for American democracy. The notion is that a lengthy period of free-market prosperity promotes social community and democratic ideals much as did our original natural frontier and the subsequent system of popular national authority.

Fast Company Magazine defines the New Economy—of course with proper literary flourish as one of its evangelistic agents—as a new way of life that involves expansion of individual opportunity, the disruptive energy of ceaseless innovation, and the transformative power of information technology ("What Is the State of the New Economy?" September 2001, accessed online at www.fastcompany.com).

Back during the presidential election campaign of 2000, candidate George Bush articulated the New Economy very effectively in consonance with the requisite sentiments of a true democratic frontiersman: "There is a new economy" and "Many of the changes in the new economy are happening in spite of government." As recounted by **Alan M. Webber** in "Vote: The New Economy's First Campaign," our President-to-be effusively cited the blessings of the new economy technology:

> "When I think about the power of the Web, I immediately think of people with disabilities and the Web, of rural America and the Web, of libraries and the Web, of education and the Web . . . The Web is freeing people . . . And when it happens, some young Hispanic kid in Texas is going to say, 'You know, this high-tech business is meant for me too. I'm going to start my own dotcom. I'm going to get an engineering degree at Texas A&M, or the

University of Texas.' It's my job and the job of the responsible citizenry of the United States, to send the message that this experience is meant for everybody. If you work for it and make the right choices, you can win." (*Fast Company Magazine*, October, 2000, accessed online at www.fastcompany.com),

However, others question the staying power and civic blessings of our turn-of-century economic boom. *Business Week Magazine*, for example, a leading national business journal, worries about sustainability and broader ramifications of the New Economy environment in a special report on "America's Future: The Boom, the Bust, Now What?" (August 27, 2001). *Business Week's* editor, apparently trying to be positive, anxiously generalizes that "we are in a very uncertain time of acute, short-term problems combined with long-term potential." (accessed online at www.businessweek.com)

• **Lee Walczak** and his team, in an article about "The Mood Now" in that special report, articulate more elaborately their editor's anxious generalization:

If history is any guide, America could have reasonably expected to slouch toward the new millennium in a fin de siecle funk. Instead the U.S. economy rocketed through the Nineties at what used to be called Internet speed. Propelled by the potent mix of information technology and ready capital, the economy broke free of the gravitational pull of slow growth and soared for the stars. The result was a virtuous cycle of prosperity that soothed deep-seated social ills even as it appeared to defy the laws of physics—and economics. The nation experienced rapid growth, plentiful jobs, glorious—or so it seemed—investment opportunities, and not even a speck of inflation for the Fed to stomp on.

Then every thing went suddenly, spectacularly wrong. With a swiftness that caught business leaders and economists off guard, the extraordinary New Economy boom flared like a supernova and went dark. The aftermath has been ugly: a year-long downturn of unexpected duration and depth, an investment-led slump that still holds the U.S. and the world economy in its grip. The Big Bust vaporized corporate profits, scorched investment portfolios, laid waste to the technology sector, and humbled scores of dot-com "visionaries." It has also inspired endless soul-searching about the meaning of the celestial fireworks we witnessed. The question on everyone's lips: Now what? (accessed online at www.businessweek.com)

• **Richard S. Dunham** and **Ann Therese Palmer**, in another *Business Week* article ("Governing a Nation Divided"), focus on the political ramifications of the New Economy, asserting that America is entering the new century with disturbingly divergent philosophies and growing frustrations:

As Election 2000 so vividly illustrated, there are now two distinct Americas—split along geographic, social, religious, and racial lines—that demand entirely different things from government. That makes forging a consensus ferociously difficult . . .

Essentially, the U.S. is now split into New Economy suburbs and rural backwaters, a development that has produced a red-zone/blue-zone political map where the two populations ask entirely different things from government—and vote in diametrically opposite ways. Meanwhile, the number of citizens who don't bother to vote at all continues to increase. (accessed online at www.businessweek.com)

- **Aaron Bernstein** acknowledges, too, in a piece on "The Human Factor," a nagging, double-edged tendency of the New Economy environment:

Absent a full-blown recession, though, skilled workers are likely to remain in short supply. The same may not hold true at the bottom of the labor market, which is unlikely to see solid wage growth without a return to the extraordinary growth levels of 2000. That leaves the U.S. facing renewed social cleavages as those on the top continue to gain while the rest struggle to keep up. (accessed online at www.businessweek.com)

- Furthermore, **Amy Borrus** frets about social and class problems related to growing immigration in "Land of Shrinking Opportunity." She notes that immigration swells the labor pool at the low end, jeopardizing wages of unskilled Americans and pushing the wage gap wider. Furthermore, in a slow-growth environment, increased immigration pressures states to expand social services just as tax receipts dwindle. "If that goes on for long, immigration may start to look less like an economic safety valve and more like a social burden" (accessed online at www.businessweek.com).

- **Others challenge the New Economy's basic, essential promise of steady, continuous growth and good times free from governmental control.** *The Economist*, for one, has labeled America's contemporary condition the "Bubble Economy"—an inflated financial bubble that could burst suddenly or turn into an economic depression; and it suggests easing inflationary pressures through governmental action ("America's Bubble Economy," April 16, 1998). **Bruce Freed**, head of a strategic public affairs and planning firm, already detects growing public unease about unchecked business power ("How the New Economy Is Reshaping Politics," *The Hill*, January 26, 2000):

What's happening is that the New Economy at long last is reshaping American politics. It is moving forward a new constellation of personal issues and concerns that are changing the political balance in the country and Congress. Already, these issues and concerns are prompting the public to look at government as a helper.

Another analyst, Philosophy Professor **Liu Ben** of the Chinese Academy of Social Sciences (People's Republic of China), dismisses the very idea of the

New Economy as a modern expression of capitalist crisis. In an interview ("Bubble Economy and Bubble Culture," *China Youth Daily*, June 6, 1999), he says:

> The Western capitalist countries issue this propaganda in order to use the so-called knowledge-based economy to hide the decline of its substantive economy, to hide the profound crisis of capitalism, and to conceal the fact that it is fighting with developing countries for resources. (accessed online at www.sinopolis.com)

Surely, America has benefited from several decades of technological restructuring, the growth of electronic commerce, the end of the cold war, and the opening of a global market. But it does not seem that the New Economy is our next democratic frontier. Besides the fact that (as I adamantly emphasized in my introduction) America means more than economic prosperity, the New Economy has not yet bolstered significantly (or permanently) the sagging systemic foundation of our national democratic experiment; and, in some ways, the New Economy is proving stubbornly oblivious to democratic ideals.

....

AMERICA'S HISTORIC DEMOCRATIC BOOM MAY—OR MAY NOT—HAVE BUSTED

In other words, our long-running democratic boom perhaps has been busting since America lurched past mid-Twentieth Century. The troubling pronouncements (by Chancellor, Galbraith, Schlesinger, and others) during the 1990s may substantiate Tocqueville's "anxiety", Turner's "shock", and Webb's "unpleasant logic" about the eventual future of American democracy.

Alternatively, however, the uncertainty and turbulence of the past half century could be viewed simply as the unavoidable trauma of systemic transformation whereby America divines its next democratic frontier. The natural environment of the Western frontier may indeed have yielded to urban crowds and civilization; and the political frontier of national public authority possibly may have reached its limits; but, just as logically, changing environments and new frontiers may still beckon future experiments in democratic ideals. In other words, turn-of-century America's national distemper could presage another real, timely, expansive democratic frontier and systemic transformation. Our uncertainty and turbulence of the past few decades may represent, not "dying" America, but the painful, vital "rebirthing" of our Great Experiment.

Arguably, numerous interesting, potential "new frontier" developments (including the New Economy) are now impacting the course of American democracy. For example (as we will discover in a later discussion on governance), rapid technological progress—in such forms as "Electronic Democracy", "Teledemocracy", and "Digital Nation"—is changing our representative system of governance in important ways; and the U.S.-Mexican border has been promoted as "La Nueva Frontera," where "our economic, cultural and political future is being forged" and where "the Century of the Americas" is being born ("The New Frontier," *Time Magazine Special Report*, 2001, accessed online at www.time.com). The list of other possible new frontiers is endless—globalism, science, space, medicine, human rights, vegetarianism, time travel—and there's even a *New Frontier Magazine of Transformation* for New Age thinkers.

But all of these developments, somewhat like the New Economy, seem less effectual or promising than one might ask of a systemically rebirthing experience; and thus the lights are still burning late in Washington and throughout the world over the future of American democracy.

TENTATIVE SYSTEMIC ASSESSMENT

It is impossible at this time to assess fully the historical nature and significance of America's systemic condition during the past few decades; we're too close temporally and emotionally to adequately characterize contemporary developments and patterns as either "busting" democracy or the beginnings of a new, vibrant, democratic frontier. However, I will attempt to summarize three tentative mainpoints of my propositional observation about the systemic condition of American democracy:

(1)   A starting-point of my transformational analysis is that American democracy began and prospered in a favorable setting, but that systemic environment has declined over time.

(2)   To be specific, our original, open, natural frontier has been closed for many years, and the subsequent popular expansion of national public authority appears to have slowed somewhat.   At the least, our favorable systemic environment has been constrained significantly.

(3)   While it is impossible to characterize our systemic condition of the past few decades as "busting" or "dying" or "rebirthing" America, it is clear that broad, sweeping, unsettling developments are transforming American democracy.

. . . .

SUMMARY COMMENT

My hypothetical argument is that Tocqueville's anxiety, and Turner's shock, and Webb's unpleasant logic have become our contemporary reality—a massive, disparate population crammed together in a fixed systemic environment, with limited room to breath or to experiment

societally, and at the same time facing stubborn challenges of philosophical nature. Gone is the free land, with its personal liberty and political opportunities. Apparently stalled, too, is the expanding force of national public authority that, with popular support, secured egalitarian benefits.

Thus have faltered (as we will see in the next few chapters) the auspicious foundations that produced a practical people with civic virtue, that fashioned political mechanisms linking these people with their leaders, and that supported a sufficiently effective and efficient government. We are sorely in need of a genuine new frontier for American democracy as the Twenty-First Century unfolds.

CHAPTER 5

PROPOSITION NUMBER TWO:

"WE HAVE ENTRAPPED AMERICAN DEMOCRACY WITHIN A PHILOSOPHICAL CIVIL WAR."

My thesis of American democracy continues with the notion that our country, besides possessing propitious original systemic conditions, also has enjoyed, historically, a conducive national mindset for expanding public authority on behalf of democratic ideals. In other words, a distinctly American national culture has been instrumental in producing the continuous blessings and benefits of American democracy for the past two centuries. Unfortunately, the most disruptive development in contemporary America is a divisive struggle over democratic ideals, cultural values, and principles of governance. In an era, ironically, of economic and international well-being, we have plunged deep into a morass of serious and stubborn philosophical questions, some of which—like the role of religion and the power of central government—have dogged our nation since its birth and now threaten the future of American democracy.

....

AMERICA IS ENGAGED IN A PHILOSOPHICAL CIVIL WAR OVER DEMOCRATIC IDEALS, CULTURAL VALUES, AND PRINCIPLES OF GOVERNANCE

The historical importance and continuity of American national culture for our democratic endeavor cannot be overstated. According to **Ronald Inglehart**, "In the long run, democracy is not attained simply by making institutional changes or through elite-level maneuvering. Its survival also depends on the values and beliefs of ordinary citizens" ("Culture and Democracy", 2000, 96). Or as University of Arizona English Professor **John Harmon McElroy** explains in *American Beliefs: What Keeps a Big Country and a Diverse People United* (1999):

> Historical cultures allow human beings to live in society with other human beings, something that requires a shared sense of a right way to live. Human beings have a "moral imagination," which is to say that we are capable of imagining right conduct and need to live with other human beings according to a right way of behaving. A set of right belief-behaviors is as indispensable to human well-being as food and water. In many instances in history, ordinary men and women have preferred to suffer death rather than violate a belief-behavior of their culture. (accessed at www.barnesandnoble.com)

A NATIONAL ARGUMENT ABOUT "WHAT AMERICA MEANS" AND "HOW AMERICA OUGHT TO WORK"

Now, despite unrivaled and acknowledged prominence as the world's leading democracy, America is engaged in a national argument over democratic ideals, cultural values, and principles of governance. I will not dwell further or extensively at this point on the contentious course of democratic ideals in general, since the continuing evolution of individualism, freedom, and justice is the broad focus of my manuscript. Shifting ideas about such ideals are an important element of the contemporary philosophical struggle; but I'm concerned here more specifically and analytically with two inter-related developments of central consequence within the philosophical civil war—our national debate over cultural values and the neopopulist movement of direct democratization—that pose different and disturbing challenges for American democracy. In fact, these dual developments now confound conventional democratic politics, distracting and detracting from the progressive pursuit of generalized democratic ideals. For example, heated cultural issues (such as abortion, homosexuality, and school prayers) and issues of representational governance (such as our recent Electoral College drama, the unsavory role of special interest money, and the politics of personal destruction) now interfere significantly with rational debate about a diversity of public initiatives such as civil rights, education, health care, welfare, and even national defense.

Of course, America has always experienced similar anxieties and cross-pressures of normative nature; what makes the contemporary argument consequential are the cumulative forces of philosophical turmoil and systemic constraints, enhanced by a technological revolution and empowered by resurgent populism, all oriented toward dramatic democratic change. Such developments increasingly disorient traditional American democracy; and, unless addressed, they could disrupt the future workings of our national democratic experiment.

In effect, we have entrapped our Great Experiment within a philosophical civil war about "what America means" and "how America ought to work". Various forces and powerful factions now struggle for control of the American experiment in terms of newly contentious ideals, substantive values, and procedural principles, presenting a national challenge that is qualitatively different from anything experienced within the past century.

GENERAL MOOD

Our philosophical civil war can best be described as an unprecedented national brawl, an anarchic streetfight, a political free-for-all among disparate forces challenging the status and course of American democracy. This is a systemic convulsion, an explosive reconsideration of democratic ideals, mixed with destabilizing cultural values, along with the possibility of rearranged governance—all during, and perhaps reflecting, increasingly adverse systemic conditions for American democracy. The contemporary war defies easy definition because there are no clear ideologies, armies, or battlelines, and because there are too many dimensions, contradictions, and inconsistencies for traditional characterization. However, I will attempt to convey my view of the basic nature and crosscurrents of the war.

The general mood of today's unsettling debate is one that supports democratic principles in general but questions, for a variety of reasons, the direction of American democracy. On one hand are hyper-champions of democratic ideals (particularly freedom) whose concept of democracy emphasizes the values of traditional, majoritarian, advantaged society. On the other hand are similar hyper-champions of democratic ideals (especially equality) whose concept of democracy emphasizes the values of an emerging, heterogeneous, disadvantaged society. More often than not, the first camp favors a private-sector route to proper ideals and values (somewhat like the situation during our original, natural environment) and finds much to dislike about the contemporary democratic experiment; and the latter camp usually finds activist government (as in the historic expansion of public authority) in keeping with their views about ideals and values, views that fit more comfortably in recent development of the democratic experiment. Obviously contributing to the anxiety of this situation is the fact that the traditional, majoritarian culture is in danger of losing its historically dominant status in an increasingly diverse and divergent America.

Now I need to backtrack—and repeat my statement that this is a superficial conveyance that misses the variety and contentiousness of this debate. My emphasis on the central clash between traditional/majoritarian and emerging/heterogeneous forces ignores a growing libertarian movement that rejects both governmental and societal control—regardless of its philosophical orientation. These rabid democrats dislike governance and authoritarianism— period. They just want to be left alone in pursuit of their democratic dream.

The contemporary scene is one of countless, disparate factions running amok with particularistic ideals, values, and principles for improving America; and every faction employs strategies and tactics befitting its immediate needs of the moment. About the only commonality among these disparate forces, beside their disrespect for civic moderation and their rejection of normal rules of the political game, is their intense determination to reshape America.

INTERLINKED STRUGGLES

It would be an incredible stretch to characterize today's philosophical civil war as a single national struggle between clear and coherent movements. There is no comprehensive framework of philosophical war; and most Americans know and care very little about such political warring. However, the dominant forces and substantive aspects of their struggles are linked together in several important ways that represent a serious challenge to America. In the first place, the various battles—over democratic ideals, cultural values, and principles of governance—are occurring simultaneously, a fact of more than casual significance. Secondly, there are some overlapping issues and constituencies, thus merging and magnifying the impact of seemingly disjointed causes. Thirdly, these various conflagrations reach beyond local and regional politics to philosophical issues of national consequence. Most importantly, these causes and issues share kinship in that they are disruptive of the prevailing direction and character of American history. After two centuries of democratic progress, values nationalization, and governmental centralization, these simultaneous, overlapping, far-reaching forces are now rebelling against an America they find increasingly unacceptable. In summary, the anarchic troops do not dress in similar, recognizable uniforms, march in lockstep unison, or chant the same slogans; but collectively, they constitute a serious threat to the continued course of American democracy.

Today's convulsion may be more disruptive than rational, and the disparate factions may or may not represent the majority of Americans; but this philosophical civil war, in tandem with our declining systemic environment, is forcing us as a nation to deal with some hard, basic questions about America's ideals, values, and governance.

MURKY HISTORICAL BACKGROUND

The average person, uninvolved directly but seriously impacted by this philosophical civil war, might reasonably ask why we are flagellating ourselves about "what America means" and "how America ought to

operate" at this late date in our country's history. Surely, one might expect, these debates were settled in the beginning, when our country was founded. But the reality is that America's historical, fundamental law, for all its strengths, is rather murky on these points.

American history and fundamental law provide mixed and muted directions about democratic ideals, cultural values, and the mechanics of governing. Our Founders created an amazing and enduring legacy in the Declaration of Independence, the Constitution, and the Bill of Rights. But, in important respects, they packaged a very loose system of democratic principles and practices in a "bundle of compromises" and on a "fill-in-the-blanks" foundation, leaving succeeding generations to deal with unresolved questions as they travel the course of history. America therefore began and has functioned without solid, consistent, coherent, comprehensive philosophical foundation.

PHILOSOPHICAL PURPOSELESSNESS

No one should be surprised that contemporary America is re-visiting its rather nebulous vision of democracy and democratic ideals. Contending concepts of philosophy and politics have been central to our Great Experiment, and those contentions have chronicled the entire history of the United States. Disputes about freedom and equality and justice dominated the founding of our country and almost tore it apart in the mid-nineteenth century.

Benjamin R. Barber provides one of the most creative and interesting treatises on American democracy in *A Passion For Democracy* (1988) by claiming that our philosophical fuzziness has been an historical blessing:

> The hypothesis offered here is that America has never had enduring public purposes and that for a long time this was properly taken to be one of the nation's fundamental strengths . . . .The constitutional solution was thus a radical and wholly untested challenge to the traditional wisdom of republican thought, one that turned the nation's early years into an unprecedented historical experiment . . . For many, many years, in many, many ways, the experiment achieved a remarkable success. (41-42)

Philosophical purposelessness was not simply an accidental cost of implementing the American experiment, Barber asserts, but was the guiding principle of its success. "What began as necessity and soon turned to virtue had by the middle of this century become an awesome American ideal—the finest product of American exceptionalism" (49). Furthermore, he says, this absence of democratic philosophy has functioned for most of our history as the foundation of American political consensus—an agreement to agree on nothing substantive, to avoid public values as defined by republican theories or collectivist ideologies. "The republic worked because it never tried to contrive a center; and thus, by eliciting the assent of the citizenry to this value default, acquired a center after all—in the acquiescence of the people to purposelessness" (50).

Over time, of course, we moved along an uneven path toward freedom and equality, nationalized values, and centralized governance. The most serious challenge to the prevailing direction of American development was settled militarily by the Civil War; and we continued along the bumpy road of democracy. Now, due to our deteriorated systemic environment and philosophical civil war, those same basic questions (not slavery but similar concerns about ideals, values, and governance) are back as purposeful challenge to traditional indefiniteness. As Barber says, "The present dilemma arises therefore not from a loss of purposes but from changes in the conditions that traditionally made public purposelessness an effective, even necessary feature of the compromises that permitted America to flourish" (41-45).

CHANGING DEMOCRATIC CALCULUS

Some suspect, however, that after two centuries of loose philosophical functionalism, America may be reconsidering and redefining its democratic soul. Michael J. Sandel, in *Democracy's Discontent: America in Search of a Public Philosophy* (1996), concludes that we have changed our definitions of liberty, public life, and citizenship over time. Our "utilitarian calculus" of the past served us well, Sandel says, but "Despite the achievements of American life in the last half-century, our politics is beset with anxiety and frustration" (accessed online at www.harvard.edu).

POLITICAL RIPENESS

The inevitable course of our democratic experiment thus has reached a state of sufficient contention, or political "ripeness", for national debate. What is surprising, I guess, is that it has taken us so long to reach our current frenzy. It will suffice here to say that we may have arrived at the quantitative and qualitative boundaries of our national democratic experiment—too many people crowded into a constrained environment wrought with philosophical tensions, thereby maximizing competitive, unprecedented, and dysfunctional claims upon the broad, democratic ideal.

Therefore, I want to move on to those critical issues—our contemporary debate over cultural values and the renewed argument about principles of governance—that pose dramatic challenge for American society.

....

WE NOW ARE CONDUCTING AN INTENSE NATIONAL DEBATE OVER AMERICA'S BASIC CULTURAL VALUES ("CULTURE WARS")

America's contemporary debate over cultural values—popularly referenced as "Culture Wars" or "The Culture War"—is a disjointed but

far-reaching development. Countless individuals, institutions, and movements now hope to determine, essentially and absolutely, America's basic values as a nation. After two centuries of functional indefiniteness, we are conducting an intense national debate over "what America means"; and we seem to be heading toward a national cultural showdown.

DIFFERENT SYSTEMS OF MORAL VISION

To many, the defining framework of the culture war is destructive partisan battling between Democrats and Republicans, or the persistent rancor between liberals and conservatives. To others, it has been simply "Bill and Hillary-versus-the vast, right-wing conspiracy." But the values struggle is broader, deeper, and more consequential than politics and personalities. As **James Davison Hunter**, Director of the University of Virginia's Institute for Advanced Studies in Culture, explains in *Culture Wars: The Struggle To Define America* (1991):

> . . . America is in the midst of a culture war that has and will continue to have reverberations not only within public policy but within the lives of ordinary Americans everywhere . . . At stake is how we as Americans will order our lives together. (34)

According to Hunter, today's culture clash is rooted in different systems of moral vision and worldviews deriving from moral authority. The war pits cultural conservatives, or those inclined toward orthodoxy, against cultural liberals, defined as those inclined toward the spirit of the modern age. (Actually, he uses the term "progressives" but I prefer the more common "liberal" appellation.)

The conservatives share a commitment to a consistent, unchangeable concept of what is good, who we are, and how we should live. They believe that moral authority comes from above and for all time. For the liberals, on the other hand, moral authority tends to be defined within the experience of contemporary society; and they view truth as a process that is forever unfolding. Even liberals of religious convictions can translate their historic faith according to the prevailing assumptions of modern life.

Hunter is emphatic about the significance of this debate:

> . . . the conflict is deeper than mere "differences of opinion" and bigger than abortion, and in fact, bigger than the culmination of all the battles being waged. As suggested earlier, the culture war emerges over fundamentally different conceptions of moral authority, over different ideas and beliefs about truth, the good, obligation to one another, the nature of community, and so on. (49)

Hunter traces the cultural struggle across numerous fields of conflict—family, education, media, the arts, law, and electoral politics; and he connects dots among seemingly disparate disputes to a struggle over national life itself:

> . . . the contemporary culture war is ultimately a struggle over national identity—over the meaning of America, who we have been in the past, who we are now, and perhaps most important, who we, as a nation, will aspire to become in the new millennium. (50)

THE CENTRALITY OF RACE

Of course, we cannot discuss American history and the current cultural struggle without focusing, directly and candidly, on the most confounding factor and flaw of our national democratic experience—race and racism. Just as slavery played a key role in earlier America (precipitating a civil war), racial factors figure prominently in today's cultural divide. It's not simply black-white animosities; America's democratic dilemma also incorporates ethnic, religious, and nationality considerations of increasing complexity. Predictably, white Americans generally feel more comfortable with conservative cultural orthodoxy while non-white Americans and other traditionally disadvantaged people quite often have a different vision of national destiny.

Also predictably, as America becomes more societally diverse, these differing philosophical orientations will contaminate an endless list of volatile political issues. Journalists **Thomas Byrne Edsall** and **Mary D. Edsall** capture the nature of this volatility in *Chain Reaction: The Impact of Race, Rights, and Taxes on American Politics* (1991):

> In a steady evolutionary process, race and taxes have come to intersect with an entire range of domestic issues, from welfare policy to civil service testing, from drug enforcement to housing regulation, from minority set-aside programs to the decline in urban manufacturing jobs, from prison construction to the globalization of economic competition, from college admissions standards to suburban zoning practices, from highway construction to Federal Communications Commission licensing procedures. In the struggle for government and private-sector resources, race has become a powerful wedge, breaking up what had been the majoritarian economic interests of the poor, working, and lower-middle classes in the traditional liberal coalition. Taxes, in turn, have been used to drive home the cost to whites of federal programs that redistribute social and economic benefits to blacks and to other minorities. (3-4)

According to Edsall and Edsall, race, mixed with taxes, and joined by a rights revolution (on behalf of, among others, criminal defendants, women, the poor, non-European ethnic minorities, students, homosexuals, prisoners, the handicapped, and the mentally ill), has created a "chain reaction" realignment of the electorate that has important ramifications for the Great Experiment:

> . . . at stake is the American experiment itself, endangered by a rising tide of political cynicism and alienation, and by basic uncertainties as to whether or not we are capable of transmitting a sense of inclusion and shared citizenship across an immense and diverse population—whether or not we can uphold our traditional commitment to the possibilities for justice and equality expressed in our founding documents and embedded in our most valued democratic institutions. (288)

REALITY OR RHETORIC?

The notion of cultural warfare has ignited a firestorm of commentary spanning the spectrum of American life and resonating with theological passion.

For example, priest and scholar **Richard John Neuhaus**, in *America Against Itself: Moral Vision and the Public Order* (1992), interprets our contemporary turbulence as a struggle between religion and secularism; and he claims that American democracy cannot flourish without a religious foundation.

Historian **Gertrude Himmelfarb** provides an equally structured intellectual framework—a thoroughly documented essay on societal culture since the beginnings of our country—in *One Nation, Two Cultures* (1999). Drawing upon the ideas of Adam Smith, Himmelfarb identifies two different schemes or systems of morality that exist simultaneously in human society, one that is strict and austere and another that is liberal and loose; and she claims that a counterculture of moral and religious relativism has overcome traditionally dominant conservative values and now dominates American life:

> In fact, the counterculture progressed far more rapidly and widely than even its most enthusiastic supporters predicted, for it proved to be nothing less than a cultural revolution. And this revolution was magnified by other concurrent ones: a racial revolution (inspired by the civil rights movement); a sexual revolution (abetted by the birth-control pill and feminism); a technological revolution (of which television was a notable by-product); a demographic revolution (producing a generation of baby-boomers and a powerful peer culture); a political revolution (precipitated by the Vietnam War); an economic revolution (ushering in the Great Society and the expansion of the welfare state); and what might be called a psychological revolution (the "culture of narcissism" as Christopher Lasch dubbed it). Each was momentous in itself and together they fed upon each other, fostering a growing disaffection with established institutions and authorities and a rejection of conventional modes of thought and behavior. (17)

Whereas the Founders addressed issues of republican governance and the mischiefs of faction, Himmelfarb says that later generations were concerned with the problems of democratic society—such as poverty, racism, unemployment, and inequality. Now, she contends, America faces an equally fundamental challenge of sustaining a culture that is morally right and good:

More recently we have confronted yet other species of diseases, moral and cultural: the collapse of ethical principles and habits, the loss of respect for authorities and institutions, the breakdown of the family, the decline of civility, the vulgarization of high culture, and the degradation of popular culture. In poll after poll, even at the height of economic prosperity, a great majority of the American people (a many as two-thirds to three-quarters) identify "moral decay" or "moral decline" as one of the major problems, often the major problem, confronting the country. (20)

Obviously, not everyone takes seriously such talk of cultural war in America. David Whitman simply dismisses the debate as cynical hyperbole. In *The Optimism Gap: The I'm OK—They're Not Syndrome and the Myth of American Decline* (1998), he calls the controversy "a kind of iron triangle of alarmism created by the media, advocacy groups, and business lobbyists" (accessed online at www.amazon.com). Similarly, **Neil J. Smelser** and **Jeffrey C. Alexander** claim that common values are still a social reality. In *Diversity and Its Discontents: Cultural Conflict and Common Ground in Contemporary American Society* (1999), they write, "we are convinced that the assertions about the death of common values are premature at best" (17). In fact, claims fellow sociologist **Alan Wolfe**, Americans agree about much more than is generally assumed by politicians and the media. Based on interviews with a couple hundred suburbanites, Wolfe concludes, in *One Nation, After All* (1999), that the American middle class is more accommodating, pluralistic, tolerant, and expansive than either side of the ideological spectrum has recognized:

> Although I cannot speak with certainty about all Americans, I am persuaded from the results of this study that there is little to the charge that middle-class Americans, divided by a culture war, have split into two hostile camps. Middle-class Americans, in their heart of hearts, are desperate that we once again become one nation. (320-321)

Furthermore, not everyone is enthusiastic about a single, idealized, national culture. In *Multi-America: Essays on Cultural Wars and Cultural Peace* (1997), Pulitzer-prize nominee **Ishmael Reed** argues the welcomed obsolescence of debate about "the American culture."

> MonocIturalism is essentially an anti-intellectual coalition . . . If white monoculturalists would make the same intellectual effort as the New White intellectuals whose essays appear in this book, then perhaps serious talk could get under way about a new, inclusive definition of the common culture. (xvii, xxvi).

Robert Wuthnow, Director of the Center for the Study of American Religion, suggests that we address our cultural struggle less confrontationally and more realistically and sensibly. In "The Culture of Discontent" (an essay in the collection edited by Smelser and Alexander), Wuthnow writes:

> In the final analysis, the current culture of discontent is both accurate and misleading. It is accurate insofar as is it registers the public's perception that all is not well in the United States at the end of the twentieth century. It is misleading insofar as it fails to recognize that social conditions themselves are the source of this discontent, more so than some failure of nerve or penchant for passivity on the part of individual Americans. (34)

Marc F. Plattner, editor of *Journal of Democracy*, more pointedly lectures that, amid such argumentation, perhaps we should focus on the fact that American democratic principles are being embraced around the globe ("Liberal Democracy, Universalism, and Multiculturalism", 1998):

> Today, as people from a multitude of cultures throughout the world are expressing their support for America's liberal democratic principles, it is not only ironic but also deeply troubling that the intellectual foundations of those principles are being eroded here at home. (162)

Apparently then, America is indeed engaged in a real national debate—of uncertain origin and mixed opinion but disturbing systemic significance— over cultural values.

....

WE ALSO ARE RE-EXAMINING OUR TRADITIONAL SYSTEM OF LIMITED, REPRESENTATIVE GOVERNANCE ("NEOPOPULIST DEMOCRATIZATION")

A less dramatic, relatively unfocused, but equally unsettling challenge of the philosophical civil war is the growing debate over "how America ought to work", or, more specifically, how we want to govern ourselves as a nation. Contemporary America—newly enamored of democratic ideals—is re-examining its historic experiment with limited, representative governance; and the forces of "neopopulist democratization"—now invigorated with technological prowess—press toward almighty direct democracy as the pre-eminent civic value and pre-destined solution to all our problems.

It is perhaps the irony of our time that democracy—carried to its frenzied extremity—may undermine the republican character of American government. The neopopulist movement, combined with contemporary cultural turmoil about "what America means", therein embodies our inherent capacity for undoing America's national democratic experiment.

THE CONTEMPORARY APPEAL OF DIRECT POPULAR GOVERNANCE

The global democratization movement is usually described in glowing terms, as the triumph of western ideals over communism and authoritarian

regimes. **Indeed, the condition of democracy as we begin a new century is remarkably improved around the world.**

In America, the centerpiece of western democracy, we have fallen head-over-heels in love, again, with the idea that unlimited virtue, wisdom, and potential reside in the individual rather than society, government, or any established institution. The direct democracy movement seeks, in effect, to achieve ultimate democracy, an idealized, unfettered public will without the bungling, broken mechanics of traditional American democracy. Energized by democracy's global ascendancy, the marvels of communications technology, and the emergence of a growing, driven force of democratic "true believers," direct democrats sense the inevitability of their revolutionary experiment. In fact, we now are flirting with a frantic, almost religious worship of pure self-governance.

The contemporary direct democracy movement views and adjudges our national democratic experiment from the compulsive, frenzied, singular perspective of "we the people." Increasingly and uncritically, we define, prioritize, and monitor democratic ideals as sacred emanations from the public. John Q. Public is courted, quoted, pampered, and pandered as never before. "Man-and-woman-in-the-street" comments are obligatory for all public issues. Town hall meetings, talk shows, public participation debates, public opinion polls, initiatives, referenda, faxes, e-mail, and the internet increasingly are the venues and staples of contemporary discourse.

More broadly, direct democrats celebrate their evolving "Free Agent Nation" and its dynamic independence from traditional society and governance. According to **Daniel H. Pink**, ("Free Agent Nation," *Fast Company*, Dec-Jan 1998):

> These groups—at once hardheaded and softhearted—are creating new communities. One part board of directors, another part group therapy, these small, self-organized clusters are part of the emerging free-agent infrastructure. Along with Kinko's, Office Depot, Staples, and Web sites too numerous to count, they are forming the new foundation of our economic and social lives. (136, 140)

Indeed, one New Agent citizen, citing Tocqueville, declares "This is going to be a new kind of democracy" (144).

A COMBINATION OF "ANTI-BIG" FORCES

America's neopopulist version of society and governance is a natural reaction to the historic growth of large, insensitive, unresponsive institutions—particularly "Big Government", which over many years concentrated power and resources and societal control in Washington. Actually, the direct democracy challenge is part of a universal movement of "anti-big" forces that have been changing our country and the world for decades.

- **John Naisbitt** introduced us to the transformational movement two decades ago in his best-selling *Megatrends: Ten Directions Transforming Our Lives* (1982). The opening sentence of his book communicates a grandiose effort to change America-as-we-know-it:

> As a society, we have been moving from the old to the new. And we are still in motion. Caught between eras, we experience turbulence. Yet, amid the sometimes painful and uncertain present, the restructuring of America proceeds unrelentingly. (1)

Naisbitt's thought-provoking analysis, especially his disparaging remarks about national government, struck a responsive tone with many Americans. He recounted our historic, growing reliance on government to provide for basic needs—food, housing, health, education—and as a buffer against the harsh realities of life. But as government became ever bigger in our lives, it failed us. Politically, he said, America has evolved into a society that is too varied for central government; "Furthermore, I would argue that decentralization is America's natural condition . . . centralization is anathema to democracy (99)."

THE CHALLENGE TO FEDERAL REPUBLICANISM

Besides questioning the general notion of a universal, centralized, national interest, the neopopulist movement specifically challenges the historic representational relationship between America's citizens and their leaders (our constitutionally-structured "republican form of government").

• Consider **John Naisbitt**'s outright dismissal of representative democracy in *Megatrends* (1982):

> Politically, we are currently in the process of a massive shift from a representative to a participatory democracy . . .

> We created a representative system two hundred years ago when it was the practical way to organize a democracy . . . For two hundred years, it worked quite well . . .

> But along came the communication revolution and with it an extremely well educated electorate. Today, with instantaneously shared information, we know as much about what's going on as our representatives and we know it just as quickly.

> The fact is we have outlived the historical usefulness of representative democracy and we all sense intuitively that it is obsolete. (160)

Of course, few suggest routine mass voting on policy issues; but the contemporary democratization movement is a serious calling—with interesting possibilities—for a growing number of American citizens and institutions.

National Policy Elections?   Some clamor, for example, for direct popular referendums on important federal issues such as taxes and abortion. Thus far, other than constitutional amendments, there have been no national policy elections; but the American people apparently would welcome such opportunity.

• "The American people want more say about their government at all levels," says **M. Dane Waters**, President of the Initiative and Referendum Institute in Washington. In a news release, the Institute reports that 58 percent of polled respondents favor establishing the citizen initiative process at the federal level, with only 21 percent opposed ("Americans Favor the Citizen Initiative," May 10, 2001, accessed online at www.iandrinstitute.org). Also, according to the website of the Coalition for National Referendum, national referendums have taken place in many countries, including Canada, England, Ireland, Italy, France, and Denmark; in South Africa, for example, apartheid was terminated through   direct   popular   vote   ("Referendums,"   undated,   accessed   at www.nationalreferendum.org).

• Knowledgeable observers, such as Pulitzer Prize-winning Columnist **David Broder**, predict its eventuality:

> I do not think it will be long before the converging forces of technology and public opinion coalesce in a political movement for a national initiative—to allow the public to substitute the simplicity of majority rule by referendum for what must seem to many frustrated Americans the arcane, ineffective, out-of-date model of the Constitution. (*Democracy Derailed*, 2000, 242)

• Already, some of my political science colleagues—namely **Theodore Becker** and **Christa Slaton**—are busily designing direct, popular policy-making through a new democratic paradigm that they call "Teledemocracy":

> From our experiences and experiments and those of many others mentioned in this book, we see that informed and deliberative citizenries are far wiser and fairer than any political elite could ever be . . . Those who hold political power today continue in the tradition of those who have held political power since the Federalist invented modern representative government.   They believe that clashing self-interests of elites produce a common good. We know that collaboration among informed representative samples of citizens does a far better job of that . . . When the general public comes to understand this, the way things are done politically will change . . . It is only a matter of time. (*The Future of Teledemocracy*, 2000, 212)

Abolition of the Electoral College? Perhaps because of our experience in Election 2000, pressure also is mounting to replace the Electoral College with direct, popular election of the U.S. President.
Public opinion polls have shown pretty consistently that Americans favor disbanding the Electoral College; and there have been more proposals for amending this historic mechanism of federal republicanism than for any other

aspect of the constitution, according to the National Archives and Records Administration ("Frequently Asked Questions on the Electoral College," undated, accessed online at www.nara.gov).

Aside from the legal issues of Florida's vote-counting controversy, there are strong theoretical and political arguments on both sides of this question.

• In the first place, Lawrence University Government Professor **Lawrence D. Longley** claims (in congressional testimony) that the Electoral College is an unfair distortion of popular will:

> The Electoral College is not a neutral and fair counting device for tallying popular votes cast for President in the form of electoral votes. Instead it counts some votes as more important than others, according to the state in which they are cast. As a result, these distortions of popular preferences greatly influence candidate strategy: certain key states, their voters, parochial interests, political leaders, and unique local factions, are favored. (quoted in James McGregor Burns, et al., *Government By The People*, Basic Version , 2002, 216)

• Former Senator **Patrick Moynihan**, citing lessons of history, counters that the Electoral College is a durable process for representing the concurrent majorities and diverse regions of our American nation:

> I would stress . . . the representation directly and indirectly of people and States . . . a principle that involved not just one majority, but in the most important sense, many majorities . . . the proposal before us (direct election of the president), in the guise of perfecting an alleged weakness in the Constitution, proposes the most radical transformation in our constitutional system that has ever been considered. (quoted in James MacGregor Burns, et al., *Government By The People*, Basic Version, 2002, 217)

It will be very difficult to abolish the Electoral College; but, as pressures mount, more and more states are altering their participation to reflect direct expression of popular will in the selection of the U.S. President.

Plebiscitary Governance? Actually, the neopopulist forces already are achieving surprising levels of success—particularly at state and local levels—through plebiscitary mechanisms such as initiative, referundum, and recall.

• **David Broder** speculates, furthermore, that plebiscites could become our nation's preferred process of governance (*Democracy Derailed,* 2000):

> At the start of a new century—and millennium—a new form of government is spreading in the United States . . . It has given the United States something that seems unthinkable—not a government of laws but laws without government. The initiative process, an import now just over one hundred

years old, threatens to challenge or even subvert the American system of government in the next few decades. (1)

Broder reports that voters in half the states and in hundreds of municipalities are passing laws and amending constitutions for a variety of goals:

> They ended affirmative action, raised the minimum wage, banned billboards, decriminalized a wide range of hard drugs and permitted thousands of patients to obtain prescriptions for marijuana, restricted campaign spending and contributions, expanded casino gambling, banned many forms of hunting, prohibited some abortions, and allowed adopted children to obtain the names of their biological parents . . . Not one of these decisions was made through the time-consuming process of passing and signing bills into laws—the method prescribed by the Constitution, which guaranteed the nation and each of the states "the republican form of government." Rather, they were made by the voters themselves—or whatever fraction of them constituted the majority on Election Day. This is the new form of government—an increasingly popular one. (4-5)

- According to news statements from the Initiative and Referendum Institute, two-thirds, or 68 percent, of polled American citizens approve of the initiative process in their states ("Americans Favor the Citizen Initiative"); and a larger proportion of state ballot items—61 percent—was approved in 1998 than in any election in that decade ("Voters Pass 37 Initiatives and Popular Referendums," November 5, 1998, accessed online at www.iandrinstitute.org).

- Columnist **Jeff Jacoby**, columnist for *The Boston Globe*, calls these citizen initiatives jewels of self-government:

> Initiatives are the last resort of desperate citizens, a way to check the power of remote or arrogant lawmakers. When politicians refuse to heed the public, when special interests block reform, when the governor is disdainful, when the courts offer no relief, voters in 24 states still have some leverage: They can bypass the Legislature and change the statute-book themselves . . .

> Citizen initiatives are good for democracy and a jewel of self-government. More often than not, they bear out Holmes's dictum that the best test of truth is the power of an idea to get itself accepted in the competition of the market. A ballot measure that wins the electorate's approval is likely to have been broadly publicized, vigorously debated, carefully analyzed, and widely discussed. If only the same could be said about all our laws. ("A Jewel in the Crown of American Self-Government," June 7, 2001)

But Broder expresses personal doubts about the wisdom of these initiatives:

> Though derived from a reform favored by Populists and Progressives as a cure for special-interest influence, this method of lawmaking has become the favored tool of millionaires and interest groups that use their wealth to

achieve their own policy goals—a lucrative business for a news set of political entrepreneurs. (1)

More fundamentally, he fears for the future of American democracy:

> Admittedly, representative government has acquired a dubious reputation today. But as citizens, the remedy to ineffective representation is in our hands each election day. And whatever its flaws, this Republic has consistently provided a government of laws. To discard it for a system that promises laws without government would be a tragic mistake. (243)

- **Alan Rosenthal**, a distinguished scholar of state legislatures, argues equally convincingly against plebiscitary governance. In *The Decline of Representative Government* (1997), he reasons:

> . . . the judgments rendered by a representative body, like those of the individual representative, derive in part from the give-and-take of discussion. More of a premium is on information, reason, commonality of interests, and even farsightedness than is the case in public judgments recorded by a poll or a referendum. Citizens are extraordinarily weak when it comes to deliberation. They are constrained by time, competing interests for whatever leisure hours they have, and the complexity that is usually involved . . . And there is little recourse once a snap judgment is reached. (40-41)

In a subsequent interview, Rosenthal laments the wilting resolve of today's leadership in the face of demofrenzied assault ("Too Much Democracy," *State Legislatures*, December 1997):

> If they were any more responsive to their constituents they'd be sleeping with them every night . . . .I think they're getting too democratic in the sense that they're too tied, they're too responsive, too worried about public opinion polls, too insistent on pleasing rather than in doing what's right. (14-15)

And he grudgingly acknowledges the success of the democratization movement:

> Government is no longer conducted with the consent of the governed, according to the original Federalist plan. It is conducted with significant participation by the governed, and by those who claim to speak for the public's interest, according to a more populist plan. The voices of elected representatives are being drowned out by pronouncements made on behalf of the public. Representative democracy, as the states had experienced it for several centuries, is now in decline. (4-5)

The neo-democracy movement articulates a pretty convincing case for progressive reform of America's political system; but it is just as easy to identify potential pitfalls such as unchecked executive power, weakened legislative performance, and unworkable public policy. Experience has shown, too, that organized special interests can easily manipulate and

dominate the plebiscitary process. Most importantly, the direct democracy movement, in conjunction with the raging cultural struggle, presents a fundamental, philosophical challenge to American democracy.

....

THIS IS A DIFFERENT
AND OMINOUS CHALLENGE.
FOR AMERICAN DEMOCRACY

The nature of the philosophical civil war demonstrates that we are dealing with something that, in several respects, is very different and potentially ominous for American democracy.

(1) Of first importance is the moral nature of today's struggle. The current conflict over democratic ideals, cultural values, and principles of governance is one of philosophical character and universal moral authority rather than a scramble for the traditional spoils—money, jobs, and power—of politics. Today's "philosofighters"—including both "culture-warriors" and "demo-fanatics"—conduct themselves as self-ordained Founding Fathers and Mothers of "New Millennium America," evangelical crusaders for an idealized society who often demonize the opposition and sometimes attack their own friends in their struggle for absolute victory. Virtually every public official in today's political process has been burned, at some time or another, by the fires of this morality war.

(2) Second is the comprehensive substantive scope of the battlefield. Some of the struggle falls along an ideological continuum, but this is not simply a Democrat-Republican fight or even a liberal-conservative competition. The range of debate is astounding—government vs. the individual, religion vs. secularism, community vs. diversity, rights vs. responsibilities, localism vs. nationalism vs. globalism—the list goes on and on. And the battle contaminates the entire universe of issues; for example, some of the most contentious debates in Congress over national defense now involve, not weapons systems, but abortion and homosexuality.

(3)   Third, this war is one of ubiquitous conflict waged in all forums and at all levels, from the power centers of Washington to the textbook committee of the local school board, and even to the playing fields of neighborhood youth sports. The combatants have no respect for established boundaries and inter-relationships of traditional institutions of governance or for the distinction between public sector and private sector activities; they fight the good fight anywhere and everywhere.

(4) A fourth distinctive dimension of this struggle is the sophistication of its

warfare. The participants are intelligent and well resourced, and they have mastered the art, weaponry, and technology of politics, thereby altering the nature and intensity of traditional American politics.

(5) Fifth, the current struggle is being waged in an intense environment of corrosive cynicism without the ameliorative influence of traditional political machinery; in fact, today's political machinery has adjusted to the civic brawl by contributing to the negativity of our times.

(6) Finally, we must take very seriously the potential long-term impact of today's philosophical civil war. Unlike other political movements or fights, this war, conducted within a declining national environment, could wreak permanent havoc on American democracy.

....

SUMMARY COMMENT

America is experiencing a philosophical civil war over ideals, values, and governance. What is new and dangerous about today's philosophical conflict is its moral nature, substantive scope, ubiquitous reach, sophisticated firepower, corrosive cynicism, and potential impact. Most Americans could care less, but for a disturbing number of activists and interests, this is an all-out survival struggle over fundamental ideals, values, and governance. Powerful forces on different sides of many divisive issues demand that whatever they want is a matter of moral imperative and public consequence which must be resolved, absolutely, now, with finality and authority, at least for themselves and perhaps for everybody in America.

Regardless of whether or not this is a case of fatal entrapment, the philosophical civil war—working in tandem with the uncertainties of a transforming system and anxious society—spells trouble for the future of American democracy.

CHAPTER 6

PROPOSITION NUMBER THREE:

"AMERICAN DEMOCRACY NO LONGER WORKS THE WAY IT HAS IN THE PAST."

Without question, America today is very different from historical America. For the past several decades, our adverse systemic environment and philosophical civil war have been impacting negatively on American democracy; and despite a healthy economy and international stability, the critical elements of our magical mix— our people, politics, and government—individually and collectively are evidencing the degenerative effects of democratic distemper.

A Quick Sketch of Transformational America. Just for the record, let's sketch a quick picture of transforming America. Historically, the elements of American democracy—our people, politics, and government—developed and functioned for a loosely structured system of limited, representative governance within a favorable environment; and, in fact, our historic system worked pretty well. The American people collectively have been a functional civic mix—self-interested, privately-oriented, publicly-disorganized, generally supportive of democratic ideals, and sufficiently engaged in a political process driven by political elites, powerful special interests, and dominant social groupings. Interaction between these politically unsophisticated people and their leaders necessitated the development of linkage organs—election campaigns, political parties, and news media, all tending toward democratic participation. Relatively unburdened, unconstrained institutions of governance functioned, efficiently enough, in pursuit of democratic policies and practices. Thus, democratic ideals such as individualism and equality thrived in a non-zero-sum game played loosely within a supportive environment of natural conditions and national authority. The magical mix worked its magic.

Now, under changed circumstances, the American people appear to be losing their civic virtue, the political machinery of American democracy is broken, and American government is malfunctioning. This manuscript is not an American government textbook or research project, so I will not attempt a fully documented presentation of the historical structures and ways of American democracy. I simply will characterize how and why our contemporary people, politics, and government are evidencing symptoms of systemic democratic degeneration; then I'll speculate in later chapters about where we're going in future America.

....

THE AMERICAN PEOPLE ARE LOSING THEIR CIVIC VIRTUE

The most discouraging aspect of contemporary America is that the American people are losing their civic virtue. Our national personality increasingly tends toward uncivic public character.

For decades, cynical notions have been replacing traditional concepts such as trust, responsibility, and participation in public life. Our cynicism has reached far beyond the political arena, infecting our relationships with virtually all institutions of society—our work, our schools, our churches, the media, sports, anything that smacks of authority and power. In the process, this growing "cyni-culture" seems to be undermining traditional American democracy.

I regret pointing my finger of blame at "we the people". It would be easier directing my attention toward popularized villains, such as crooked politicians and the special interests, as the dysfunctioning elements of American democracy. However, governmental and political reform will be meaningless and unattainable unless "we the people"—including both the public and our leaders—admit and address our unhealthy civic condition.

CIVIL SOCIETY AND AMERICAN DEMOCRACY

It has long been recognized that the nature of a country's government and politics depends, in important ways, on the basic societal ways and norms of its people. Certain civil associations, attachments, and principles must exist among the population in sufficient degree for sustained self-governance. In short, a healthy civil society provides a favorable foundation for stable democracy.

Civic Culture. **Although the ancient Greeks and successive philosophers deliberated extensively about civil society and democratic citizenship, systematic investigation and documentation is a relatively recent endeavor.**

Gabriel Almond and **Sidney Verba** conducted the definitive statement of functional civil society in their behavioral study of "civic culture" in the United States, England, Germany, Italy, and Mexico (*The Civic Culture: Political Attitudes and Democracy in Five Nations*, 1963).

Almond and Verba differentiated civic culture from more conventional ideas about "civics" and democratic life. While civics implies idealized notions about how citizens ought to behave, civic culture defines a situation in which real-world facts-of-life temper the civics ideal and make it work in actual political practice. Their commentary is so instructive that I want to quote fragmentarily and extensively from their concluding chapter on "The Civic Culture and Democratic Stability":

> The civic culture, which sometimes contains apparently contradictory political attitudes, seems to be particularly appropriate for democratic political systems, for they, too, are mixtures of contradictions . . . the democratic citizen is called on to pursue contradictory goals; he must be active, yet passive; involved, yet not too involved; influential, yet deferential . . . The comparative infrequency of political participation, its relative lack of importance for the individual, and the objective weakness of the ordinary man allow governmental elites to act . . . Yet the very fact that citizens hold to this myth—that they see themselves as influential and as obligated to take an active role—creates a potentiality of citizen influence and activity . . . This balance between consensus and cleavage is managed within the civic culture by a mechanism similar to the one that managed the balance between activity and passivity; that is, an inconsistency between norms and behavior . . . the civic culture allows a balance between apparently contradictory demands through the mixture of a set of norms . . . .and actual behavior . . . that are themselves in contradiction one with the other . . . In sum, the most striking characteristic of the civic culture as it has been described in this volume is its mixed quality . . . There is political activity, but not so much as to destroy governmental authority; there is involvement and commitment, but they are moderated; there is political cleavage, but it is held in check . . . The mixture of attitudes found in the civic culture, we have argued in this chapter, "fits" the democratic political system. It is, in a number of ways, particularly appropriate for the mixed political system that is democracy. (340-360)

Civic Virtue. **American democracy, according to this model of mixed cultural dynamics, thus requires that its citizenry possess, among its diverse inclinations and activities, a sufficiently positive level of collective, connective balance between personal, private interest and responsible public life.** It is necessary that we as a society adequately understand that our individual self-interest generally abides in and is consistent with the broader public good; we also must recognize that good citizenship sometimes must tilt the balance in favor of the public good.

This is not to connote anything negative about individualism or personal pursuits; nor does it suggest that we all must subscribe to official standards of noble motivation and civic purity. It certainly does not require that we have to agree with each other politically. In fact, very few of us ever contemplate, and many of us never demonstrate such "civic goodness". But, according to precepts of traditional democratic theory, we must subscribe sufficiently to ideas such as duty, trust, efficacy, and community. This collective civic virtue—a healthy balancing between private, personal, self interest and public citizenship—provides a vital ingredient to American democracy.

THE EMERGENCE OF UNCIVIL SOCIETY

Almond and Verba's version of civic culture may have been an acceptable description of America in the 1950s. Unfortunately, we have seen in the latter half of the past century a dissipation of civil society and civic life. There is obvious disconnect, among a growing proportion of the American people, between their personal, private lives and the public good. Increasingly, we seem to view the broader societal endeavor as irrelevant or contradictory to our own self-interests.

A Deficit of "Social Capital". **Robert Putnam,** Professor of Public Policy at Harvard's John F. Kennedy School of Government, pinpointed this disconnect in a 1995 article calling attention to America's potentially disastrous deficit of "social capital". In "Bowling Alone: America's Declining Social Capital" (*Journal of Democracy*, 1995), he unfavorably compared contemporary society with Tocquevillian democracy:

> When Tocqueville visited the United States in the 1830s, it was the Americans' propensity for civic association that most impressed him as the key to their unprecedented ability to make democracy work. "Americans of all ages, all stations in life, and all types of disposition" he observed, "are forever forming associations. There are not only commercial and industrial associations in which all take part, but others of a thousand different types— religious, moral, serious, futile, very general and very limited, immensely large and very minute . . . Nothing, in my view, deserves more attention than the intellectual and moral associations in America." (65)

Putnam's thesis was that Americans have withdrawn from civic life in the past few decades—from the simple act of voting to their affiliations with religious, labor, school, and fraternal organizations. Whereas Americans used to bowl in bowling leagues, Putnam said, now they're bowling alone.

Putnam's ideas drew a mixture of positive reviews and angry attack by reputable analysts; and even he admitted that his idea lacked sufficient documentation. In his more ambitious, comprehensive project—*Bowling Alone: The Collapse and Renewal of American Community* (2000)—Putnam addresses that deficiency with straightforward, voluminous data showing that Americans are indeed becoming civic truants (at least in terms of traditional public life):

> For the first two-thirds of the twentieth century a powerful tide bore Americans into ever deeper engagement in the life of their communities, but a few decades ago—silently, without warning—that tide reversed and we were overtaken by a treacherous rip current. Without at first noticing, we have been pulled apart from one another and from our communities over the last third of the century. (27)

Now, Putnam explains, societal changes have denigrated community and public interests:

> Over the last three decades a variety of social, economic, and technological changes have rendered obsolete a significant stock of America's social capital. Television, two-career families, suburban sprawl, generational changes in values—these and other changes in American society have meant that fewer and fewer of us find that the League of Women Voters, or the United Way, or the Shriners, or the monthly bridge club, or even a Sunday picnic with friends fits the way we have come to live. (367)

Putnam has compiled a bulging catalogue of such lost causes throughout the country, like the Glenn Valley Bridge Club in Pennsylvania, the Roanoke, Virginia, NAACP, the Berwyn, Illinois, VFW Post, Washington DC's Vassar alumnae, Dallas' Charity League, and Boston's Tewksbury Memorial High School marching band. Because of these developments, Putnam says, "Our growing social-capital deficit threatens educational performance, safe neighborhoods, equitable tax collection, democratic responsiveness, everyday honesty, and even our health and happiness."

Affirming Observations. **I can attest to Putnam's concerns with some observations and developments here in my own part of the world.**

•   **Most appropriate is the following one-paragraph item, buried in *USA Today*, about an incident in my home state of South Carolina:**

> SOUTH CAROLINA: Greenville — The Greenville County Library no longer has a community events bulletin board. Director Phil Ritter ordered it removed, saying his staff was caught in the middle of sniping from both sides of the political spectrum about what was on it. (July 29, 1997)

The Greenville County Library community events bulletin board is rich as Tocquevillian metaphor for civil America. Substantively and procedurally, it represents the essence of grassroots democracy—a voluntary forum open to anyone in the community to post announcements and read information of public interest. The unseemly demise of that bulletin board is a quiet declaration by ordinary citizens that their civic ideals and principles no longer sustain a community bulletin board in a public building; and it sends a subtle but profound message about the state of our civic health.

• **More recently, I noticed in my own home area of Alabama a newspaper headline declaring: "Next Meeting May Be Last For COUL"** (*The Anniston Star*, January 16, 2000). The Committee Of Unified Leadership) is a bi-racial group that has provided a constructive forum for discussing issues of local race relations in Calhoun County for the past three decades. COUL was formed voluntarily in 1971 by black and white residents from every part of the community. During its active years, about 50-75 members of COUL would meet twice monthly; as many as 175 people attended its annual meetings.

Now the organization seems to have lost its way. In recent years, attendance has fallen to ten or fewer persons; and fewer than twenty attended the annual meeting last year. According to Acting President Eddie Williams, "I think it's a shame those discussions aren't going on, but if we can't get a good crowd to come, maybe the organization should be dissolved."

Incidentally, at the advertised "next" and perhaps "last" meeting of COUL two weeks later, eighteen people raised their hands to continue its work. "We're going to try to generate interest in the younger people," said the acting president. But my local friends tell me privately that it's a lost cause.

• **Another recent Alabama headline posed similar but more generalized sentiments about the fading role of historically important African-American churches in southern society: "Are Black Traditional Churches Losing Their Relevance?"** According to *The Montgomery Advertiser* (July 13, 2000), the pastor of one of the South's most historic black churches—Dexter Avenue King Memorial Baptist Church—says that the nation's traditional black churches may be losing their missions because of changing society.

"There are scores of traditional African-American churches that continue to struggle with the issue as to how to remain relevant in the changing tide of the religious market," says the Rev. Michael Thurman; "This is a critical issue for us."

Rev. Thurman bases his concern on a just-completed study of traditional black churches throughout the country—such as his own church in Montgomery, First African Baptist Church in Savannah, Ebenezer Baptist Church in Atlanta, and Sixteenth Street Baptist Church in Birmingham—churches that in the past have served as the bedrock of their communities but now experience serious decline in membership and influence in southern society.

POLITICAL ESTRANGEMENT

Current research demonstrates unfortunately that we also are moving further away from the political responsibilities of democratic citizenship. According to the National Commission on Civic Renewal, our uncivic inclinations have led to startling estrangement from politics and public life.

The Civic Renewal Commission (headed by former Democratic Senator Sam Nunn and former Republican Education Secretary William Bennett) monitors a combination of indicators—such as civic trust, political participation, associational memberships, personal security, and family components—the kinds of things that Tocqueville would have considered if he had possessed such data and methodology. Their composite index of civic participation (using estimated figures for 1960-71) has plunged from a score in the high 120s in 1960 to the low 80s during the 1990s; and their index shows particularly notable estrangement from political activity such as voting, signing petitions, working for a political party, and running for office.

Although the Commission takes heart in recent data indicating that this plunge may have bottomed out, its report—*A Nation of Spectators* (1998)—concludes that America's public life is weaker than a generation ago:

> Civic health may be measured along several dimensions—participation in electoral politics, political and social trust, voluntary sector activity, and attitudes and conduct bearing on the moral condition of society, to name a few . . .

> Not all of these trends move in the same direction. Political participation and all forms of trust have declined significantly in the past generation, although there is some evidence of stabilization and perhaps even modest improvement during the past two years . . .

> But when most Americans evaluate our civic condition, their point of comparison is not the late 1980s or early 1990s, but rather their sense of how things were a generation ago. In this key respect, the Index of National Civic Health is consistent with the beliefs of most Americans: our overall civic condition is weaker than it was—and in need of significant improvement. (June 26, 1998, accessed online at www.puaf.md.edu)

DECLINING VOTER TURNOUT

Of course, the simplest, most direct indication of our depressed civic condition is voter participation—or nonparticipation—in national, state, and local elections over the past several decades. Only half of the voting age population actually took part in the hotly contested 2000 presidential election between Vice-President Al Gore and Governor George W. Bush. As a matter of fact, the 1998 (midterm) and 1996 (presidential) elections represent turnout low-points since World War II.

Furthermore, voter turnout decreased during the latter half of the Twentieth Century despite the dramatic influx of potential voters among women, blacks, and young people, and despite an apparently richer and more educated polity. According to data from the Federal Election Commission, the following proportions of voting age Americans have participated in presidential elections over the past half-century:

1952	1956	1960	1964	1968	1972	1976	1980	1984	1988	1992	1996	2000
62%	59%	63%	62%	61%	55%	54%	53%	53%	50%	55%	49%	51%

This pattern of extended electoral depression is such a commonly documented phenomenon as to merit little discussion here other than to quote **Curtis Gans**, Director of the Committee for the Study of the American Electorate:

> Every biennium American politics seems to produce new modern records for citizen political disengagement. And every year, the nation seems further and further from the political comity, cohesion, and consensus that makes possible the constructive address of citizen needs. In the 1998 election, only 11 percent of the 18-19 year olds eligible to vote for the first time bothered to go to the polls. The United States now stands 139th out of 163 democracies in the rate of voter participation. And the nation that prides itself on being the best example of government of, for, and by the people is rapidly becoming a nation whose participation is limited to the interested or zealous few. ("Table for One, Please: America's Disintegrating Democracy," *The Washington Monthly*, July/August 2000, accessed online at www.washingtonmonthly.com)

WHAT ABOUT YOUNG AMERICA?

These gloomy assessments would be less troubling if America's young people were maturing toward responsible citizenship. But available evidence indicates that they are not so inclined. Study after study indicates that the new generation of citizens has very little interest in American government and the democratic process. Consider the following recent news reports:

- "A Record Low—and No One's Cheering: A Census Survey Shows that Fewer Young Voters Are Going to the Polls"

According to most recent census data, slightly less than a third of all 18-24-year-olds voted in the 2000 elections, a record low turnout for this age group. According to **Richard Morin**, director of polling for *The Washington Post*, this anemic showing is distressing because overall turnout increased slightly in the latest election; furthermore, he notes:

> Even more ominous is the fact that the long-term decline in political participation among the young has occurred when other evidence suggests just the opposite should be happening . . . Yale political scientist Don Green notes that over the past 35 years, education levels have soared among young Americans. Participation dropped even in particularly competitive election years such as 2000. And across the country, it's never been easier to register to vote or to cast a ballot. (*The Washington Post National Weekly Edition*, January 14-20, 2002)

- "Harvard Goes to Washington? Not Anymore"

Perhaps the most direct message from young America is the fact, as pointed out in a Harvard University newspaper column, that today's graduates seem disinterested in working for their government:

> Harvard may once have nurtured public men and women, but the number of students from the Class of 2000 who are heading to D.C. next year to begin political or governmental careers can be counted on the fingers of your hands—with maybe a few toes thrown in . . . Apart from Harvard's plentiful crop of Truman scholars— who are obliged to take a governmental job in D.C. for the summer, at least—it's difficult to find anyone who'll be working inside the Beltway. (**Caitlin E. Anderson**, *Harvard Crimson*, June 8, 2000)

- "What Political Scientists Should Know
  About the Survey of First-Year Students in 2000"

Researchers at the UCLA Higher Education Research Institute (which has conducted surveys among our nation's college freshmen for the past 30 years) report a broad pattern of growing indifference among many students to important issues in American society . . . The proportion of students who keep up with political affairs is "the lowest percentage since HERI began reporting on first-year students in 1966"; and the data on free speech "ought to chill the blood of civil libertarians" (**Stephen Earl Bennett** and **Linda L. M. Bennett**, <u>PS: Political Science and Politics</u>, June, 2001).

- "College Freshmen Have The Blahs, Survey Indicates"

In an earlier story on the Higher Education Research Institute series, the Class of 2001 is depicted as "more bored with school, less interested in politics or social issues, and just plain lazier than any class in a generation."   UCLA Professor Alexander W. Astin characterizes these trends as "part of a larger pattern of disengagement of the American people from political and civic life in general" (**Rene Sanchez**, *The Washington Post,* January 12, 1998).

- "Survey: Young Voters Uninterested"

Another survey, conducted in 1998 for the National Association of Secretaries of State (to which I once belonged), finds widespread cynicism among Americans aged 15-24. The study's executive summary says that "young people today lack interest, trust, and knowledge about American politics, politicians, and public life generally. In these and other respects, the future for American democracy seems gloomy, indeed" (**Will Lester**, Associated Press, February 10, 1999).

- "Survey: Students Fail History Test"

Similarly, the younger generation demonstrates dismal comprehension of the historical fundamentals of American democracy. According to an American Council of Trustees and Alumni study at 55 top colleges and universities (including Harvard and Princeton), nearly 80 percent of seniors received a D or F on a high-school level American history test. Sen. Joseph Lieberman, D-Conn., quoting Thomas Jefferson, laments that "if a nation expects to be ignorant and free it expects what never was and never will be" (**Caren Benjamin**, Associated Press, June 27, 2000).

- "The Civics Deficit"

The situation among high school students is much the same, says Columnist **E.J. Dionne,** who notes a National Assessment of Educational Progress finding that most high school seniors are not proficient in civics. Editorializes the *St. Louis Post-Dispatch:* "When students in the world's most powerful democracy cannot see the value of representative government, we need to rethink the culture we have created" (*The Washington Post*, November 30, 1999).

A CIVIC CRISIS?

Logic tells us that such localized sentiments and developments—if indeed occurring increasingly throughout the country—spell trouble for the more formal, functional aspects of America's national democratic experiment.
Oxford University's **John Gray** harshly criticizes American culture for denigrating communal attachments and civic engagement; and he raises the possibility of an ungovernable, criminalized, violent society ("Does Democracy Have a Future?" *The New York Times Book Review*, January 22, 1995):

> Now that the Soviet collapse has deprived the American Government of the legitimacy it borrowed from the cold war, it is difficult not to foresee a further weakening of the civic culture in the United States, whose eventual result can only be economic decline. In a worst-case scenario, we may even glimpse a sort of Colombianization of the United States, in which failing political institutions become increasingly marginal in an ungovernable, criminalized and endemically violent society. (25)

Just as is the case in our cultural war debate, however, some dispute these cries of alarm. For example, columnist **E.J. Dionne** and a group of knowledgeable essayists claim that, contrary to the thesis of civic crisis, America is experiencing a boom of civic mindedness (*Community Works: The Revival of Civil Society in America*, 1998); and **Robert Wuthnow** purports that, while certain kinds of civic engagement may be declining, innovative new forms are taking their place (*Loose Connections: Joining Together in America's Fragmented Communities*, 1998).

We can argue subjective hypotheses and quantitative data all day, but it seems to me (based on my reading of research data and my own personal experience) that there has been a definite qualitative decline in civic behavior and civil society over the past few decades. Americans may be participating in new and different social activities in ways and at levels that compare, on the surface, with past patterns; but sustaining a supportive culture for American democracy requires that we engage, not simply dabble, in the civil community. There must be some degree of allegiance to the broader idea of citizenship (conveyed in such concepts as "civis", "demos", and "polis") in addition to our individual human need for personal enrichment, social interaction, economic gain, or racial-religious-ethnic attachment. Our new-found habits of connecting with somewhat similar but unknown beings in an electronic chat room, participating with business friends in a stock-trading group, enrolling in a neighborhood health club—these are not the essence of democratic citizenship; and such actions do not represent sufficient investment of social capital in civil society for the long run.

I believe **Theda Skocpol** and **Morris P. Fiorina** accurately depict the deficiencies of our current situation in *Civic Engagement in American Democracy* (1999):

> In personal lives and local communities, contemporary Americans are finding new ways to relate to one another and accomplish shared tasks. But if we look at U.S. democracy in its entirety, and bring issues of power and social leverage to the fore, then optimists are surely overlooking the downside of our recently reorganized civic life. Too many valuable aspects of the old civic America are not being reproduced or reinvented in the new public world run by memberless organizations. (499)

And they correctly define our civic assignment:

> Since the 1960s many good things have happened in America. New voices are heard, and there have been invaluable gains in equality and liberty. Vital links in the nation's associational life have frayed, though, and we may need to find creative ways to repair those links if America is to avoid becoming a country of detached spectators rather than fellow democratic citizens. (506)

It is debatable whether or not we can describe our problem as a crisis of virtue; however deteriorating civic life over the past few decades helps explain our contemporary democratic distemper; and the restoration of civic spirit will have to be an important priority for transforming American democracy. Just as importantly (as the following discussion will demonstrate), we also must devote considerable attention to the malfunctioning machinery (the media, political parties, and elections) of our Great Experiment.

....

THE POLITICAL MACHINERY
OF AMERICAN DEMOCRACY
IS BROKEN

Historically, there has existed in America an organic arrangement of political mechanisms—election campaigns, news media, and political parties—linking our people with their government. These mechanisms, working together as the political machinery of American democracy, have been critical to the success of our national democratic experiment. However, for several decades now, our political linkage system has suffered disrepair and disrepute. In short, the political machinery of American democracy is broken.

AN ORGANIC SYSTEM
OF REPRESENTATIONAL LINKAGE

America's elections, parties, and media were not designed originally as fully functioning organs of American representative democracy; they evolved, over time, from necessity. Some of these mechanisms developed integrally as formal interactions between the public and government (such as the electoral system); some developed consequentially (such as political parties); others simply coincided (such as the news media). But, collectively, they constituted an organically functioning support system linking the functional elements of our national experiment in democratic ideals.

The linkage machinery of American politics has worked in almost miraculous ways for over two centuries in translating public opinion into public policy (and just as importantly, in shaping public opinion on behalf of national policy goals). Normally, these political mechanisms transmit popular preferences to political officials (upward linkage) and, conversely, to relay the sentiments of those officials to their constituents (downward linkage). In the course of this essential mediating service, these linkage institutions perform the equally valuable function of bringing together diverse segments and moderating the divergent tendencies of American society. Sometimes unintentionally, inefficiently, and ironically, this complex system has made American national government sufficiently responsive to the varying special interests of its citizens while at the same time allowing the government to exercise responsibility for the broad public interest.

In simpler times, these vital linkage organs worked reasonably well. America needed intermediary mechanisms because direct democracy was inappropriate and impractical. Within a favorable and democratic environment, they served the needs of a relatively unsophisticated, uninterested, and disorganized people and their relatively unstructured government. Our organic system of elections, parties, and media worked well for our limited, representative system of governance.

A BROKEN SYSTEM

There is virtually universal agreement that the historic capacities of our parties, media, and elections have deteriorated; and the representational linkages between our people and our government have weakened.

Political Parties.   In the first place, our political parties have fallen into disrepair and disrepute. The political party system still dominates American politics, but the two major parties do a poor job of pulling us together or linking the people with their government; instead, they too often serve the interests of partisan hackdom and as conduits of special interest money and influence.

The contemporary American two-party system therefore is experiencing institutional decline—or "dealignment"—of systemic consequence, as described by **Ted Halstead** and **Michael Lind** in *The Radical Center: The Future of American Politics*, 2001):

> This striking dealignment suggests that our Democratic and Republican Parties have failed the two most important tests of American politics: the ability to unite a majority of citizens in a lasting coalition, and the ability to find workable solutions to the problems of our time. Having been captured by their own extremes, both parties are increasingly incapable of promoting majority views across a wide range of issues. Second, both remain so wedded to the ideas and institutions of the last century that neither has proven itself capable of rising to the challenges of the next.   Our nation's politics are dominated by two feuding dinosaurs that have outlived the world in which they evolved. (1-2)

The House Judiciary Committee hearings regarding the possible impeachment of President Clinton illustrate this point.   The impeachment hearing was a process of partisan harangue and bipartisan disgrace. Columnist **Tom Teepen**'s analysis during that distemperate period was directly on target:

> Both groups misrepresent the nation. You'd be hard pressed to find an outfit as monolithic as the GOP's even in a Moose hall these days. The Democrats look like a parody of diversity . . . these two Americas sit in judgment of an errant president and of one another . . . Power will end this business, of course. Will it be power giddy with opportunity and driven by its own indignation: or power, informed by wisdom instead, that seeks a resolution in political compromise that can be, as well, socially reconciling? ("Cultural Battle Rages in House over Clinton and United States," *The Monterey Herald*, October 10, 1998)

It is hard to imagine American democracy without parties, according to **Paul Allen Beck** and **Marjorie Randon Hershey,** but political life in the United States without the dominance of the Democratic and Republican Parties is no longer unthinkable (*Party Politics in America*, 2001):

The American parties face a range of difficult problems. The American electorate is more and more varied. The breakdown of traditional group ties encourages greater individualism. Voters respond with more differentiated loyalties. The great majority of voters maintain an identification with a political party but they also respond to candidates and issues, stylistic matters and ideologies. The result is a more diverse, complicated politics that no single set of loyalties and no single set of political organizations can easily contain. (331)

News Media. **The mainstream news media likewise have lost their historic role in providing information and ideas to the American people, bringing us together, and mediating/moderating public debate.** The people and public officials have figured out how to bypass the traditional press; and what's left today is very little news and even less public dialogue.

An unusually frank inside assessment of the media comes from **James Fallows**, former news magazine editor and author of *Breaking the News: How the Media Undermine American Democracy* (1996):

> Americans have never been truly fond of their press. Through the last decade, however, their disdain for the media establishment has reached new levels. Americans believe that the news media have become too arrogant, cynical, scandal-minded, and destructive. Public hostility shows up in opinion polls, through comments on talk shows, in waning support for news organizations in their showdowns with government officials, and in many other ways. The most important sign of public unhappiness may be a quiet consumers' boycott of the press. Year by year, a smaller proportion of Americans goes to the trouble of reading newspapers or watching news broadcasts on TV. This is a loss not only for the media but also for the public as a whole. (3)

University of Virginia Political Scientist **Larry J. Sabato** complains also that contemporary media coverage of politics too often savages politicians, the public, and good journalism *(Feeding Frenzy: How Attack Journalism Has Transformed American Politics,* 1991):

> Alexis de Tocqueville celebrated news organizations because "they maintain civilization." As press conduct during feeding frenzies has proved repeatedly, they can also decivilize politics. The legions of responsible and dedicated newsmen and –women must work to moderate the excesses that destroy confidence in their profession and threaten support for press freedoms. Journalists and journalism must feed less at frenzies and more at the table of fairness and civility. (246)

Elections. **Complementary to the wayward ways of the political parties and news media, our elections too often have become empty and demeaning experiences.** Campaigns and elections are held, but public participation and support are declining. Money and nastiness dominate as never before. Voters and candidates are disgusted with each other and the system.

Kathleen Hall Jamieson, Dean of the Annenberg School for Communication at the University of Pennsylvania, has rolled all these distasteful habits into a terse, cynical comment on contemporary elections *(Dirty Politics: Deception, Distraction, and Democracy*, 1992, 204): "Increasingly, campaigns have become narcotics that blur our awareness of problems long enough to elect the lawmakers who must deal with them." Consider also the end-of-career thoughts of campaign consultant **Ed Rollins**, one of the most feared, criticized, and knowledgeable men in American politics over the past few decades. In *Bare Knuckles and Back Rooms: My Life in American Politics* (1996), Rollins says our political system has gone haywire because of attack ads, the insatiable media, dysfunctional campaign financing, confrontational politics, the power of special interests, and the lack of term limits:

> The cumulative effect of these six factors is that voters don't like or trust any of the people they send to Washington. They believe instead that politicians and parties have developed tin ears—and they're right. Our representatives don't listen to the people as they're charged to do; instead, they heed the loudest and most seductive voices. Even the most highly regarded officeholders are deemed long on rhetoric and short on substance. They don't seem to have the best long-term interests of the country uppermost in their minds. (355)

To summarize, the traditional machinery of American politics is worn out. The forces of changing America are undermining the health of our elections, parties, and media; and these organic mechanisms increasingly are unable to link the American people with their representatives. Obviously, furthermore, these developments are creating serious problems for American government.

....

AMERICAN GOVERNMENT
IS FUNCTIONING IN UNACCEPTABLE MANNER

The clearest example and most maligned element of distempered America is its national governance. Broad changes—especially the deteriorated systemic environment and our philosophical civil war, combined with unhealthy developments among our people and political machinery—are pressuring American government adversely. Consequently and unarguably, our system of governance has changed significantly, and not for the better, during the latter half of the Twentieth Century.

In short, American government is functioning—or malfunctioning— unacceptably. Our traditional institutions of governance are very poorly performing their central, requisite, historic functions; and our touted model of democratic governance appears to have run seriously off-course.

THE CASE AGAINST AMERICAN GOVERNMENT

A full body of analytic literature demonstrates that American government, particularly American national government, is functioning in unacceptable manner. The case against government—against our governmental institutions, against our political leaders, and against their collective public performance— has been made repeatedly during the past decade by practitioners, academicians, and journalists, with each pitching his or her own theoretical, methodological, political, or personal angle. I'll reference a few of these efforts, in rough chronological order, to convey the substantive nature and variety of their indictment against American government.

****

EDITORIAL NOTE: I will not over-burden this essay with extensive theoretical and methodological discussion other than to note the difficulty of conceptualizing and measuring governmental performance. The simplest and most simplistic assessment, of course, is popular support as measured in public opinion polls and electoral returns. Another approach is to examine quantitative governmental outcomes, such as public expenditures, growth, unemployment, and poverty. A third approach is procedural, evaluating governmental operations in terms of service provision, bureaucratic efficiency, and, of course, "waste, fraud, and abuse." Finally, we can look normatively at broad policy dimensions such as progressiveness or regressiveness in individual freedoms, civil rights, and social welfare. The material referenced here draws upon all four approaches.

****

• As the Cold War dramatically drew toward closure, *Time* magazine bluntly asked "Is Government Dead?" in a cover story employing such terminology as "a costly irrelevancy", "a kind of neurosis of accepted limits", and "a frightening inability to define and debate America's emerging problems" (October 28, 1989). This scorching assessment asserted, among other things, that "Washington no longer seems capable of responding to its growing challenges" and that "politicians are letting America slip into paralysis."

• Enterprising consultants **David Osborne** (a veteran governance writer) and **Ted Gaebler** (a former city manager) tapped into mounting public concern about governmental performance "from schoolhouse to statehouse and city hall to the Pentagon." In *Reinventing Government: How the Entrepreneurial Spirit Is Transforming the Public Sector* (1992), they addressed the "Is Government Dead?" issue:

As the 1990s unfold, the answer—to many Americans—appears to be yes. Our public schools are the worst in the developed world. Our health care system is out of control. Our courts and prisons are so overcrowded that convicted felons walk free. And many of our proudest cities and states are virtually bankrupt . . . Eastern Europe and the Soviet republics overthrow the deadening hand of bureaucracy and oppression. But at home we feel impotent . . . We do not need another New Deal, nor another Reagan Revolution. We need an American perestroika. (1-2, 24)

- Shortly thereafter, **David Osborne** (the same governance writer) helped lay the political groundwork for governmental reform by contributing a chapter on "A New Federal Compact" to the pro-Democratic Progressive Policy Institute's *Mandate For Change* (edited by **Will Marshall** and **Martin Schram**, 1993). Osborne was direct and forceful in his introductory paragraph:

> The Federal government is in crisis. The American people believe Washington doesn't work. The typical American believes nearly half of every federal tax dollar is wasted. Only 17 percent of the public approves of Congress . . . And 17 of every 20 Americans want radical change . . . (237)

- Governmental types found find this language insulting, but (as is usually the case in our political system) they responded. Shortly after taking office in 1993, President Bill Clinton announced an initiative—a National Performance Review—derived from his successful political campaign; and a few months later, Vice President **Al Gore** unveiled "Creating a Government That Works Better and Costs Less" (published as *The Gore Report on Reinventing Government,* 1993). Relying on a team of experienced federal employees, the Report acknowledged the past sins of the federal establishment and included an extensive series of bureaucratic recommendations designed to improve "how" government works; in the introductory words of President Clinton:

> Our goal is to make the entire federal government both less expensive and more efficient, and to change the culture of our national bureaucracy away from complacency and entitlement toward initiative and empowerment. We intend to redesign, to reinvent, to reinvigorate the entire national government.

- Despite Gore's high-profile efforts at reinvention, the National Academy of Public Administration six years later bluntly stated through a panel of outside experts that the American people simply don't trust their government to govern right (*A Government to Trust and Respect: Rebuilding Citizen-Government Relations For the 21st Century*, June 1999):

> In America today, the relationship between citizens and government is in disarray. Many Americans do not believe that their government delivers reliable or effective public programs nor to they believe that they get much value in return for their tax dollars. For many Americans, government is a large and distant entity from which they feel disconnected and disaffected. Americans love their country and its Constitution, but many do not like and do not trust their government. (4)

- Journalists **Haynes Johnson** and **David Broder**—who have covered our democratic journey up-close for decades—saw the mid-1990s healthcare debacle as illustrative of American government's failing performance (*The System: The American Way of Politics at the Breaking Point*, 1996):

> The failure of The System on Health care reform might not loom so large if other great challenges facing the society were being met. They are not. Personal safety, economic opportunity, international peace, and health care are the four great security questions by which the American people judge the quality of their lives. On all but one of these, international peace, the last quarter of the twentieth century has witnessed the failure of The System to meet the legitimate expectations of the people it is supposed to be serving. (604)

Johnson and Broder also interpreted the healthcare wars as indicative, perhaps, of a broader governmental debility:

> Founders of The System, as we have noted several times, made it difficult for major changes to occur. But they surely did not foresee the self-destructiveness and distrust that now hobble American government and politics: the hatred of government; the demonization of elected officials from President down; the belittling of career civil servants who do the public's business, sometimes at risk of their lives. The bombing of the federal center in Oklahoma City in the spring of 1995 provides a warning of how strong these antigovernment feelings are becoming—and of the dangers from those who deliberately foment them. It was this acrimonious backdrop to the health care debate that led Dr. Reed Tuckson of the King/Drew Medical Center in the Watts section of Los Angeles to rail against those who fragment the political marketplace by trading on societal divisions and differences of class, race, ethnicity, religion, and political ideologies. The danger we face, Dr. Tuckson said, is that "we will become so fragmented and unable to discuss complex issues" that we will be incapable as a nation of addressing the major long-term problems facing the society. (638-639)

- In comparable tone, **Jonathan Rauch** of the *National Journal* defined the ills of contemporary government as "demosclerosis", or the progressive loss of ability to adapt to change. The problem, Rauch explained—in *Demosclerosis: The Silent Killer of American Government* (1994) and in *Government's End: Why Washington Stopped Working* (1999)—is that we tend to form more and more groups demanding more and more benefits and then selfishly defend them to the detriment of our nation. As a result, government has lost its ability to make things work and to solve problems effectively:

> By definition, government's power to solve problems comes from its ability to reassign resources, whether by taxing, spending, regulating, or simply passing laws. But that very ability energizes countless investors and entrepreneurs and ordinary Americans to go digging for gold by lobbying government. In time, a whole industry—large sophisticated, professionalized,

and to a considerable extent selfserving—emerges and then assumes a life of its own. This industry is a drain on the productive economy, and there appears to be no natural limit to its growth. As it grows, the steady accumulation of subsidies and benefits, each defended in perpetuity by a professional interest group, calcifies government. Government loses its capacity to experiment and so becomes more and more prone to failure. (*Government's End* , 18)

• Columnist **Richard E.Cohen** suggested that perhaps American government is suffering democratic overload, and that the real culprit may be the American people ("When There's Too Much Of A Good Thing," *National Journal*, June 18, 1994):

> Have we created a "hyper-democracy" in which public and private-sector advocates alike have overloaded the political circuits, making it difficult for elected officials to address obvious national problems in a deliberate, thorough way? Are there so many pressures that government has gone haywire? In short have excesses in political responsiveness produced new barriers to democracy?
>
> Governing is inevitably messy, of course . . . But a case can be made that the problems are just the opposite: that rising public demands for services have collided with government's eroding ability to respond, producing a form of mob rule driven by the work of lobbyists and pollsters and by pressures from a variety of interests notable for their short-term perspectives. (1477)

• **Hugh Heclo,** George Mason University Public Affairs Professor, similarly stated the problem as "hyperdemocracy" in an article of the same title in *The Wilson Quarterly* (Winter, 1999).

> The political system has become sensitive—indeed hypersensitive—to the public's opinions and anxieties. The traditional parties and interest groups, as well as the Constitution, have been pushed into the background, as polls, the media, and ideological activists and advocacy groups have moved to the forefront. American democracy is more open and inclusive than ever before, and citizens have unprecedented access to information about the workings of their government and the issues before it. Yet instead of becoming more engaged in democratic politics, the public has grown alienated from it. (Accessed online at http.wwics.si.edu)

• Diametrically different was the biting charge of "elite distemper" leveled by **Thomas R. Dye** and **Harmon Ziegler** (*The Irony of Democracy: An Uncommon Introduction to American Politics*, 2000). Theirs was a damning account of American government and its political leaders:

> Thirty years ago, when *The Irony of Democracy* was first written, a majority of Americans believed that their government was being run for the benefit of all; the elitist view was expressed by relatively few people. Today an

astounding 80 percent of Americans believe that their government is run "by a few big interests looking out for themselves." The elitist perspective, which we developed as an analytic model of American politics, has now become part of the popular political culture! (xiii)

And to Dye and Zeigler, there was no question about the nature and cause of governmental dysfunction:

This Millennial Edition of *The Irony of Democracy* . . . reflects, first of all, our increasing distress over current elite distemper—corporate greed, media arrogance, interest group gluttony, big money political influence, and, above all, the self-serving and shortsighted behavior of today's governmental leaders.

It is not only the sordid tale of "Presidential Sex, Lies, and Impeachment" on which we base our critical assessment, or even the "Ambition and Ambivalence" of the Clinton presidency. It is also the sanctimonious, self-serving, and arrogant behavior of members of Congress, federal bureaucrats, and federal judges. (xiv-xv)

• **Susan J. Pharr** and **Robert D. Putnam** provided the most comprehensive analysis—a comparative, empirical, multi-national assessment—in *Disaffected Democracies: What's Troubling the Trilateral Countries?* (2000). These Harvard professors and their associates built a strong case, based on solid research in the United States and other established democracies, that the main problem of government is government itself.

According to Pharr and Putnam, (a) the capacities of governmental institutions here and elsewhere have been diminished in an interdependent world and (b) there has been a decline in actual performance by those institutions. Conceptualizing governmental performance through the eyes of the citizenry— because "their subjective appraisal of governmental performance is what ultimately matters"—they find dramatic evidence of unacceptable governance and cause for worry at the end of the Twentieth Century:

Some commentators may tell their fellow citizens that the problem is "just in your head"—a function of unrealistic expectations rather than deteriorating performance—but we are inclined to think that our political systems are not, in fact, performing well, although perhaps for reasons beyond their immediate control. (27)

• Particularly pertinent for our Great Experiment, public dissatisfaction with American government—our sense of "anger, frustration, and betrayal"—seems to be more real and persistent than in other democracies. According to **Anthony King** ("Distrust of Government: Explaining American Exceptionalism" in the Pharr-Putnam collection *Disaffected Democracies,* 2000):

That there has been a decline in trust and confidence in government in the United States is not in dispute and has been amply documented in this book and elsewhere . . . The available evidence comparing the United States with other countries . . . does suggest that the decline in confidence in America is indeed more "real" than in most other comparable countries. (76-77)

In summarizing this discussion, we should note that talk about such things as "the crisis of governance" and "the failure of leadership" has been an easy and common endeavor for many years; but the diverse analyses presented here argue pretty convincingly that something is fundamentally wrong with American government as we begin the Twenty-First Century.

OUR FUNDAMENTAL PREDICAMENT

My "dying" proposition goes beyond all the common criticisms, ailments, and explanations—beyond such things as "disaffected citizens", "irresponsible elites", "interest group politics", "bureaucracy", "demosclerosis", and "hyperdemocracy". The great threat to American government is bigger than unhappy constituents, bigger than bad leaders, bigger than special interests, bigger than red tape, bigger than our inability to reassign resources, bigger than overly responsive democracy.

Our current governmental predicament, however, is a problem of much greater consequence and danger than conventional political wrangling. Our fundamental predicament is the cumulative combination of unpopular, poorly led, gridlocked, bureaucratized, demosclerosed, hyperdemocratic governance — AND — constrained systemic environment, intense philosophical turmoil, weakened civic culture, and broken political machinery. The combination of these civic, political, and governmental developments certainly handicap and complicate American democracy.

Moreover, in conjunction with the emerging, exciting, frightening power of electronics and computers (which I will discuss in the next few pages), these developments are altering the very nature of our historic Great Experiment.

. . . .

WE ARE WITNESSING
THE REVOLUTIONARY RISE OF "ELECTRONIC DEMOCRACY"

It is no coincidence that, just as our people, politics, and government suffer simultaneous debilitation, we are undergoing a techno-political revolution that is altering the traditional relationship between our people and our government. We are witnessing the coming of "Electronic Democracy!"

Among the most important developments in contemporary America is a dramatic technological revolution—through electronics and computers—similar to earlier transformations in agriculture and industry. America has been electronically "wired" and American democracy has been programmed for revolutionary communication, and innovation. In fact, we have entered an electronic world—an "E-World"—of unprecedented capabilities and unknown consequences for the totality of human existence.

These new technological capabilities have proven powerfully effective and rampant in American democracy. Just as radio and television impacted our lives in earlier eras, so are contemporary government and politics being transformed by super computers, home computers, personal computers, hand computers, laptops, universal data sets, interoperable programs, interactive television, teleconferencing, direct mail-tv-radio, cell phones, phone banks, faxes, e-mails, beepers, the internet, the world wide web, satellites, C-SPAN, CNN, and other technologies constantly evolving in rapid and revolutionary nature.

These developments are altering virtually every aspect and the very nature of American democracy. Upward and downward linkage via new technology is more diverse, direct, personal, immediate, continuous, and voluminous—and increasingly unfettered by mediating bureaucracies of the past. Without question, traditional linkage mechanisms such as parties, media, and elections are becoming less relevant; alternative technicians and their toys increasingly handle all forms of political transaction—fundraising, campaigning, communications, office operations, constituent relations, research, analysis, advocacy, lobbying, even voting and policy-making. Quickly and surely, America's entire political process is transitioning into "electronic democracy".

"DIGITAL NATION"

Journalist Jon Katz declared the powerful reality of electronic democracy in "Birth of a Digital Nation" (*Wired Magazine*, April 1997, accessed online at *http://wwics.si.edu*). After studying the role of the Web on the 1996 elections, he declared the beginning of a postpolitical world:

> I saw the primordial stirrings of a new kind of nation—the Digital Nation—and the formation of a new postpolitical philosophy. This nascent ideology, fuzzy and difficult to define, suggests a blend of some of the best values rescued from the tired old dogmas—the humanism of liberalism, the economic opportunity of conservatism, plus a strong sense of personal responsibility and a passion for freedom.

> There are paradigm-shifting changes afoot: the young people who form the heart of the digital world are creating a new political ideology. The machinery of the Internet is being wielded to create an environment in which the Digital Nation can become a political entity in its own right.

How important is this movement to America's future? Katz says that Digital Nation possesses the resources to dominate the Twenty-First Century:

Here is a growing elite in control of the most powerful communications infrastructure ever assembled. The people rushing toward the millennium with their fingers on the keyboards of the Information Age could become one of the most powerful political forces in history. Technology is power. Education is power. Communication is power. The digital young have all three. No other social group is as poised to dominate culture and politics in the 21st century.

If they choose to form a political movement, they could someday run the world. If they choose to develop a common value system, with a moral ideology and a humane agenda, they might even do the world some good.

The ideas of the postpolitical young are fluid, Katz says, but their common values are clear—"They tend to be libertarian, materialistic, tolerant, rational, technologically adept, disconnected from conventional political organizations." And they are politically restless:

They are not afraid to challenge authority. They take no one's word for anything. They embrace interactivity—the right to shape and participate in their media . . . The digital young, from Silicon Valley entrepreneurs to college students, have a nearly universal contempt for government's ability to work; they think it's wasteful and clueless. On the Net, government is rarely seen as an instrument of positive change or social good. Politicians are assumed to be manipulative or ill-informed, unable to affect reform or find solutions, forced to lie to survive. The Digital Nation's disconnection from the conventional political process—and from the traditional media that mirror it—is profound.

"TELEDEMOCRACY"

Political Scientists Theodore Becker and Christa Slaton tell us that the restless forces of direct democracy already are reworking the conventional political process—and they themselves are leading the charge.

In *The Future of Teledemocracy* (2000), Becker and Slaton preach the virtues of "Teledemocracy", which they define as empowerment of the people, through modern electronic communications and information technology, over public agendas, priorities, and policies.

Becker and Slaton urge their readers "to break free from the theoretical bondage that has defined and constrained democracy in the last few centuries" (1); and they provide a thoughtful and comprehensive argument for their "New Democratic Paradigm" (158) whose core elements are the global direct democracy movement, democracy communications systems, the modern mediation movement, and the organizational power of the Internet.

Furthermore, at an accompanying website for their Global Democratic Movement (they call it "Teledemocracy Action News & Network" or TANN), Becker and Slaton provide theoretical underpinnings and an electronic forum for transforming representative democracy into participatory democracy. They refer to themselves and their associates as an army of different drummers who subscribe to a belief in the philosophical values and practical benefits of electronic self-governance. "Serious experiments in teledemocracy" they assert, "repeatedly reveal the capacity, interest, and willingness of ordinary citizens to function democratically to produce the common good."

Interestingly, Becker and Slaton (academic colleagues, personal friends, and former constituents of mine) warn electronic democrats that entrenched politicians will attempt to destroy or usurp the Teledemocracy movement:

> American history has some valuable lessons for those of us seeking to advance democracy. A little over two hundred years ago, a small group of wealthy and ambitious men met behind locked doors to write the United States Constitution. They kept the media and citizens out and kept no public record of the proceedings . . . So now, more than two hundred years after the ratification of the United States Constitution, there is discussion among the ruling elites around the world about a new world order and the global economy . . . The question for modern day democrats around the world is who will design this new world order (if there is to be one) and how are the issues of the global economy impacting the struggle for democracy at the nation-state level? . . . It is not necessary that we have a masterplan that we all embrace enthusiastically. However, it is essential that we are far more unified in our efforts to advance democracy since our goals are intensely opposed by most of those who hold political power. (accessed online at www.auburn.edu/tann)

THE PROMISE AND PERIL
OF "ELECTRONIC DEMOCRACY"

The rise of "Digital Nation" and "Teledemocracy" may indeed represent, as their champions proclaim, the beginning of a great revolution, the rebirth of love for liberty, new kinds of community, more civil society, citizen empowerment, and participatory democracy.
We may be creating in E-World a vastly different and progressive American democracy. We now have available to us technology that can serve the needs of our national republic more efficiently than can old-fashioned political operatives and outdated campaign, party, and media mechanisms. In the future, liberty, equality, and all the other benefits of democracy can be pursued under changed institutional conditions. For example, our technological revolution may lead us to a different magical mix of people and their government, a mix devoid of intermediating political machinery. Or, maybe, it will lead us to reject both traditional political machinery and republican governmental arrangements in favor of direct, democratic self-government. And who knows where this could lead in terms of new ideals, values and governance?

In effect, we may be experiencing a technological mini-frontier— "electronic democracy"—comparable in some ways to our previous natural and political transformations. Perhaps we have entered a technological version of our original natural environment, an open, adventurous experience that will radically alter opportunity and society and government. Perhaps, like the expansion of national public authority, this mini-frontier will enable us to revisit and perfect the political arrangements of our democratic experiment.

But this technological revolution also evokes anxiety about the central question of our Great Experiment: "How far can we pursue democratic ideals through limited, representative government without succumbing to the inherent, destructive tendencies of democracy?" Regardless of its noble sentiments, electronic democracy envisions a political system far different—theoretically, socially, economically, technologically—from the origins of our democratic experiment and what we now know as American democracy.

Most importantly, from a theoretical perspective, is the fact that electronic democracy is a broad, basic challenge to the essential concepts and critical elements of our historic American experiment. The objective of electronic democracy is direct democracy. It presumes the ultimate "goodness" of ultimate democracy. It rejects the role of partisan, media, and electoral linkages between the people and their government. It actually contradicts the notion of representative governance. (And I seriously doubt that it ever considers or comprehends the concepts of "inspired nationalism", "the pursuit of democratic ideals", or "limited, representative governance" as I have presented them in this manuscript.)

Just as importantly from a political perspective, electronic democracy complicates and compounds the burden of our democratic experiment by atomizing the American community. The technology that facilitates communication also can divide us into disparate groups, depersonalize our individual commitment to the broader community, and reorient us around and away from our collective national endeavor. To be specific, for example, there's already a definite "digital divide" between the "haves" and "have-nots" of American society. A recent Commerce Department report documents the growing technological gap between whites and nonwhites in America. The national survey shows that whites are more than twice as likely to own a home computer as blacks or Hispanics. As the top White House telecommunications adviser warns, "The political, cultural and economic gaps in our society are only going to get exacerbated . . . we've got a problem as a nation" ("Report: Race Divide Over Technology," The Associated Press, July 28, 1998).

We must be very careful with this revolutionary development in American democracy. The increasing use and eventual course of political technology in E-world pose critically important and iffy challenges to the future of our Great Experiment. Electronic democracy is an attempt to achieve a more perfect union by replacing traditional, weakened linkages between the people and their government with a volatile new process of policy-making that involves direct but unproven capacity for democratic deliberation.

I sometimes felt, as a national policy-maker, that we in Washington were overly responsive to disaggregated Americans while minimally responsible to America. I now wonder whether the technological revolution may, unfortunately, be moving us perilously closer to the inherent, destructive tendencies of democracy. And I worry that electronic democracy may be pushing our historic fuzziness about democratic ideals (such as freedom-vs-equality) toward ultimate, unhealthy, undemocratic resolution.

If, as I have proposed, America is suffering from a deteriorated systemic environment, a philosophical civil war, an uncivic public, broken political machinery, and a poorly functioning government, electronic democracy could prove to be divine inspiration—or the work of democratic demons.

....

DEMOGRAPHIC, ECONOMIC, AND TECHNOLOGICAL TRENDS ARE EXACERBATING OUR POLITICAL TROUBLES

Our discussion thus far in this chapter has focused on the deteriorating elements (our people, politics, and government) of American democracy and the revolutionary rise of electronic democracy over the past few decades. But it is impossible to conclude this discussion without considering the impact of other important societal developments on our magical mix.

Demographic Divergence. **It is no secret, for example, that demographic trends are changing America into a more diverse and divergent nation.** For some time now, American society has been moving in ironic dual directions: (a) on one hand, we are undergoing dramatic social diversification due to birth rates and immigration patterns; (b) at the same time, we have been segregating ourselves in terms of age, race, wealth, social status, and other cultural characteristics. Furthermore, demographers predict that our nation's historic (and aging) white majority will yield to ethnic heterogeneity over the coming decades, thereby exaggerating and aggravating societal differences about "what America means" and "how America ought to work." My Alabama political science colleague and futurist **Konrad M. Kressley** (*Living in the Third Millennium: Forecasts To Master Your Future*, 1998) has projected clearly this trending pattern of American society in the new century:

> We've always thought of America as a country dominated by people from North European stock, with a smattering of other races . . . Visit Miami, San Francisco, or San Antonio to get an impression of our population in the next century. Since the relation between ethnicity and socioecomic status still persists, a disproportionate number of well-to-do elder whites will be juxtaposed with a growing number of relatively deprived young Hispanics and African Americans in the next century. (29)

I will elaborate further on this idea in a later chapter; but, for now, I simply will note that diversity is a generally healthy aspect of the American experience; however, pronounced societal divergence can pose significant challenges to our national democratic experiment.

Economic and Technological Distraction. I have similar concerns about the impact of economic globalization and the technological revolution on our collective pursuit of democratic ideals. The end of the Cold War and the "retooling" of America—particularly in terms of computers and communications and international commerce—have opened a world of opportunity and benefits to all of us. Obviously, too, "electronic democracy" promises healthy invigoration of traditional politics. But there are also atomizing ramifications of global and technological society for American democracy. These developments have the potential to further divide the American people (socially, physically, and psychologically) and to deter us from our collective democratic experiment.

Increasingly, many Americans are reorienting themselves toward the global economy and the international community—with particular affinity for our northern (Canada) and southern (Mexico and the Caribbean) neighbors. With the Cold War over, the transnational economy beckoning, and transcending technology readily available, we now locate wherever suits our cultural fancy, earning our livelihood and living our lifestyles without regard to what happens in Washington or our commitments to the national community.

Thus some of the central and normally positive dynamics of American life—demographic fluidity, economic expansion, and technological progress—may be interfering with our national democratic experiment. Those who are relatively advantaged—socially, economically, technologically—seem to be backing away from our historic national experiment, retreating into regional constituencies and gated communities, with privatized schools, security, recreation, social services, and other important functions normally provided by government. Others, saddled with mirrored disadvantages, clearly are insisting upon expansion of the governmental arena. Such exacerbated divisions obviously do not bode well for America's Great Experiment.

. . . .

DECLENSIONAL TENDENCIES OF AMERICAN DEMOCRACY

The multiple ills identified in this chapter underlie the declensional tendencies of American democracy. While my portrayal of public life may not qualify as a democratic crisis, it appears, from the perspective of progressive democratic history, that our magical mix of people, politics, and government may be losing some of its magic.

(1) Most importantly, the American people are suffering civic depression—a disturbing pattern of political estrangement, declining turnout, and uncivic society.

(2)   The political machinery of American democracy is worn out. Our organic system of political parties, news media, and election campaigns needs repair or replacement.

(3)   American national government is not performing satisfactorily. Our basic problem, of course, is bigger than popularized villains such as crooked politicians and the special interests; but it is clear that American government has not worked very well for several decades.

(4)   We are witnessing the revolutionary rise of "electronic democracy". A technological revolution poses serious hopes and fears for American democracy.

(5)   Demographic, economic, and technological trends are exacerbating our political troubles. Americans seem to be segregating themselves in unhealthy manner; and they may be negatively re-orienting their allegiance to the democratic experiment.

As a result of all these declensions and complications, the substantive and procedural functions of our national experiment are mixed at best, an unhealthy combination of inconsequential democratic muddling; at worst, our principal output is democratic distemper that demeans the nature and endangers the future of American democracy.

....

SUMMARY COMMENT

Without doubt, we live in an increasingly democratic world; and as never before in our history, "the people" now participate in America's national experiment in democratic ideals. However, we also are experiencing the combined, simultaneous impacts of a constrained systemic environment and philosophical civil war; consequently, our historic magical mix is losing its magic. Even if we extract my dramatic references to lost civic virtue, broken political machinery, and malfunctioning government, we are left with the reality that our civic culture is suffering, our political institutions are worn out, and our government is not working very well.

Considering the fundamental disruptions of the past several decades, it is not surprising that American democracy no longer works the way it used to work. Nor should we be shocked to discover, in the next chapter, that the American people may be tiring of their Great Experiment.

CHAPTER 7

PROPOSITION NUMBER FOUR:

"AMERICA SEEMS TO BE TIRING OF ITS HISTORIC GREAT EXPERIMENT."

As the previous discussion demonstrated, the elements of American democracy are still functioning during these transformational times—but unacceptably so; and, as I will suggest in this chapter, the American people—although generally patriotic and supportive in many ways—may be tiring of the Great Experiment.

....

My final proposition incorporates the cumulative impact of multitudinous democratic ills. Despite relative peace and prosperity (and a surge of patriotism generated by the terrorist "Attack on America"), troubling constraints fundamentally shackle contemporary public life: America's favorable systemic environment has disappeared, we have entrapped our national democratic experiment in a philosophical civil war, and American democracy no longer works the way it used to work. Furthermore, after two centuries of evolutionary progressive governance, the forces of centrifugal democracy now drive American politics in strange and contradictory directions.

Upon close examination, consequently, we seem to be tiring of our historic experiment. Contemporary America evidences surprisingly mixed commitment to the traditional, essential concepts of our system of governance (along with uncertainty about its future); and we increasingly incline toward alternative ideas about American governance (and, in some ways, we actually have begun reexamining and redirecting our historic democratic endeavor).

Of course we must exercise caution in such talk. Historical comparisons are methodologically imprecise; and it is impossible to prove cause and effect through chronology. But we can survey the contemporary political scene, compare it to our understanding of earlier public life, and speculate about the developing course of our Great Experiment

Therefore, in this chapter I first will explore contemporary society's mixed commitment to national democratic principles; I then will assess some important devolutionary developments in current American politics; and, finally, I'll conjecture pertinent ramifications for the future of American democracy

....

THE AMERICAN PEOPLE EVIDENCE MIXED COMMITMENT TO THEIR NATIONAL DEMOCRATIC ENDEAVOR

It is easy to document troubling patterns of disarray in America's democratic ethos. Solid data show that the American people for the past few decades have evidenced mixed commitment to the Great Experiment.

****

EDITORIAL NOTES:

(A) We could focus simply on uncivic culture as conclusive evidence of "tired" America. Such evidence is valid and extensive. The average American appears to be minimally interested or concerned or virtuous enough to participate in the basic aspects of American democracy. But since I've already covered this subject in an earlier chapter, I'll just note it here for the record and move on with other, more pertinent indicators of my "tiring" proposition.

(B) The following gleanings come from major news services and national public opinion polls conducted within the past few years by such reputable organizations as The Gallup Poll, The Harris Poll, CBS News Poll, CBS News/New York Times Poll, Gallup/CNN/USA Today Poll, CNN News/Opinion Dynamics Poll, CNN/Time Poll, Fox News/Opinion Dynamics Poll, NBC News/Wall Street Journal Poll, ABC News/The Washington Post Poll, The Los Angeles Times Poll, Bloomberg News Poll, The Tarrance Group/Lake (R) Snell, Perry & Associates (D) "Battleground" Survey, Wirthlin Worldwide, Market Strategies, Rasmussen Research, The Freedom Forum's First Amendment Center, The Council for Excellence in Government, and The Pew Research Center for the People and the Press. The specific wording and figures vary from time-to-time and poll-to-poll; but taken collectively these surveys provide a rough outline of contemporary American opinion. (The data presented in the following pages, unless referenced as a printed source, may be accessed online at www.pollingreport.com or at the variously cited poll websites.)

(C) I have excluded from this analysis polling data reflective of the Sept 11, 2001, terrorist "Attack on America"; whether patriotic emotions extend beyond flag-waving celebrations remains to be seen and will have to be considered within the contest of long-term patterns.

****

DEMOCRATIC DISSENSUS

Although there's no reason to question the basic allegiance of America's citizenry, a growing body of public opinion data clearly reveals, alongside our patriotic and supportive orientations, surprisingly mixed sentiments— or democratic "dissensus"—regarding the Great Experiment.

Obviously, American democratic theory has never required full democratic consensus; and no serious analyst of American democracy would depict rigid adherence to national democratic ideals throughout American history. As pointed out in an earlier discussion, the American people have always been a mixed, fluid society, and they have never really debated nor affirmed their full, uniform commitment to an "American ideology;" and certainly no pollsters took America's precise political pulse during the Eighteenth and Nineteenth Centuries.

Nevertheless, modern techniques of opinion research show that we fall far short of democratic consensus on the important principles underlying our national public endeavor; and we exhibit surprisingly dissensual strains of disinterest, discontent, and disaffection among our otherwise positive attitudes. I have hinted at these tendencies throughout this manuscript; now I'll identify specific points of dissensus and provide a few recent and pertinent polling citations for each dissensual orientation.

National Identity. In the first place, we fall short of consensus on a central normative concept—sense of national identity—of our historic democratic experiment. In actuality, we have never been a consensual society of universally like-minded Americans. But broad, popular subscription to notions of inspired nationhood—as divined by our Founders and nurtured for generations—certainly has played a prominent role in the successful furtherance of our Great Experiment over the past two centuries.

Current uncertainty and dissensus regarding our national identity are obvious and noteworthy. Available evidence suggests, for example, only mixed agreement on the fundamental idea that "we're all in this together" as expressed in our original identity as "E Pluribus Unum" (declared America's national motto by Congress in 1782). Consider the 1999 Portrait of America survey by Rasmussen Research, which shows slightly less than half (48%) of the American people saying that the U.S. should be a "melting pot" and more than a third (35%) feeling that the U.S. should be a "mosaic". In another poll (Gallup) in 1998, the majority (59%) say that we should encourage new immigrants to blend into American culture, but about a third (32%) feel that new immigrants should "maintain their own culture more strongly, even if that means they do not blend in as well."

Furthermore, despite our opposition to desecration of the American flag, we seem skittish about its place in our lives. Within the past year, state and local officials in various parts of the country have refused to pledge their allegiance to the flag of the United States at official meetings; and some local school systems have prohibited its recitation in classrooms. In one case, the appointed chairman of a local planning committee was dismissed for leading an unauthorized pledge of allegiance to an unauthorized American flag ("Sparks Fly over Recital of Pledge at Meeting," *Santa Barbara News-Press*, October 19, 2001).

We've grown especially uneasy with our alternative national motto of "In God We Trust" (as inscribed on American currency by congressional direction since 1954). Just as with the flag and the pledge, numerous leaders and institutions have prohibited such statements as unduly divisive ("Motto: School Board Votes Against 'In God We Trust' Posters," *Naples Daily News*, August 24, 2001).

Apparently, there's no strong consensus in increasingly diverse and sensitive America about whether we should continue as "E Pluribus Unum" or as "Ex Uno Plures; and contemporary society seems uncertain about traditional symbols and sentiments of American nationalism.

<u>Democratic Ideals.</u> **More substantively, while most Americans today say that they value historic democratic ideals such as freedom of speech, press, religion, and assembly, they often disagree with the actual implementation of those important principles.**

Recent nationwide polling by the Freedom Forum's First Amendment Center reveals for example that, although about nine in ten respondents assert that people should be allowed to express unpopular opinions, more than four in ten think the First Amendment goes too far in the rights granted to American citizens ("Poll: More Americans think First Amendment goes too far," Associated Press, June 27, 2001). Among the other findings:

-- Almost eight in ten Americans say that people should not be allowed to burn or deface the American flag in a political statement;

-- Two-thirds of our citizens would ban public remarks that racial groups find offensive;

-- Two-thirds say teachers or others should be allowed to lead prayers in school and over public address systems at school sporting events;

-- Almost as many people think the government should be able to place restrictions on the money an individual can contribute to someone else's political campaign;

-- Over half think the press has too much freedom;

-- About half say art should not be put in public places if it may offend some members of the community;

-- About half thing that speech that offends members of a religious group should not be allowed.

This gap between enlightened theoretical principles and popular attitudes is not new, but it is strikingly wide and obvious. "It appears many Americans are having second thoughts about the First Amendment," says Kenneth Paulson, executive director of the First Amendment Center. "They treasure it as part of this nation's heritage, but they become uncomfortable when it allows others to speak out in offensive ways" ("Americans say they value First Amendment, with reservations," Associated Press, June 30, 2000).

Attitudes Toward Government. **While the American public expresses mixed opinions on national identity and democratic ideals, striking evidence of "tired" America emerges when we focus on the governance element of our Great Experiment. The picture turns from ambivalence to outright antagonism as pollsters probe our attitudes toward American national government.**
According to the previously cited Portrait of America Survey (1999), a majority of the American people view Washington as "the government" (55%) rather than "our government" (42%); and they feel that we do not have a government that is "of, by, and for the people" (54%). Almost two-thirds (61%) of Americans contend that the federal government does not reflect the will of the people (21% say it does and 18% are not sure); and just 44% believe elections are fair to voters.
Our citizens trust the government in Washington to do what's right "only some of the time" (63%), compared to "most of the time" (25%) or "all of the time" (4%). Not surprisingly, the public rates the President (54%) and Members of Congress (46%) much lower than "the ordinary man and woman" (71%) when it comes to telling the truth, attributing to the national government about the same lowly standing as business leaders, journalists, and pollsters.
While a large majority (83%) of Americans think that government has the potential to contribute positively to their lives, almost as many people think that the actual impact of government is negative (29%) as positive (37%). Many more express preference for a smaller government with fewer services (56%) than a larger one with more services (38%).
This disaffection is revealed more personally in questions probing the relationship between individual respondents and their government. About half (52%) say that people like themselves have "not much" say about what the government does. Consequently, most Americans report that they are "fairly disconnected" (34%) or "very disconnected" (29%) from national government

(and they have less confidence in the federal government than their state or local governments). As might be expected, the American people maintain that "we deserve better" (49%) as opposed to "we get what we deserve" (38%). And whom do they blame?—in various polls they target "the politicians" (65%), "the special interest groups" (38%), "the media" (29%), "elected officials" (24%), "political parties" (24%), instead of "the public" (14%).

Contemporary society also is inclined to suspect the worst about American government and our political leaders. Over two-thirds (68%) in a VOTE.com internet poll (June 2000) agreed that federal agents recklessly abused their power, causing the deaths of over 80 people at the Waco Branch Davidian conflict (accessed online at www.vote.com); and a slight majority (51%) in a CBS Poll (April 2000) think there was an official cover-up by the government or the FBI to keep the public from learning the truth about Waco (accessed online at www.pollingreport.com).

Many also think that their government may be a mass murderer, or a drug dealer, or a presidential assassin ("Poll Shows Most Believe In Government Conspiracies," Scripps Howard News Service, July 25, 1997). A shocking 51 percent of the public believes it is very likely or somewhat likely that federal officials were directly responsible for the assassination of President Kennedy in 1963. A majority believe it the CIA may have permitted Central American drug dealers to sell cocaine to inner city African American children. More than one-third of the respondents suspect the U.S. Navy shot down TWA flight 800 near New York City.

Direction of the Country. Furthermore, many Americans are skeptical about where our national experiment is heading as we begin the Twenty-First Century.

During the turbulent 1990s, almost half of the American people in an NBC-The Wall Street Journal national poll (January 1994) believed that America was in a state of decline; 49% agreed and 44% disagreed ("Opinion Outlook," *National Journal*, February 2, 1994).

More recent polling demonstrates divided confidence regarding whether our country is heading in the "right direction" or "wrong direction," with directional variations from poll to poll. For example, an NBC News/Wall Street Journal Poll (May, 2001), tends in the "right" direction by a margin of 47%-39%; so does a Bloomberg News Poll (June, 2001) by a count of 48%-44%. But a Pew Research Center Poll (June, 2001) tilts in the "wrong" direction by a margin of 52%-44%, as does a Gallup/CNN/USA Today Poll (May, 2001) by a count of 50%-46%.

By combining data from all available polling sources, I calculate that the public has been fairly evenly divided on this question for some time. The aggregated tally for the past five years (1997-2001) shows that 47% of Americans think our country is proceeding along the right course and that 44% think we are heading in the wrong direction.

CAUSE FOR CONCERN

Obviously, anyone can design virtually any interpretative pattern by selectively picking and choosing among behavioral statistics and public opinion data. But most analysts conclude that our contemporary political culture is cause for concern.

• For example, **E.J. Dionne,** writing at the beginning of the turbulent 1990s, cited our somber mood and political laziness as "an advertisement against self-government" (*Why Americans Hate Politics*, 1991):

> Over the last three decades, the faith of the American people in their democratic institutions has declined, and Americans have begun to doubt their ability to improve the world through politics . . . True, we still praise democracy incessantly and recommend democracy to the world. But at home, we do little to encourage citizens to believe that public engagement is worth the time. Our system has become one long-running advertisement against self-government. For many years, we have been running down the public sector and public life. Voters doubt that elections give them real control over what the government does, and half of them don't bother to cast ballots. (10)

• More recently, **Eugene Steuerle** and associates argue, in *The Government We Deserve: Responsive Democracy and Changing Expectations* (1998), that today's alienation is markedly different from historical distrust of government:

> Americans have always been ambivalent about government—distrusting its powers but eager for its services. But something is indeed different today— not the argument but the context in which it is taking place. Citizen distrust of government has been unusually high while voter turnout has been low. Even the rising optimism and satisfaction that accompanied the long economic expansions of the 1980s and the 1990s raised levels of trust only modestly and voter participation not at all.
>
> What underlies this current period of political alienation? Our conclusion is that more Americans than ever do not feel that they own their own government. It is there. They identify with its symbols and believe passionately in its constitutional character. They constantly interact with it as taxpayers and program beneficiaries. But it is not theirs . . . (1)

We can quibble about the precise nature and causes of our democratic dissensus. However, undeniably America is an increasingly diverse and divergent society; and judging from a lengthy statistical and anecdotal review (here and in the previous chapter on dysfunctional American democracy), our political culture appears to be decidedly different from what was presumed and observed in the past. Furthermore, our overall mixture of attitudes and orientations seems seriously problematic for our

national experiment in democratic ideals. Concomitantly, as the following section demonstrates, the American people and their leaders are reconsidering the historic nature of our democratic experiment.

....

THE AMERICAN POLITY INCREASINGLY INCLINES TOWARD ALTERNATIVE IDEAS ABOUT GOVERNANCE

After two centuries of evolutionary democratic nationalization, various constituent elements of the American polity have become dissatisfied with the tone and direction of public life; and powerful dynamics now strain American democracy.

Clearly many Americans are now inclined toward alternative ideas about governance; and they're considering different ideals, exploring different versions, attempting strange new arrangements of our traditional democratic experiment. A survey of contemporary public life provides case after case—at federal, state, and local levels—of various endeavors outside the historical norms and ways and trends of American democracy.

RADICAL VENTURES

We have already talked about some revolutionary, violent deviations—the Oklahoma City bombing and the Waco tragedy—from the traditional course of American democratic governance. In addition, numerous peaceful but unusual and extreme ventures have escaped public attention.

For example, a black religious group from New York City, claiming to be descended from Egyptians, has set up shop as the United Nuwaubian Nation of Moors on a 476-acre tract east of Atlanta; their spiritual leader, by the way, says he's an extraterrestrial being ("Space Invaders: Strangers from the North Send a Southern Town into a Tizzy," *Time Magazine*, July 12, 1999). Also, a Texas border town has adopted Spanish as its official language and even passed a resolution firing any public employee who cooperates with the U.S. Border Patrol ("Border Battle Centers on 'Spanish-Only' Town," *USA Today*, December 17, 1999). Alabama's former governor went to court to challenge the Bill of Rights as an unconstitutional imposition on his state ("Alabama Governor to Courts: 'En Garde'," *The Christian Science Monitor*, September 10, 1997). And a Southern independence group scored its first electoral victory in the drive to secede from the United States ("Southern Party Gets a Reluctant First Victory in Movement to Secede," Associated Press, September 9, 2000).

These radical developments represent no real threat to conventional government in America. But they prove, dramatically and sometimes tragically, the presence of festering infections here in our own civic body. They are like canker sores—unsightly, embarrassing, painful, and symptomatic of underlying conditions that bedevil our **Great Experiment** as we close the Twentieth Century.

Aside from these strange ideas and endeavors, however, there is a serious alternative movement—as we will see in the following discussion—that is indeed changing the historical course of democratic governance.

THE DEVOLUTIONARY MOVEMENT

The most significant development in contemporary American public life (and my illustrative example of tired America) is the popular movement—known as devolution—to reconsider the nature and re-order the arrangements of national governance. In some very important ways, we seem to be reversing the course of our historic democratic experiment, pushing power and resources away from Washington back to the states, back to the private sector, back to the people.

- The official opening statement of contemporary devolutionary philosophy was delivered by our "Great Communicator," President **Ronald Reagan,** in his inaugural address—"Government is not the solution!"—two decades ago:

> In this present crisis, government is not the solution to our problem. From time to time, we have been tempted to believe that society has become too complex to be managed by self-rule, that government by an elite group is superior to government for, by, and of the people. But if no one among us is capable of governing himself, then who among us has the capacity to govern someone else. ("Inaugural Address," January 20, 1981)

- **George Bush** followed with kinder, and gentler, but similar remarks in his inaugural speech celebrating the bicentinnial of the American Constitution:

> The old solution, the old way was to think that public money alone could end these problems. But we have learned that is not so. And in any case, our funds are low. We have a deficit to bring down. We have more will than wallet; but will is what we need. We will make the hard choices, looking at what we have and perhaps allocating it differently, making our decisions based on honest need and prudent safety. And then we will do the wisest thing of all. We will turn to the only resource we have that, in times of need, always grows—the goodness and the courage of the American people. ("Inaugural Address," January 20, 1989)

- Even **Bill Clinton,** surely one of the most successful, popular, and articulate Democratic leaders of modern times, expressed similar acknowledgement— "The era of big government is over!"—in a startling State of the Union Message midway of his eight-year tenure in the White House:

> We know big government does not have all the answers. We know there's not a program for every problem. We have worked to give the American

people a smaller, less bureaucratic government in Washington. And we have to give the American people one that lives within its means. ("State of the Union Address," January 23, 1996)

- Most recently, **George W. Bush,** speaking as a compassionate conservative, articulated this same prevailing notion of federal devolution on the occasion of his presidential inauguration:

> Government has great responsibilities for public safety and public health, for civil rights and common schools. Yet compassion is the work of a nation, not just a government. Some needs and hurts are so deep they will only respond to a mentor's touch or a pastor's prayer. Church and charity, synagogue and mosque lend our communities their humanity, and they will have an honored place in our plans and in our laws. ("Inaugural Address," January 20, 2001)

These are not glib, throwaway lines from minor politicians spoken in isolated quarters to narrow special interest groups. These are measured articulations by the past four American Presidents speaking clearly and directly to the American people; they signal significant rearrangement of our historic national democratic experiment; and, predictably, they provoke contrarian response from the loyal opposition.

- Journalist **John B. Judis**, for example, decries federal timidity during an era of progressive challenge (*The Paradox of American Democracy: Elites, Special Interests, and the Betrayal of Public Trust*, 2000):

> In America, periods of massive industrial consolidation and dramatic technological innovation have always been followed by periods of political and social reform. One eventually creates the need for the other, as the economic changes produce social conditions that come into conflict with democratic ideals. The United States has now had thirty years—comparable to the post-Civil War decades—in which the structure of industry and America's relation to the world have been thoroughly transformed. During the Bush administration and during Clinton's first years in office, some new and some older social problems have emerged. In the past, the nation did not seem to have the resources to deal with them. With budget deficits soaring, how could it afford to complete the funding of Headstart, reduce teacher-student ratios, make college education affordable, subsidize urban rapid transit systems, broaden access to health care and improve antipollution technology? Now it does have the resources, but still nothing happens. (252)

- **Robert Reich**, Clinton Administration Labor Secretary, similarly skewers his Democratic colleagues for doing nothing in times of apparent opportunity ("The Era of Great Social Rest," *The American Prospect*, July 17, 2000):

> Scholars of American political history will one day look back upon the summer of 2000 as the oddest of times . . . The world's richest nation ever also has the widest inequality of income and wealth of any advanced

country—wider than it has experience in more than a century—but no strategy for how to reduce it, and none is being discussed. (Accessed online at www.prospect.org)

• My former colleague, Senator **Charles E. Schumer**, actually calls for larger federal government—the new "New Deal"—in response to terrorist threats in the new century. "The changing times present President Bush with what could be the greatest challenge of his presidency . . . The president can either lead the charge or be run over by it." ("Big Government Looks Better Now," *The Washington Post*, December 11, 2002)

• Civil-libertarian **Eric Foner** perhaps best articulates the hopeful thinking of those troubled by trending devolution (*The Story of American Freedom*, 1998):

> No one can predict the ultimate fate of current understandings of freedom, or whether alternative traditions now in eclipse—freedom as economic security, freedom as active participation in democratic governance, freedom as social justice for those long disadvantaged—will be rediscovered and reconfigured to meet the challenges of the new century. All one can hope is that in the future, the better angels of our nature (to borrow Lincoln's words) will reclaim their place in the forever unfinished story of American freedom. (332)

REARRANGING DYNAMICS

The rearranging dynamics of alternative ideas are revealed and reflected in federal policies and politics of contemporary America.

• Political Scientist **David G. Lawrence** (*America: The Politics of Diversity*, 1998) characterizes contemporary dynamics as an interesting but logical stage in the developing story of American diversity:

> At the beginning of a new century, we find reshuffling of roles in this system. Subnational governments still must lobby Washington for federal aid and grants. They must also contend with those preemptions and mandates. But federal policymakers seem intent on shift major responsibilities from Washington to the states, even those that seem to be—and some critics claim, out to be—federal responsibilities. This re-sorting is nothing new; it has been going on since the Founding. What makes it all the more interesting today is that our federal structure reinforces American diversity and makes our political system even more hyperpluralistic than would otherwise be the case. (79)

• According to **John D. Donahue**, an ex-Clinton Administration official who teaches public policy at Harvard University, Washington has been a willing partner in this devolutionary process (*Disunited States*, 1997):

As advocates of state primacy found their voice, the nationalist side of the argument was strangely muted. Washington acquiesced in the ascendancy of the states, and not only because of Republican dominance of both Congress and the statehouses . . . Clinton seemed quite comfortable with the broad devolutionary theme. The administration proudly noted, in a report on labor-market trends, that federal government employment had fallen by over one-tenth on its watch (from January 1993 to March 1996) while state and local government employment had grown . . . Federal domestic spending (aside from transfers and interest) fell from around 3 percent of the economy at the start of the 1990s to less than 2 percent in 1996. (34-35)

Donahue also predicts that the federal role will shrink further in the new century:

Aside from sending checks to health-care providers, Social Security claimants, and debt holders, the federal government will be a shrinking presence in most Americans' lives well into the early years of the twenty-first century. (37)

• Actually, devolutionary philosophy targets more than just the size and shape of federal governance. **Lynn A. Staeheli, Janet E. Kodras, and Colin Flint** maintain, in *State Devolution in America: Implications for a Diverse Society* (1997), that contemporary rearranging dynamics are creating new policy relationships between the American people and American government:

At the heart of this ongoing debate is the issue of geographically distributing power and resources within the federal hierarchy . . . Devolving federal responsibilities to states and localities or shifting functions to a highly fragmented private sector greatly accentuates spatial variations in government provision. Although the pieces of legislation enacted subsequent to the 1994 election will have complex and even contradictory effects, the clear message of the Contract, and the prevailing direction of change, is to shift power from Washington, DC, to the states, thus removing the traditional leveling role of the national government accentuating differences in the economic competitiveness and social well-being of Americans, depending on where they live.   In short, the 1994 elections brought to the forefront of political debate questions related to the role of the government within the larger society. (xiii)

• Or, as stated somewhat differently and more specifically by **Colin Flint** in his concluding contribution ("Regional Collective Memories and the Ideology of State Restructuring") in *State Devolution in America*:

As the federal scale loses its desire and ability to act as provider, legitimation of the system will increasingly have to be undertaken through discursive channels as material safety nets are scaled back. The three-pronged strategy of devolution, privatization, and dismantling will benefit those places with both the adequate material foundations and a suitably oriented civil society to foster both economic growth and social cohesion.   Those places that can integrate themselves into the global economy will be able to proclaim the success of "common sense" and "pragmatism," whereas less fortunate locations must ponder on the means of building social capital when capital has passed them by. (269)

• The most dramatic comment on the rearranging dynamics of contemporary American government is **Thomas R. Dye** and **Harmon Zeigler**'s advice to their students in the closing paragraph of *The Irony of Democracy: An Uncommon Introduction to American Democracy* (2000):

> Maintain a healthy distrust of government and assume responsibility for your own life. Personal freedom is most endangered when we place too much trust in government, see great idealism in its actions, and have unquestioning faith in our public leaders. Democratic values—individual dignity, freedom of speech and press, rights of dissent, personal liberty—are safer when we are suspicious of government's power and worry about its size and complexity . . . If we look to government to resolve all our problems, our social dependency will increase, and we will assume less responsibility for our lives. The traditional democratic value is to encourage individuals to shape their own destinies. (477)

CONTINUING RHETORICAL CROSSFIRE

Speaking realistically, of course, American government is not going to shrink much if at all. Societal demands keep our national agenda full, forever growing, even while sparkling with the rhetorical gunfire of competitive ideas about proper governance. Every day that agenda stretches larger—in clear new directions and shadowy forms—through strategically manipulated budgets. In this environment of continuing rhetorical crossfire, however, Washington is reluctant to tackle head-on—through full national public authority and institutions—persistent social ailments such as racism, drugs, crime, and violence. "Big Ideas" are out, and little things—such as staged town meetings about race, photo opportunities about school uniforms, and compassionate calls for faith-based initiatives—are in. There are no serious federal initiatives or proposals, from either the White House or Congress, comparable to Social Security, the New Deal, or the Great Society. The federal judiciary, unlike progressive activists of yesteryear, seems content to tinker with established policies. Nor does there appear to be sufficient interest outside government for anything resembling the civil rights movement of the 1960s.

Even internationally, with no economic or military or ideological competitor in sight, Washington seems to have lost its way. The Clinton Administration searched frantically for a coherent, comprehensive "Clinton Doctrine", and the Bush White House has yet to define, clearly, our responsibilities as the world's singular super-power. Furthermore, many Members of Congress seem proud of the fact that they have no passports. Despite a slew of combat, humanitarian, and peacekeeping actions, our foreign engagement more often resembles a "911" service rather than international policy. Apparently out of the question is any grand new effort—such as the Marshall Plan or the Peace Corps—for the global pursuit of democratic ideals.

Something Different. **Over the course of many generations, America has seen its share of alternative, rearranging movements; and American democracy has taken such challenges in stride while moving forward on its progressive course. However this review of contemporary public life suggests that we now are experiencing something significantly different from politics-as-usual. Devolutionary inclinations—in tandem with observed patterns of civic decline and democratic dissensus, and within a broader framework of systemic, philosophical, and political change—have important ramifications for the future of our Great Experiment.**

....

TIRED AMERICA APPEARS TO BE QUESTIONING THE GREAT EXPERIMENT AT A CRITICAL POINT IN AMERICAN HISTORY

The important matter, of course, is whether our contemporary civic decline, democratic dissensus, and devolutionary inclinations have serious consequence for the future. Are these developments passing digressions, or permanent distemper? In other words, is America giving up on the historic Great Experiment of American democracy?

In attempting to answer this question, I should reiterate my earlier warning about historical comparisons and future projections—such analysis is imprecise and highly speculative. But I think that some judgments—particularly an observation about critical timing—are in order.

Clearly, America historically has demonstrated a relatively healthy mindset about our collective endeavor, and American society has conducted itself in general accord with the progressive norms our national democratic experiment. Just as clearly, however, contemporary Americans evidence surprising levels of civic disengagement and dissensus in their attitudes toward American government; and we now seem inclined toward some alternative arrangements for our historic experiment.

A MATTER OF CRITICAL TIMING FOR AMERICAN DEMOCRACY

What makes all of this timely and critical is that America seems to be tiring of the Great Experiment simultaneously, cumulatively, and interactively with other important developments. As posited in the preceding propositional observations, (a) the American systemic environment is not as favorably aligned as it has been for most of our history; (b) we have engaged ourselves in an intense philosophical debate

about American culture and governance; and (c) American democracy no longer works as well as it used to work. **Further, contemporary America evidences civic disengagement, democratic dissensus, and devolutionary governmental inclinations.**

DISTEMPERED DEMOCRACY
AND SYSTEMIC VOLATILITY

Of particular significance to this unsettling analysis is the fact that public commitment to the essential concepts of our original national democratic endeavor appears increasingly mixed and unsteady during fundamentally turbulent times. We seem unsure about American nationalism, democratic ideals, and republican governance at the same time that our political system is reshaping itself in unpredictable ways. Most importantly, the American people may be tiring of their historic experiment while assuming immense popular control over the workings of American democracy. This setting of distempered democracy and systemic volatility invites uncomfortable discussion about the aforementioned "ultimate, unhealthy authority" inherent in our Great Experiment.

Undoubtedly, America has functioned successfully in the past without full, popular, national consensus, engagement, and commitment to the Great Experiment; but just as undoubtedly, our historic functional success is no guarantee that we can and will perform as well in the future. Our original democratic experiment allowed elites and powerful interests to run a loose, limited, representative framework of governance—within a pretty favorable environment—in pursuit of vague democratic ideals for a cooperative, collective society. In time, that simple experiment evolved in much more formally structured, highly developed, politically complex, and progressively democratic directions; but its progressive development also guaranteed that, sooner or later, systemic constraints, philosophical debates, and political realities would prove disruptive and challenging to the historical order of elitist democracy.

The term "elitist democracy" may strike some as an ideological oxymoron, but it accurately describes the American system and conveys an interesting irony of American political life over the past two centuries. As stated by **Thomas Dye** and **Harmon Zeigler** (*The Irony of Democracy*, 2000):

> It is the irony of democracy that the survival of democratic values—individual dignity, limited government, equality of opportunity, private progress, freedom of speech and press, religious tolerance, and due process of laws—depends on enlightened elites. The masses respond to the ideas and actions of elites. When elites abandon democratic principles or the masses lose confidence in elites, democracy is in peril. (16)

This is not a political defense of elite rule, according to Dye and Zeigler; it is a realistic explanation of how democracy actually works in the real world:

Democratic values thrive best when the masses are absorbed in the problems of everyday life and involved in groups and activities that distract their attention from mass political movements. Political stability depends on mass involvement in work, family, neighborhood, trade union, hobby, church, group recreation, and other activities. When the masses become alienated from home, work, and community—when their ties to social organizations and institutions weaken—they become vulnerable to the appeals of demagogues, and democratic values are endangered. (20)

Now—at a critical time in the course of American democracy—"We the people" are taking our place among traditional elites and powerful interests in the arena of public power; and in this volatile, transformational environment, surprising patterns of public disengagement, dissensus, and devolution become more than academically interesting.

In short, the American people seem to be tiring of their historic experiment at the same critical time that they are assuming significant power and responsibility for the future of American democracy.

RADICAL POSSIBILITIES

The danger of these critical times is that eventually, without corrective action, an impatient populace may—democratically and incrementally— exercise its ultimate authority and alter our historic version of America in radical ways. I share the sentiments of **Jean Bethke Elshtain**, who despite her faith in "democracy's enduring promise," says in *Democracy On Trial* (1995):

As an American who has passed her own mid-century mark, I have never known the loss of independence, foreign armies, or occupations, but I have joined the ranks of the nervous generation. I believe we are in the danger zone. No outside power will take us over and destroy our freedom. We are perfectly capable, my nervousness tells me, of doing that to ourselves, all in the name of more freedom. (XIV-XV)

I would like to think that today's developments constitute a case of temporary distemper, or a simple pause, or a few targeted adjustments, or a sharing of some of the burden of democratic progress between the federal government and a broader, supportive society. In the long run, some of these developments may be inconsequential or even therapeutic for America. Furthermore, a strong economy over the past decade has relieved some of the more superficial strains on American democracy. But there is a reasonable chance that, early in this new century, we will have to deal with daunting new public problems; and we may have to ask ourselves the final, uncomfortable question posed in my definitional discussion about "America", "American democracy", and "dying": "How far can we pursue democratic ideals through limited, representative governance without succumbing to the inherent, destructive tendencies of democracy?"

My "dying" speculation is an extremely unlikely outcome, but it serves as useful, sobering background for assessing our present predicament. It is

worthwhile analysis, not idle speculation, to conclude that these are subtly unhealthy times for America—and to worry about our Great Experiment.

A GENERAL PATTERN OF DISTURBING INCLINATIONS

Therefore, if we view historic America as an acceptable model of democratic life (that is, as a public process incorporating the practical capacity for continuous, progressive march toward democratic ideals), and if we acknowledge the distempered condition of contemporary America at this critical transformational juncture in American history, then we have to be concerned about the future of our Great Experiment.

In my opinion, and drawing from the propositions and observations presented in this section, "tired" America generally tends in patterned fashion and disturbing directions. Increasingly we seem to be revisiting and revising—sometimes consciously but often unthinkingly—the original, essential, conceptual elements of our Great Experiment:

(1)   First, the American people are experiencing and evidencing a declined sense of American nationalism. Societal divergence, centrifugal democracy, and economic globalism are reorienting and diminishing our traditional national community.

(2)   Secondly, while popularly-expressed support for democratic ideals in general remains strong, in-depth study and public referenda reveal that Americans are developing reservations about the specific application and advancement of these ideals through national government; on the other hand, some want to elevate cultural values (such as the family, religion, community, and diversity) as central elements—alongside or above traditional democratic ideals—of our national experiment.

(3)   Thirdly, we seem increasingly impatient with our national experiment's difficult, contentious balancing of inconsistent, contradictory, confusing democratic ideals. "Culture-warriors" and "demo-fanatics" drive public debate in troubling philosophical and political directions; and too often we talk about re-arranging the historic framework of limited, representative governance—through uncertain mechanisms such as direct initiatives and teledemocracy—to accommodate contemporary inclinations.

(4)   Finally, we seem insufficiently concerned as a nation about the danger of these unsettling tendencies for our democratic endeavor. A sense of civic irrelevancy—combined with the above-mentioned ailments—appears to have weakened our commitment to the national experiment in democratic ideals; and there is a disturbing propensity—both "inside the beltway" and "out here"—for individuals, institutions, and communities to simply walk away from our historic democratic experiment in favor of less inspired alternatives.

Thus America, at a critical juncture, may be questioning its Great Experiment, moving—quite often consonant with democratic principles and processes—in ways and directions that are contradictory to the historic spirit and course of American democracy.

....

SUMMARY COMMENT

In short, despite having enjoyed perhaps the greatest period of peace and prosperity in memory, our magical mix is losing its magic. **Transforming American democracy no longer works the way it used to work, and we seem to be tiring of our national democratic experiment.** We evidence surprising civic disengagement and democratic dissensus in our beliefs and attitudes; and we increasingly incline away from the traditional ways and norms of democratic governance. Sometimes violently and tragically (as in Oklahoma City), sometimes openly and messily (as in California's governance by plebiscite), but, of most significance, often democratically and effectively (as in Washington's devolutionary retreat from "Big Government"), we appear to be drifting outside the basic currents of American history and American democracy.

Furthermore, the preliminary prognosis—absent full analysis of our transformational distemper—has to include, in theory, more seriously negative consequences, even national demise. Theoretically, America, as we have known it, may be dying!

_____
_____
_____

SECTION THREE

IS AMERICA GOING TO DIE?

My analysis thus far has suggested that contemporary America is changing in ways that are important and unsettling for the future of American democracy. I began with a set of four propositional observations and an analytical framework positing that, if all four propositions are true, then America may indeed be dying. While it would be inaccurate to affirm these propositions, it is clear that serious systemic, philosophical, political, and societal problems afflict American democracy. Contemporary America is undergoing a transformational experience of historic significance unprecedented except during the Civil War era. Ironically, in times of obvious fortuity and civic irrelevancy, the historically magical mix of American democracy is turning into a divisive, disruptive, debilitating family feud.

Distempered Pursuit of a More Perfect Union. Victimized in the crossfire of our family fight are not only routine functions of government and civil society but also, and of critical importance, perhaps the survival of our Great Experiment. Ironically, in a sense, we may be stifling the pursuit of democratic ideals with our distempered pursuit of "a more perfect union."

What Can We Do? In this section, I want to deal with some important questions about the future of American democracy. Have we reached a critical point of systemic overload? Has our democratic experiment run its course? What awaits America if we continue our current course? What can we do to enhance the future of American democracy?

_____

_____

_____

CHAPTER 8

HOW SERIOUS IS
AMERICA'S DEMOCRATIC DISTEMPER?

SYSTEMIC REALITIES
AND ALTERNATIVE SCENARIOS

Clearly we have reached an important point in American history. Furthermore, it really is not surprising that America has come to this point. Our historical origins inclined us toward systemic overload sooner or later.

. . . .

AMERICA APPARENTLY HAS REACHED
A CRITICAL JUNCTURE OF SYSTEMIC DESTINY

American government and American democracy developed originally to accommodate a loose, unstructured, diverse society, which enjoyed sufficient room to breathe and experiment with different ideas about "the good life." The Founders designed a decentralized federal system for pursuing vague, indefinite democratic ideals and material benefits within the framework of open opportunity and limited, representative government; and they wisely avoided the resolution of contentious inclinations into national absolutisms.

In time, with relatively successful, satisfactory operation of that loose system, we evolved into a tradition of majoritarian democracy that accommodated minority rights. Modern America may not be exactly what the Founders had in mind, and it certainly is not perfect; but it has proven remarkably progressive and resilient. Other than the 1860s civil war, the system worked fairly well for two centuries.

IRRESISTIBLE FORCES OF DEMOCRACY

However, considering the original, restrained, representative framework of governance established by our Founders and the developing, popular, irresistible forces of our national journey, America perhaps was destined to reach the point at which (a) public demands for policies, services, and benefits might nationalize and centralize the federalist democracy to the maximum of its progressive capabilities and (b) conflicting democratic ideals, cultural values, and principles of governance would disrupt the Great Experiment.

In a sense, contemporary America is being victimized by the historic success of its Great Experiment. While no society will ever complete its pursuit of democratic ideals, America's march has progressed far beyond the Founders' aspirations for economic stability, national security, and political democracy. We have demonstrated very well (to use the terms of my original, provocative, three-part question) that our nation—a people of cultural diversity, with divergent ideals, values, and principles of governance—"can" pursue freedom, equality, and justice within the traditional framework of limited, representative government. We also have shown "how" to continue this pursuit of democratic ideals under such conditions for an extended period of history.

In fact, America has addressed these concerns over the past two centuries sufficiently well enough to consider turning its attention to more challenging philosophical ideals. But we now come face to face with the third part of my provocative question: "How far can America pursue the Great Experiment without succumbing to the inherent, destructive tendencies of democracy?" We now find ourselves somewhat in the position of **Francis Fukuyama**'s "Last Man"—enjoying the triumph of liberal democracy while staring into a brave new world of possible democratic chaos and conflict (*The End of History and the Last Man,* 1992). Or perhaps, as **Russell Jacoby** complains in *The End of Utopia: Politics and Culture in an Age of Apathy* (2000), we face something worse: "No one even pretends to believe in a different future" (180).

RISKY REDEFINITION

Now, while basking in worldwide democratization, America is attempting to deal anew with difficult democratic ideals, values, and governance (ironically, at the same time, our "boundless continent" in many ways resembles an old world society of crowded peoples struggling in fixed time and place for the same limited philosophical resources). Thus, the irresistible forces of democracy, by their very success, are pushing us toward a fundamental, traumatic, risky redefinition of our historic system;

and the systemic realities of today's debate seriously jeopardize the continued, collective, national pursuit of democratic ideals. The search for democratic ideals in general—with its necessary balancing of alternative strains among those ideals—is a precarious venture by itself. Our Great Experiment can never achieve full resolution of competing democratic ideals; and mixing moral and religious values and new ideas of governance into that experiment is a toxic, explosive reformulation that makes a positive outcome virtually impossible. The philosophical civil war weakens the drive toward democratic ideals by pitting warring faction against warring faction, with neither side interested in furthering general freedom or equality (or various other democratic ideals) because they now see specific democratic ideals as integral to their particularistic cultural values and principles of governance. Their continued warring distracts and derails the democratic movement as a common endeavor.

Benjamin Barber, in *A Passion For Democracy* (1998), provides a rather lengthy but panoramic statement of the mounting problems of our Great Experiment:

> When the Constitution was first fashioned, America stood at the threshold of a century of growth, material prosperity, and burgeoning national power. Heterogeneity provided room to operate, privatism was an invitation to speculation and growth (personal gain publicly legitimized), continental power was an unexploited promise as seductive as the frontier seem endless, inequality appeared to be a remediable condition which, even unremediated, nurtured ambition and (upward) mobility. The threshold has long since been crossed, however . . . The irresistible force embodied in the endless American frontier has encountered the immovable object embodied in the limits of growth. The American nation, frozen between these awesome pressures, seems in danger of failing both as a republic and an empire . . . Under these changed conditions, the very institutions that once fostered success now catalyze failure. They represent a governmental chemotherapy which, though it long sustained the nation's republican health against the twin cancers of anarchy and tyranny, is now itself imperiling the body politic. (50-51)

A STUDY IN DISORDER

Philosophical order has never been a rigid rule of American democracy, but as a result of today's constricted systemic environment and intense wrangling over ideals, values, and governance, the political process has become a study in disorder and dysfunction. Philosophical warriors of all types—Democrats and Republicans, liberals and conservatives, even libertarians, all hell-bent on promoting their immediate pet missions—are trashing traditional democratic icons such as the First Amendment and the Bill of Rights. Radical reformers are short-circuiting representative government in favor of direct democracy. Affirmative action, immigration, gun control, abortion, homosexuality, and pornography dominate our policy agenda, exacerbating more conventional democratic pursuits. Day-to-day government plods along, but important questions of public policy—such as long-term budget problems, national defense, and healthcare—suffer collateral damage. In the absence of acceptable progress on pressing issues, the governmental forum too often is filled with finger pointing, symbolism, and other political games.

Our political free-for-all is not limited to politicians and the governmental forum. Various segments of the American people have joined the fray in unconventional and ironic manner. We see grandparental senior citizens, permanently dependent upon a structurally defective governmental transfer payments program, angrily warning elected public officials to "keep your blankety-blank hands off social security." We see farmers, philosophically conservative and culturally apolitical, protesting the termination of public subsidies. We see minorities, historically victimized by official discrimination, parading for governmentally decreed racial arrangements. We see religious groups, fundamentally supportive of religious freedom, fighting for governmentally sanctioned religious activity. In fact, we see a large portion of Americans simultaneously benefiting from governmental action and schizophrenically dog-cussing government. It's not a very pretty picture, somewhat like watching a hatchet fight between Siamese twins.

OUR DEMOCRATIC EXPERIMENT
MAY HAVE RUN ITS COURSE

It appears that America's Great Experiment may simply have run its course, that American democracy may have outlived (or outgrown) its historic foundations. Our Great Experiment was designed to allow a national society's pursuit of fuzzy democratic ideals in a favorable systemic environment and through a loose framework of limited, representative governance. Our federal republic was not designed to work as a democratic Leviathan—nor can it survive in today's constrained setting as a Seinfeldish sit-com about civic nothingness.

The notion that our Great Experiment may have run its course is not new. Besides the usual political rant of run-of-the-mill doomsayers, serious concerns and questions have been raised over the past half-century. Actually, Journalist **Peter Schrag** proposed a variation of my thesis in *The End of the American Future* (1973). Schrag, a long time newspaper editorialist, suspected during the 1960s that "an American age" was coming to its end:

> There was no way to be certain just what had changed or why the language of conventional American politics no longer worked . . . The language of American politics had always assumed an inevitable rise in the conditions of American life . . . But what if a growing number of people no longer believed in that inevitability—if their very demands were based on doubt? . . . It was as if the country had begun looking for itself, as if its perceptions of time had changed, and as if the interwoven strands once inadequately labeled "the mainstream," "the future," and the "American dream" had become increasingly unreliable or unattractive. (12-15)

Concerned about civil rights, Vietnam, and a slew of other social wars, Shrag visited every region of the country, talking to people in schools, factories, and union halls about what was happening and about our growing intellectual despair. Afterwards, he sounded less than enthusiastic in concluding that the alternative to utopia was not necessarily apocalypse:

> The country would never be as wonderful again, never as grand in its expectations or its innocence—and was, therefore, less of a country—but neither was it likely to be so demanding and pretentious . . . As the country approached its bicentennial in 1976 it was, in a way, like starting all over. (306)

The turbulent sixties and seventies dragged on into the anxious eighties, then into the roller coaster nineties, when a post-Cold War economic flourish bought some relief to weary America. Now, at the beginning of the Twenty-First Century—as the economy recedes and international tensions arise anew—we need to address the reality of democratic distemper that has challenged our nation for the past half century; and we must ask whether our Great Experiment has run its course.

....

CONVENTIONAL ASSURANCES OF AMERICAN DEMOCRACY'S ENDURING STRENGTH

Of course, many serious, intelligent people disagree with my assessment. Some contend that historic liberal democracy will endure with time, patience, and perhaps some adjustments.

Harper's Senior Editor **Michael Lind**, for example, says that the most significant development in contemporary America is an emerging, multiracial, middle-class majority united by traditional principles of American democracy (*The Next American Nation: The New Nationalism and the Fourth American Revolution,* 1995). Rejecting various tenets of both the left and the right, Lind preaches the inevitable union of cultural and economic nationalism in the interest of a multiracial middle-class in "Trans-America" (15).   This is not a prophecy, he declares, but an observation of American and world history:

> Self-conscious Trans-Americans are the prophets and pioneers of a new, more inclusive community, in the same way that pan-German and pan-Russian and pan-Italian intellectuals in the nineteenth century were forerunners of nationalisms that seemed alien at first to people accustomed to thinking of themselves as members of tiny, parochial peasant communities. They are harbingers of the next stage in the development of American society: the national awakening. (300)

Additionally, a quartet of impressive end-of-century analyses by very competent scholars—all deriving, interestingly, from Princeton University Press—provide differing but relatively positive interpretations of American democracy's enduring strength.

A FLEXIBLE REPUBLIC

An especially strong case for America's enduring democratic destiny is Benjamin R. Barber's *A Passion For Democracy* (1998)—which I have already cited as one of the most interesting treatises on American democratic history. In a collection of essays written over the past three decades, Barber (Professor of Political Science and Director of The Walt Whitman Center for the Culture and Politics of Democracy at Rutgers University) places America's contemporary predicament within a history of paradoxical democracy. What makes this book worthwhile is Barber's personal, poetic, meandering explanation of the contradictory intricacies of American democracy—especially his essay about our artificial "crisis of purposelessness." He optimistically predicts that America will continue its unique democratic journey:

> But, history shows, America is a rare and not so fragile nation—forever exhibiting its exceptionalism in new and startling ways. It found the way in its compromised republic to reconcile republic and empire; now it must compromise the compromises and find a way to preserve the republic in a strange new world of finitude, boundaries, and interdependence. If it can again improve the formula, it may once more confound the great tradition out of which it arises by proving that a flexible, well-made, republic responsive to changing American conditions can survive the most pernicious of its modern enemies: modernity itself. (57)

Despite the limitations of a collection spanning the past quarter century, Barber possesses the credentials and skills for such passionate optimism.

HISTORICAL STABILITY

John A. Hall and Charles Lindholm argue, in *Is America Breaking Apart?* (1999), that America will endure because of its historical institutions and classless society. Hall (a sociologist from McGill University) and Lindholm (an anthropologist from Boston University) examine our apparent distemper and pronounce America in basically good health.

> The main burden of our argument is clear: America is not in any danger of breaking apart. Historical processes have worked to solidify and stabilize powerful central institutions, while suppressing possible sources of resistance. Class loyalties, so important in European politics, have been eclipsed in America, where the vast majority lump themselves together as

> "middle class" and assume themselves to be in general agreement on fundamental principles. (149)

Interestingly, furthermore, Hall and Lindholm belittle the nature of such inquiries into the future of American democracy:

> If warnings of disintegration are useless as analyses, they do tell us something about an aspect of the American experience. Most obviously, the rhetoric of breakdown has inherited its moralistic tone from the first American intellectuals: Calvinist preachers. Modern critics, whether on the left or the right, tend to sound like Jeremiahs, self-righteously calling on Americans to rise above their sinful natures. More generally, behind the discourse of disintegration lie elitist fears of democracy as practiced by real people . . . We believe that Americans have less to fear from the messiness and occasional violence of popular protests and movements than they do from the machinations of anti-democratic elites. (151-152)

Despite their "more hopeful and less evangelical" perspective (or perhaps because of that approach), the Hall and Lindholm analysis overemphasizes the historical institutions and shared cultured values of the American experience without considering the transformational impact of fundamental change in the American systemic environment. By ignoring or denying the altered realities of the broader world, their essay begins and concludes with the premise that American democracy will persevere because it always has persevered.

CONTINUITY OF COMMON VALUES

Neil J. Smelser and Jeffrey C. Alexander provide more balanced analysis about America's anxious democracy in *Diversity and Its Discontents: Cultural Conflict and Common Ground in Contemporary American Society* (1999).
Smelser (Director of Stanford's Center for Advanced Study in the Behavioral Sciences) and Alexander (Sociology Professor at UCLA) report in this edited collection that the contemporary sense of decline is nothing new: "From the beginnings of the Republic, institutional and social change has been constant, creating periodic crises of confidence and spasms of concern about national stability, social cohesion, and democracy itself" (8). They offer assurance that common values are still a social reality: "National surveys report that Americans continue to believe in democracy, in the opportunity for social mobility, and in the value of American life" (9). They also identify a variety of structural developments—affecting such institutions as family, sexuality, education, religion, and voluntary organization—that have led to a sense of cultural crisis.
Most importantly, the authors balance their explanations for our cultural discontent alongside an acknowledgement of real, important societal change:

In a word, the Tocquevillian specificity of American society remains in place, but it has been given a different structure . . . Those working at the grass roots of American society have created new, normatively sanctioned organizational arrangements and new ways to negotiate conflicts. Traditional American values, rather than being fragmented or deconstructed, have not only provided a stabilizing anchor for these pragmatic responses but have stimulated them . . . In identifying the misdiagnoses of both the left and the right we are far from claiming that "all is right with the world." But we are convinced that the assertions about the death of common values are premature at best. (16-17)

PRUDENT CONCERN (BUT NO CRISIS)

The most rigorous and useful analysis among this series is *Disaffected Democracies: What's Troubling The Trilateral Countries?* (2000) edited by Susan J. Pharr and Robert D. Putnam. Pharr (Professor of Japanese Politics at Harvard University) and Putnam (Professor of International Peace at Harvard University) attempt to assess the state of governance in democratized societies a quarter century after a controversial Trilateral Commission report portraying a crisis of democracy and questioning the future of democratic governability.

The editors discount talk of "democratic crisis" this time around, focusing instead on how and why contemporary democracy struggles amid its success over alternative ideologies:

Indeed, it is a remarkable irony that just at the moment when liberal democracy has defeated all its enemies on the battlefields of ideology and politics, many people in the established democracies believe that their own political institutions are faltering, not flourishing. The larger issue today, at the outset of the twenty-first century, is not whether democracy will survive or, indeed, whether it is in crisis, but how well leaders and institutions in democracies can meet the expectations and needs of their citizens. (xviii)

Pharr, Putnam, and their colleagues find no reason to believe that American democracy is at risk of being supplanted by undemocracy; but they present substantial evidence of mounting public unhappiness with government and the institutions of representative democracy throughout North America, Western Europe, and Japan; and they consider these patterns of serious consequence:

These criticisms of governments and leaders do not necessarily translate into a "crisis of democracy' that threatens constitutional and representative government. Nevertheless, the fact that representative democracy per se is not at risk does not imply that all is well with our political systems. Indeed most of our fellow citizens believe that all is not well. Due regard for their view, as well as a prudent concern for the future, suggests that we should explore the sources of this democratic discontent. (27)

The contributions of this latter book to our discussion of American democracy are numerous. First, it is comparative analysis, drawing from international experts and focusing on systems throughout the established democracies. Secondly, it presents significant original and timely research.　But most importantly, while stating the obvious primacy of democracy as the standard ideological framework for the modern world, the authors acknowledge that something is fundamentally wrong in America and other societies as we enter a new century.

....

UNCONVENTIONAL INTERPRETATIONS OF DEMOCRATIC DESTINY

Despite American democracy's historic resiliency, many intelligent and passionate observers assert serious discontent and acknowledge the unpleasant possibility that our Great Experiment may have run its expansive course; and they present a diversity of unconventional analysis and commentary about our democratic destiny.

THE THIRD WAVE?

Perhaps the premier futurist of the past few decades has been Alvin Toffler, whose best-selling books, articles, and speeches continuously fascinate and irritate those of us concerned with society and change. *The Third Wave* (1980) was published years before our turn-of-century frenzy regarding the future of American democracy; but I include it here in my 1990s collection because of its pertinent insights.

After discussing mounting pressures on the nation-state, Toffler penned an imaginary letter "To the Founding Parents":

> . . . I want to thank you, the revolutionary dead, for having made possible for me a half-century of life as an American citizen under a government of laws, not men, and particularly for that precious Bill of Rights, which has made it possible for me to think, to express unpopular views, however foolish or mistaken at times—indeed, to write what follows without fear of suppression.
>
> For what I now must write can all too easily be misunderstood by my contemporaries. Some will no doubt regard it as seditious. Yet it is a painful truth I believe you would have quickly grasped.　For the system of government you fashioned, including the very principles on which you based it, is increasingly obsolete, and hence increasingly, if inadvertently, oppressive and dangerous to our welfare.　It must be radically changed and a new system of government invented—a democracy for the twenty-first century. (396)

Toffler suggested several heretical principles of "Third Wave Government," including minority power (replacing the previously legitimizing principle of majority rule), semi-direct democracy (eliminating representatives from the representational process), and decision division (sharing decisions more widely and switching the site of decision-making appropriate to the problems themselves). Toffler foresaw no single massive reorganization or single revolutionary change imposed from the top; he predicted instead thousands of conscious, decentralized experiments at the local level which then could be applied nationally and transnationally. The responsibility for change, he said, lies with the people:

> Above all, it means starting this process of reconstruction now, before the further disintegration of existing political systems sends the forces of tyranny jackbooting through the streets, and makes impossible a peaceful transition to Twenty-First Century Democracy.
>
> If we begin now, we and our children can take part in the exciting reconstitution not merely of our obsolete   political structures, but of civilization itself.
>
> Like the generation of the revolutionary dead, we have a destiny to create. (421)

AN OPEN-ENDED FUTURE?

William Strauss and Neil Howe suggest an equally imaginative and open-ended future in *The Fourth Turning: An American Prophecy* (1998). Drawing upon a cosmic interpretation of historical eras, or "saeculums," they predict that, early in the new century, we may see a national crisis on par with the Revolution, the Civil War, and World War II.
Among their projected possibilities are "the end of our nation" (closing the book on the political constitution, popular culture, and moral standing of America), "the end of modernity" (a complete collapse of Western Civilization), or "the end of man" (an omnicidal armageddon).
In their final chapter, Strauss and Howe also see the possibility of a reborn nation—but not necessarily the same America:

> The new saeculum could find America a worse place. As Paul Kennedy has warned, it might no longer be a "great power." Its global stature might be eclipsed by foreign rivals. Its geography might be smaller, its culture less dominant, its military less effective, its government less democratic, its Constitution less inspiring. Emerging from its millennial chrysalis, it might evoke nothing like the hope and respect of its "American Century" forbear. Abroad, people of goodwill and civilized taste might perceive this society as a newly dangerous place. Or they might see it as decayed, antiquated, an Old New World less central to human progress than we are now. All this is plausible, and possible, in the natural turning of saecular time. (331)

Or, they project, we could see a more positive future:

Alternatively, the new saeculum could find America, and the world, a much better place. Like England in the Reformation Saeculum, the Superpower America of the Millennial Saeculum might merely be a prelude to a higher plane of civilization. Its new civic life might more nearly resemble that "shining city on a hill" to which its colonial ancestors aspired. Its ecology might be freshly repaired and newly sustainable, its economy rejuvenated, its politics functional and fair, its media elevated in tone, its culture creative and uplifting, its gender and race relations improved, its commonalities embraced and differences accepted, its institutions free of the corruptions that today seem entrenched beyond correction. People might enjoy new realms of personal, family, community, and national fulfillment. America's borders might be around an altered but more cogent geography of public community. Its influence on world peace could be more potent, on world culture more uplifting. All this is achievable as well. (331)

TEMPER OUR EXPECTATIONS?

Veteran Foreign Service analyst Graham Fuller suggests, in *The Democracy Trap: Perils of the Post-Cold War World* (1991), that we think less creatively and expansively; instead, he recommends that we temper our expectations of American democracy:

> No system—a few occasional benevolent dictatorships aside—other than liberal democracy is more systematically reliable in bringing about the well-being of society. But this belief, this faith, does not guarantee that the path will be permanently sustainable. It has also been the cardinal thesis of this book that our democratic values are creating increasingly severe operational dilemmas in their wake. Particular social problems, including the handling of race and ethnicity, morality, and maintenance of the social order are daunting; they may even be exacerbated by the systematic furthering of democratic practice . . . If the social problems become critical enough, and the democratic order becomes paralyzed, it may result in a sharp pendulum swing toward an authoritarian solution in order to preserve society. (266-277)

Fuller warns that "our greatest enemy is no longer overseas but lies in the inherent contradictions of ourselves and our system" (267). Democracy becomes a trap, Fuller says, by stimulating the erroneous belief that the end of the Cold War signals an automatically perfect and democratic world:

> The Democracy Trap is the possibility that democracy may not simply go on getting better, but may contain the seeds of its own decline, possibly spurring an eventual authoritarian response from within our own society. Indeed, the Democracy Trap may lie in the very nature of postindustrial American democracy itself—its tendency to intensify the disorders of an unstructured and possibly decaying society—one in which the traditional binding social institutions of the past are falling by the wayside. Uncritical extension of the frontiers of democratic society and practice could mark the deterioration, rather than the maturation, of American society. (2)

Fuller predicts that America's faith in democracy will be tested in the next few decades as we confront mounting problems and unusual challenges to the current order:

> But what about our Union? Washington indeed fought four bloody years in order to attain a settlement at Appomattox that preserved the Union . . . Could George Bush today call in federal troops and go to war against our own population if, say, the South decided that economically and culturally it no longer wished to remain in the Union? If it undertook a referendum and freely voted for independence? Or if the Spanish-speaking parts of the United States voted for autonomy or separation? Can anyone imagine American troops today killing tens of thousands of Americans—in front of TV cameras—in order to prevent regional separation? I submit that the Appomattox solution—the use of military force to preserve the Union—is no longer tenable. Should a new attempt at regional autonomy or separation ever emerge in America—supported by a local referendum—it could no longer be stopped by force from Washington. American and world values have changed too much for that kind of violence to be wreaked ever again— at least in America—simply in the name of preserving the Union. (99)

JUNK THE CONSTITUTION?

Daniel Lazare rejects outright the limited, representational wisdom of our historic institutional arrangement. He proposes, in *The Frozen Republic: How the Constitution Is Paralyzing Democracy* (1996), that America junk its constitutional republic:

> The problem with the Constitution as it has developed over two centuries is that rather than engaging in a fundamental reordering, Americans have tried to democratize a predemocratic structure . . . The electorate, as a consequence, is locked in a desperate internal struggle, which, as long as Madisonian checks and balances remain in effect, can never end. The results are tortuous, yet ultimately only two outcomes are possible. Either the body politic will keel over from exhaustion or it will explode. (301)

Lazare claims that the Constitution was designed, purposively by its founders, to be counterdemocratic; and he proposes that we start over with different objectives:

> What Americans need is less faith and more thought, less willingness to put their trust in a bygone political order and a greater realization that they, the living, are the only ones capable of maneuvering society through the storm. Instead of beginning with the Constitution as the essential building block, they should realize that there are no givens in this world and that all assumptions, beginning with the most basic, must constantly be examined and tested. (4)

Lazare recommends that somebody—specifically California—start the revolutionary process by challenging the undemocratic nature of the U.S. Senate. He states the case for a political ultimatum: "No taxation . . . without equal representation" (286-287). If America accepts the change to a democratic Senate by either constitutional or political means, he says California should stay in the United States. "If not, it will go . . ." (287). And he's confident that such a successful challenge would be followed by the toppling of an outdated constitution and system of governance.

Americans should cast off their chains, Lazare says. "They have nothing to lose—except one of the most unresponsive political systems this side of the former Soviet Union" (9).

ALREADY TOO LATE?

Patrick Kennon, recently retired after 25 years with the Central Intelligence Agency, says that it is already too late to save American democracy. Democracy has become marginal as a way of governance, he writes in *The Twilight of Democracy* (1995):

> Far from being a divinely ordained arrow in the blue, beyond gravity, destined to rise to ever-greater heights, democracy is an earthbound, human creation subject to the entropy of all such creations. It now travels a course of declining relevance much like that of European monarchy from the power of Elizabeth I to the impotence of Elizabeth II . . . Democracy, like the queen, is gradually ceasing to be a force and becoming a symbol. (255)

Kennon, declaring that the very completeness of democracy's victory as an ideology constitutes a threat, offers an exceedingly cynical preview of American democracy:

> The citizen who once found the meaning of life in work now finds it in consumption and leisure and "respect" . . . .The individual ceases to be an individual and becomes an oilman, a doctor, a woman, a black, a lesbian, an automobile worker, a teacher—a member of a group that has a claim on the national treasury, a group that is not going to have its rights trampled upon, a group that is suspicious of all other groups, a group that is willing to shut down the country if necessary. The bureaucracy is privatized, captured by special interests. It ceases to be a machine for progress and becomes a conduit for passing out subsidies. The politicians, now with no other function than to pander to the groups, mud-wrestle for a cardboard crown and a meaningless title. (260-261)

Kennon's pessimistic prediction is that "Those societies that continue to allow themselves to be administered by individuals whose only qualification is that they were able to win a popularity contest will go from failure to failure and eventually pass from the scene" (263).

BORN TO DIE?

Robert Kaplan, an imaginative seer who has roamed America and the ends of the earth in search of the future, takes an equally disconcerting view of our destiny. In periodic *Atlantic Monthly* articles, best-selling books, and personal appearances, he preaches a "Mad Max" message of unraveling civilization; and he maintains that "America is born to die" in the course of transfiguring into an international nation (speech accessed online at www.calvin.edu/january/1999). Despite his cataclysmic ramblings, Kaplan's creative analyses are worth more than passing attention.

Transnational Junction Point. Our country will not be conquered and will not collapse as did earlier civilizations, Kaplan explains; instead the United States will turn into a transnational junction point for the world's most talented people. Kaplan travels extensively throughout the country, observing a nation that is polarized ethnically, economically, and politically, where technological progress moves privileged society forward with a radically different world-view from that of their less privileged neighbors.

We get some idea of Kaplan's vision of transnational America in *Atlantic Monthly's* introduction to its series on "Travels Into America's Future" (August, 1998, accessed online at www.theatlantic.com) and in the subsequent booklength publication of *An Empire Wilderness: Travels into America's Future* (1998):

> Imagine a land in which the dominant culture is an internationalized one, at every level: in which the political units that really matter are confederations of city-states; in which loyalty is an economic concept, when it is not obsolete; in which "the United States" exists chiefly to provide military protection. That is the land our correspondent glimpses, and it is no longer beyond the horizon. (*The Atlantic Monthly*, August 1998)

Disconnection and Evolution. While visiting Orange County, California, Kaplan asked a routine question of political reporting—"Where's the power?" He found his answer not in any governmental building or political machine—but in the restaurant where he was having lunch:

> Power now was here, in this restaurant, dispersed among many more people and much less accountable, for the issue was simply profit, disconnected from political promises or even geography. Orange County's global corporations were merely home bases—which could be moved in an instant in response, for example, to tax increases. (*An Empire Wilderness*, 1998, 99)

Intrigued by this idea of disconnection, Kaplan bluntly asked "Will this place fight for its country? Are these people loyal to anything except themselves?" Rick Reiff, a Pulitzer Prize winning reporter from Ohio and now editor of the *Orange County Business Journal*, was equally direct in his response: "Loyalty is a problem . . . People came here to make money. In the future patriotism will be more purely and transparently economic. Perhaps patriotism will survive in the form of prestige, if America remains the world economic leader" (*An Empire Wilderness*, 100).

The gist of what Kaplan heard in his west coast encounters is that our country must change—actually it must evolve—in ways, directions, and destinations very different from the past:

> They believed that federal power was waning, that the massive ministry buildings of Washington, D.C., with their oxen armies of bureaucrats, are the product of the Industrial Age, when society reached a level of sheer size and complexity that demanded such institutions, and are not necessarily characteristic of the decentralized American future. Somehow, this leaden federal colossus must slowly evolve into a new, light-frame structure of mere imperial oversight—for the sake of defense, conservation, and the rationing of water and other natural resources—allowing, as I have suggested, for a political silver age if not another golden one. (*An Empire Wilderness*, 335)

Sober Realization. In his latest account of American destiny (*The Coming Anarchy: Shattering the Dreams of the Post Cold War*, 2000), Kaplan says that America probably will not survive in its present form because of its multi-ethnic character and international tensions:

> This and many other factors will make the United States less of a nation than it is today, even as it gains territory following the peaceful dissolution of Canada. As Washington's influence wanes, and with it the traditional symbols of American patriotism, North Americans will take psychological refuge in their insulated communities and cultures. (56)

And he predicts the decline of national community:

> As the size of the U.S. population and the complexity of American life spill beyond the traditional national community, creating a new world of city-states and suburbs, the distance will grow between the citizens of the new city-states and the bureaucratic class of overseers in Washington. (97)

In a final burst of inspiration, Kaplan delivers his futuristic punchline:

> And that brings us to a sober realization. If democracy, the crowning political achievement of the West, is gradually being transfigured, in part because of technology, then the West will suffer the same fate as earlier civilizations . . . I do not mean to say that the United States is in decline. On the contrary, at the end of the twentieth century we are the very essence of creativity and dynamism. We are poised to transform ourselves into something perhaps quite different from what we imagine. (98)

. . . .

ALTERNATIVE SCENARIOS FOR AN UNCERTAIN FUTURE

Apparently, then, we have reached a critical juncture in American history, a political and philosophical crossroads, a transformational struggle for the body and soul of America.

To reiterate, my rhetorical question ("Is America Dying?") is designed to dramatize my contention that, despite an unprecedented period of economic expansion and international power, these are not the best of times for American democracy. America is experiencing systemic constraint and philosophical turmoil; the American people are losing their civic spirit; the political machinery of American democracy is broken; and American government is not functioning very well. The bottom-line result is that American democracy no longer works the way that it is supposed to work, and thus we are questioning our basic democratic ideals, our historic framework of governance, and our commitment to the Great Experiment. This is a democratic sickness of spirit and body.

Our Hopes and Fears. I do not believe that America is going to die. But it is time for us to call time-out, to discuss our transformational condition, where we are going, and what we want America, eventually, to be. We need to determine, in Tocqueville's terms, our hopes and fears for the Great Experiment. I can envision in future America, for example, several alternative scenarios representing various emphases and combinations of wayward currents in contemporary public life—disintegration, deformation, transition, and transformation (all as defined below):

Alternative Scenario No. 1:
Disintegration ("Death of America")

Conceivably, the battle for the body and soul of America could lead to the disintegration of the United States—through either peaceful or violent means—resulting in a unitary state or a confederation of mini-states. "Dying", of course, is an unthinkable option; but who, simply a decade or so ago, really comprehended or predicted developments in the Soviet Union, Yugoslavia, and countless other disintegrating entities around the globe.

Alternative Scenario No. 2:
Deformation ("Amerika" or "USSA")

It is also possible that America could change—perhaps democratically—into a far different nation from what exists today. Simple constitutional amendment, accompanied by statutory contortions, could create deformed, polar versions (or something in between) of our present system, such as a majoritarian, nationalistic, centralized ethnostate—the "United State of Amerika", with conservative ideas about freedom and right-wing cultural values. Or we could become the "Union of Socialist States of America", representing an ultimate confederation of heterogeneous, egalitarian, left-wing sentiments. Of course, "Amerika" or "USSA" (or any other deformation) likely would incorporate extreme interpretations, variations, and mixtures of our historic democratic principles in their refashioned Great Experiment.

Alternative Scenario No. 3:
Transition ("The American Federation")

It is highly possible that America will proceed along its current course, without seriously considering the important and unsettling changes of contemporary public life, and eventually transitioning into "The American Federation". Our divergent, diverging populace may simply re-arrange the federal system—through the normal political process—thus modifying our Great Experiment to accommodate the growing forces of democratic decentralization. But transitional America will not further our experiment along its historic path of progressive democracy; indeed, such accommodation may simply be a compromised step in an unpredictable and risky direction. (More on "The American Federation" in the next chapter.)

Alternative Scenario No. 4:
Transformation ("New America")

"New America" envisions a more aggressive and progressive adjustment to a fundamentally transformed America, democratically strengthening the structure and process without changing the basic principles of our historic national experiment. Transformation obviously requires that we rethink the democratic essence of our nation and that we redesign our Great Experiment if we are to continue our pursuit of democratic ideals. The important question is whether we can address our problems—consciously and rationally—without succumbing to destructive tendencies. (More on "New America" in my concluding chapter.)

****

*EDITORIAL NOTE: Because of the progressive course of American history, futuristic discussion often reflects reactionary and doomsday thinking; but there are important, intriguing insights in polemics about America's possible demise. For example, **Andrew McDonald/William L. Pierce** (The Turner Diaries, still being reprinted since first appearing in 1976) and **Thomas Chittum** (Civil War II, 1997) provide first-person versions of America's violent death. **Wallace Henley** depicts the coming of national sovietization (Escape from America, 1993), and **Wilmot Robertson** (The Ethnostate, 1993) makes a strident case for ethnological nationalization. Far-fetched accounts of "disintegration and "deformation" merit passing mention here simply because these scenarios provide interesting and useful points of reference in the current discussion. However, the scenarios of transition and transformation suggest more plausible variations in our national democratic experiment; therefore, I will explore "The American Federation" in the next* *chapter before concluding with some transformational observations about "New America" and the future of American democracy.*

****

. . . .

SUMMARY COMMENT

How serious is America's democratic distemper? Serious enough to prompt words of caution and reform from conventional analysts and talk among unconventionalists about toppling the constitution, the end of democracy, and the death of the United States.

America's history has shown that we "can" successfully pursue democratic ideals within the framework of limited, representative government. Our history has demonstrated also "how" we can conduct this pursuit. But now we may be in the unpleasant position of finding out "how far we can"—or, more accurately, "how far we cannot"—pursue democratic ideals without succumbing to the inherent, destructive tendencies of democracy.

The progressive evolution of the American system is remarkable; but we may have to acknowledge that today's cumulative challenges—a declining systemic environment, philosophical civil war, and an unmagical mix of people, politics, and government—is straining our progressive capacity. Powerful forces of cynicism, frustration, and resignation have been building for the past half-century; and, at the same time, too many of our citizens seem to have succumbed to civic irrelevancy. Particularly if America were to experience additional political turmoil or enter prolonged civic deterioration, we may come face-to-face with the inherent, destructive tendencies of democracy.

We must now ask ourselves whether our Great Experiment can continue—and in what form and manner—or will America fall to those inherent, destructive tendencies.

CHAPTER 9

WHAT MIGHT AMERICA LOOK LIKE
—IF WE CONTINUE OUR CURRENT COURSE—
IN 2050?

A SPECULATIVE PROJECTION:
"THE AMERICAN FEDERATION"

Most of my readers should be around to enjoy America's democratic blessings and benefits throughout the coming century. But I think that it may be worthwhile to ask what might happen if we fail to consider—consciously and rationally—our long term future. In other words, "Where are we heading if we stay on our current course?" Accordingly, in this chapter, I want to speculate about what America might look like midway—say, in the year 2050—of our Twenty-First Century journey.

<u>Heuristic Speculation.</u> No one can say for sure what the long term future holds; but I am prepared to speculate here—by and with the full authority of my self-invoked literary license—about where we may be heading in the next few decades if we continue our current course. This transitional projection, of course, is neither my prediction nor my recommendation; it is a speculative discussion of how contemporary conditions and developments might play out in the years ahead. It is an heuristic artifact designed simply to stimulate thinking and discussion.

My projective premise is that our fundamental condition—an unfavorable systemic environment and philosophical civil war—is not going to change magically or overnight; and we may simply adjust our civic formula in piecemeal fashion, with minimal consideration of the future of our Great Experiment. The trending dynamics of American society and politics, as projected in the following discussion, suggest the possible nature of such adjustments.

....

CENTRIFUGAL DYNAMICS ARE RESHAPING THE AMERICAN POLITICAL SYSTEM

My speculation is that, within a constrained systemic environment and philosophical civil war, relentless centrifugal dynamics are pushing us toward popular decentralization of the American political system. The cumulative, powerful forces of contemporary cultural and public life are reshaping American society and could necessitate serious adjustments in our national democratic experiment.

Clearly, America will look and act differently as the Twenty-First Century proceeds. It is no secret that demographic trends are turning America into an older nation; and over the next few decades, the American populace will experience the "Aging Baby Boomer" syndrome, increasingly evidencing the changed perspectives, needs, and demands of an older society. But more importantly for my analysis, population growth patterns will create a new social order—with the historically dominant (and aging) white population losing its numerical majority by mid-century; and the emerging majority-of-minorities will be an eclectic lot, thereby further splintering American society. Thus America of the future could be even more diverse, divergent, and democratically dissentient than has been the case historically, eventually exerting powerful new pressures—pressures of less nationalistic and more decentralistic nature—on the American political system.

SOCIAL DIVERSITY

Census 2000 data demonstrate changing America and our increasing social diversity. Our population continues to grow (now approaching 300 million persons), fueled in great part by increases in Hispanic residents who now match the black citizenry (with each classification accounting for about 35 million persons).

Actually, our national family portrait will be even more and differently crowded in the next decade. Our Asian population, for example, is surging just as has the Hispanic community:

If last year's census reflected a decade of Hispanic growth, expect the 2010 headline to be an Asian boom.

One of the fastest growth rates in the 1990s belongs to those with Asian ancestry. With the population growing 74 percent to 11.5 million last year, demographers expect them to help give America a much different look a decade from now. ("Looking Ahead to a More Asian-Influenced America," Associated Press, April 18, 2001)

Census data indicate too that our diversity trend is likely to become more complex as America's younger citizens swell the new "multiracial" category:

A glance at the latest national statistics of the American population under age 18, released Monday, shows the country is on its way to becoming even more racially and ethnically diverse, demographers say.

A prime clue: of the 6.8 million people identified as being more than one race, about 2.9 million, or 42 percent were under 18 . . . In comparison, 26 percent of the total U.S. population of 281 million are under 18 . . . As these multiracial youths grow older and start raising their own families, there is a greater likelihood of seeing more people identifying their diverse backgrounds and making America's statistical portrait even more complex, said Hilary Shelton, executive director of the Washington Bureau of the National Association for the Advancement of Colored People. ("Data on America's Youth Shows Country Could Get More Diverse," Associated Press, March 13, 2001)

Moreover, foreign-born persons now account for about one in every ten Americans (up from 4.7 percent born outside the country in 1970); and almost a fifth (18 percent) of children in America speak a language other than English at home (up from 14 percent a decade ago).

SOCIETAL DIVERGENCE

Along with this increasing diversity, various currents of American society seem to be running in divergent directions. In particular, Americans appear pretty clannish about where and how they live their lives. Independent analysis of the 2000 census shows, for example, that residential segregation is a continuing reality of American society:

Blacks and Whites in the United States remain geographically divided despite population shifts for both groups during the 1990s, new analyses of the 2000 census data showed Monday . . . From the figures which will have broad political and economic implications in the coming decade, the bureau found that whites, whose proportion of the total U.S. population dipped to 77 percent in 2000 from 80 percent in 1990, were most concentrated in counties in the northern half of the country . . . By contrast, blacks were highly concentrated in the southern states, comprising 50 percent or more of the total population in 95 southern counties but 6 percent or less of the population in 64 percent of counties nationwide. ("Census 2000 Analysis Shows U.S. Melting Pot Elusive," Reuters, August 13, 2001)

An academic analysis finds similar patterns for both race and ethnicity:

The United States is more racially and ethnically diverse than ever before, but an independent analysis of the 2000 census data suggests that people still live in largely segregated neighborhoods.

The analysis, conducted by researchers at the State University of New York at Albany, found that from 1990-2000, even as virtually every corner of the country adopted a slightly darker hue, whites, blacks, Asians and Hispanics still tended to live apart ("Analysis of Census Finds Segregation Along With Diversity," *The New York Times*, April 4, 2001)

Other studies indicate correspondent patterns in America's schools:

Segregation in U.S. schools increased during the last decade, despite the nation's growing racial diversity, according to a Harvard University study. The study, released Tuesday, found that 70 percent of black students and more than one-third of Hispanic students attended predominantly minority schools during the 1998-99 school year, the latest data available from the National Center of Education Statistics.

The study also found that white students were more segregated from other minorities . . . "White children are growing up in a society that is going to become more than half minority, and they are almost totally isolated from those minorities," said Gary Orfield, a Harvard professor and co-director of The Civil Rights Project that conducted the study. "These suburban kids are vastly unprepared for the future." ("Harvard Study Finds Segregation in Schools Increasing Despite Country's Growing Diversity," Associated Press, July 18, 2001)

POLITICAL DISSENTIENCE

It's no secret either that these societal patterns already extend to our political mentality and voting behavior. For example, tracking polls preceding Election 2000 identified marked gaps or chasms between sizeable segments of the American electorate, including the Marriage Gap, the North/South Gap, the City/Country Gap, the Union Gap, the Income Gap, and the Race Gap ("Beyond Gender, Polls Reveal Wide Gaps," *The Washington Post*, October 25, 2000). Additional study revealed the religious complexities of our political dissentience:

A post-election poll of adult voters showed that more than ever, the Republican religious coalition consisted of solid majorities of weekly churchgoers among white Protestants, white Roman Catholics, and Mormons.

The heaviest Democratic religious categories were, in order: black Protestants, Jews and other non-Christians, Hispanic Catholics, Hispanic Protestants, people who consider themselves completely secular, and Catholics who don't attend Mass each week. ("U.S. Voters Religiously Polarized," Associated Press, January 25, 2001)

Post-election polling further confirmed the dissentient relationship between social characteristics and voting preference. For example, men favored George Bush 54-43 percent while women voted 55-43 percent for Gore; and while whites leaned toward Bush 54-43 percent, blacks overwhelmingly preferred Gore by a 90-9 percent count (The Los Angeles Times Poll, November 7, 2000, accessed online at www.pollingreport.com).

Furthermore, as studies of that election demonstrate, the American people have splintered into distinct geo-political patterns. A newspaper analysis of actual voting data and exit polling shows clear divisions among the American electorate:

The map tells the story. Vast stretches of red across the rural heartland, all Republican George W. Bush country. A coastal perimeter and urban patches of blue, where Democrat Al Gore prevailed.

Geography is perhaps the most striking yardstick by which to measure the gulf between those who voted for Bush and those who voted for Gore. The election results might be inconclusive as to who won the presidency, but they are clear when it comes to who was won over by the presidential candidates . . .

The cultural differences between Gore's voters and Bush's, as illuminated by exit polls, were striking. Bush attracted people who go to church more than once a week, who think it's more important that the president be a moral leader than a good government manager, who oppose stricter gun laws and who believe that if a school is failing, the government should pay for private school. Honesty is the quality they value most in a leader, followed by leadership and likability.

Gore drew heavy majorities of gay and Jewish voters, those who rarely or never attend church, who support stricter gun laws and who say a school should be fixed if it is failing. Their paramount value is experience, followed by competence to handle complex issues and caring about "people like me." (**Jill Lawrence**, "Country vs. City, Spelled in Red, Blue," *USA Today*, November 9, 2000)

We used to view the rural white South ("Appalachia") as America's singularly important subculture; then we discovered urban black culture. Now we speak prophetically of important new, subcultural configurations and movements, such as "Red Country versus Blue Country;" we identify "multiple melting pots" in California, New York, Florida, and Texas; we see "Amexica" crawling along the southwestern border; we read about "Cascadia" in the Pacific Northwest; and we hear stirrings from the wired, restless, unpredictable community of "Digital Nation".

Whatever their reasons, Americans seem to be settling, residing, working, and conducting their public lives in subcultural enclaves (regions, communities, and groupings) distinctly defined by their demographics, lifestyle, philosophical outlook, and voting behavior. After two centuries of American assimilation and nationalization, we seem to be experiencing centrifugal democracy in terms of our social and political culture. Our national family now seems intent upon subcultural segregation of a subtle nature; and the gap between "us" and "them", by many measurements, is becoming more consequential for our Great Experiment.

DIVERSITY, DIVERGENCE, DISSENTIENCE AND AMERICAN DEMOCRACY

Obviously, democracy does not require complete societal assimilation, nationalistic convergence, and political consensus.   David G. Lawrence expresses an essential principle and the reality of American democracy in his comment that "The American notion of government of, by, and for the people has actually been a contest of competing visions of self government . . . diversity in large measure explains how politics is done in the United States" (*America: The Politics of Diversity*, 1998, 2, 8).

But a certain degree of cultural commonality apparently enhances the environment for democratic institutions and politics. As Freedom House President **Adrian Karatnycky** notes in that organization's annual survey (*Freedom in the World*, 2000, accessed online at www.freedomhouse.org):

> Indeed, democracy is, as a rule, significantly more successful in mono-ethnic societies (that is, societies in which there is a single dominant majority ethnic group representing more than two-thirds of the population) than in ethnically divided and multiethnic societies . . . When this year's Survey data are examined through the prism of ethnic composition, they offer some revealing findings. For example, of Free countries, 64 (74 percent) have a dominant ethnic majority representing more than two-thirds of the population, while 22 (26 percent) do not . . . In short, a state with a dominant ethnic group is some three times more likely to be Free than a multiethnic state.

Clearly, then, subculturalizing society, in concert with the centrifugal dynamics of a constrained systemic environment and philosophical civil war, could further alter the way that American democracy works in the Twenty-First Century.

For example, **William Frey**, a demographer with the University of Michigan's Population Studies Center, has identified and documented a "new demographic divide" that is sharply different from what happened for most of the twentieth century (*New Demographic Divide in the U.S.*, 1999). Frey says that America is dividing into "multiple melting pots" (states such as California, Texas, Florida, and New York with high numbers of new racial and ethnic minorities) and much of the rest of the country that is older, whiter, and more middle class. This phenomenon has important consequences for the future of America as a national experiment in democratic ideals because it divides America into cultural regions with differing views of America and American democracy. According to Frey, these emerging "multiple melting pots" will produce a different kind of "Americanization" for new immigrants in the twenty-first century (as contrasted with the assimilation process of the current century). But just as important is what Frey sees happening in the rest of the country:

> New region-based political constituencies will emerge that place greater emphasis on middle class tax breaks and the solvency of the Social Security system, and that cast a wary eye on too much federal government regulation. Already these regions are becoming more conservative and more likely to vote Republican. Their residents will become far less energized over issues such as preserving affirmative action laws, extending the federal safety net to new foreign-born generations or maintaining bilingual education in the schools. (35)

Political Science Professors **Philip A. Klinkner** and **Rogers M. Smith** are concerned, specifically, that societal and political trends could impede progress on civil rights *(The Unsteady March: The Rise and Decline of Racial Equality in America*, 1999):

> To be sure, the United States is not headed back to formal Jim Crow laws, much less slavery. But it is not so unlikely that Americans of different races, and especially blacks and whites, will live in different regions, attend different schools, concentrate in different occupations, and be governed by policies that reinforce these patterns, especially when they serve the interests and values of affluent whites and their closest allies. If so, the result is likely to be that extensive de facto segregation will be accompanied by severe inequalities in economic, educational, and political statuses and chronically fractious, sometimes explosive, racial and ethnic relations. It is not unlikely that this result will occur, we think, because despite real progress that is more or less where we are now. Moreover, many politically potent current policy positions seem likely to move us further in these directions. (319)

Where Are We Going? Fortunately, this issue (so often mired in harsh ideological arguments) has moved into a cautious stage of realistic deliberation; and many now ask, appropriately, "Where are we going?" Distinguished Constitutionalist **Walter Berns** (Emeritus Professor at Georgetown University) for example, cautions that our national future depends upon full understanding of the historic relationship between multiculturalism and constitutional democracy; and equally eminent Historian **C. Vann Woodward** (Emeritus Professor at Yale University) encourages debate about multiculturalism as envisaged in historic principles of integration and assimilation rather than unbridled separation (see their respective essays,

"Constitutionalism and Multiculturalism" and "Meanings for Multiculturalism", in **Arthur M. Melzer, Jerry Weinberger**, and **M. Richard Zinman**, *Multiculturalism and American Democracy*, 1998). University of Virginia Government Professor **James Ceaser** says, too, that the debate entails very consequential options for American democracy ("Multiculturalism and American Liberal Democracy," also in *Multiculturalism and American Democracy*):

> Will multiculturalism strengthen or weaken American liberal democracy: It is quite possible, even likely, that the multicultural movement has contributed to achieving some goals sought by previous reformers. But at what cost? That cost, I would hazard is to undermine some of the important props of liberal democracy, without offering any coherent idea of what alternative might replace it . . . The time, regrettably, may soon be approaching when each person may face the choice of attempting to save his or her own "culture" first. Any victory on these terms cannot be a victory for American liberal democracy. (154-155)

In short, while both community and diversity have always been competing strengths of American democracy, the prudent course is one which consciously balances "pluribus" and "unum" (and considers the possible consequences of "ex uno plures"). Certainly cultural developments, in conjunction with related systemic dynamics, pose interesting challenges for future American democracy; and we must now engage in coherent discussion about how changing America might re-orient or replace its historic experiment.

....

A CONTEMPORARY VISION OF OUR DEMOCRATIC FUTURE (THE CALIFORNIA ANALOGY)

My unconventional, provocative thesis rests thus far on theoretical premises and sketchy propositions. However, West Coast America presents a handy, real-world analogy for the unfolding future of our Great Experiment.

California: America's Future. Some may disagree, but there is merit to the oft-stated idea that California is America's future. As a media strategist commented prior to Election 2000, "In fact, California, more than any other state, represents where America is headed. It is as close to being the heartbeat of America as any place in the country" ("Where America Is Heading," *U.S. News and World Report*, December 7, 1998). In that same publication, Reporter **Betsy Streisand** writes that the Golden State represents the shape of politics to come in both its ambience and its raw power: "California's growing status as the model for the next millennium goes far beyond the symbolic. For the first time, California voters may actually wield the type of early political clout that the state's size and makeup demand" Furthermore, as **Peter Schrag** proclaims in *Paradise Lost* (1998), California issues (such as the 1970s tax revolt) seem to resonate especially well at the national level; they may not originate in California, but that area generally serves as a forum for launching important ideas and actions.

CALIFORNIA SOCIETY

Clearly, California is at the forefront of America's demographic future. In both size and population, this state will shape and reflect our changing nation throughout the coming century. According to census data, about one in every eight Americans (33.9 million persons) lives in California; and there is no racial or ethnic majority in the state. Non-Hispanic whites now comprise less than half (47 percent) of that total (down from about 80 percent in 1970); Hispanics account for 32 percent, followed by Asians (11 percent) and blacks (7 percent). Furthermore, immigrants and visitors from numerous foreign countries now call California home.

For the most part, California public officials (particularly Democratic politicians) celebrate their state's increasing social diversity. According to Governor Gray Davis, "A more diverse population creates some potential discomforts and even potential conflicts but it also brings great strengths" ("Whites in California Will Be In Minority," *Electronic Telegraph*, accessed online at www.telegraph.com). Adds Hispanic Lt. Governor Cruz Bustamante, "If there is no majority, maybe there are no minorities . . . The time has finally come for us to simply refer to ourselves as Californians" ("Whites in Minority for First Time," Associated Press, March 3, 2001). The San Diego City Council has even voted to strike the term "minority" from official use ("San Diego Council Bans the Word 'Minority'," Associated Press, April 3, 2001).

CALIFORNIA POLITICS

However, academicians and journalists characterize California politics in different tone.

- For example, California Political Scientist and ex-City Councilman **David Lawrence** says, in very pointed style, that his state is a compelling example of "hyperpluralism" in a multicultured democracy (*California: The Politics of Diversity*, 2000):

> In California politics, a single public interest and a single majority seem to be endangered political species. In a sense, "minorities" already rule in the Golden State. On a statewide basis, a relatively small number of individuals and groups set legislative agendas and determine which issues make it to the ballot. A relatively small percentage of Californians who qualify to vote actually register in order to do so; an even smaller percentage bother to turn

out on election day; and only a simple majority of those determine election outcomes . . . Ironically, while majority rule means less and less, some political ground rules require supermajorities to enact public policy. The state legislature must approve the annual budget by a two-thirds vote, and similar majorities are required for voters to raise taxes or amend the state constitution. Such numbers are increasingly difficult to achieve. (17)

• **Mark Baldassare,** another Golden State political scientist, also reports that Californians enter the new century with societal division and fundamental political disengagement (*California in the New Millennium: The Changing Social and Political Landscape*, 2000). Based on extensive polling and focus group research for the independent, nonpartisan Public Policy Institute of California, Baldassare concludes that several powerful undercurrents are transforming the political character of California.

For starters, according to Baldassare's research, California's fragmented social dynamics are hampering the state's ability to chart appropriate and acceptable public policy:

> Record levels of immigration for more than two decades have transformed California from a state where a vast majority were white to a multiracial society with a large and growing Latino population. The racial and ethnic change under way is having profound effects of the ability to reach consensus on crucial state issues. Divisions over racial and immigration policies have already surfaced in initiatives . . . creating social tension and conflicts. Another troubling issue is the political nonengagement of the fastest growing and soon-to-be largest ethnic group in California. (Research Brief, Public Policy Institute of California, April 2000)

Californians also are congregating regionally in areas and ways that interfere with the development of popular consensus and cooperation among political leaders:

> The ongoing regional population changes add further complications, shaping how the political power in the future will be shared among the various regions . . . These regions all differ dramatically in their populations, economy, geography, politics, and public concerns. The policy challenges facing each often have little in common, and the lack of political consensus by elected officials representing these major regions impedes public dialogue at a time when there is a great need to reach a statewide consensus on social, environmental, land use, and infrastructure issues. (Research Brief, Public Policy Institute of California, April 2000)

• Secessionist developments in the Los Angeles area parallel and illustrate the Golden State's growing political problems with size, diversity, and divergence. Seven regions are considering official withdrawal from California's most populous city (actually the second largest city in the nation) for a variety of social, economic, and political reasons. While most current Los Angeles residents oppose secession (according to a Los Angeles Times Poll), they also say the city is heading in the "wrong direction," that their children's public education is "inadequate or very poor," and that race relations in the city are "poor or not good." Almost half think their neighborhoods are getting shortchanged from the city, and more consider the growing immigrant population "bad" rather than "good."

Ethnic strife contributes to secessionist fervor, according to the newspaper; "Many African Americans have expressed fear of being pushed out of their homes and jobs, and many new immigrants have said they feel they aren't welcomed by their new neighbors" ("Many in L.A. Feel Upbeat," *Los Angeles Times*, March 5, 2001).

Furthermore, and curiously, many city residents—both inside and outside the breakaway regions—support secession even if it hurts Los Angeles. One West LA resident, speaking of the San Fernando Valley (where 60 Percent favor secession), says "If they want their own community, they should have it. Culver City is its own little thing, and so is West Hollywood. Why shouldn't the valley get to be its own city?" ("Los Angeles: 60% of Valley Voters Favor City Secession," March 31, 1999, *The Los Angeles Times*)

• In another localized account of California's social and political problems, Journalist **John Mercurio** chronicles tensions between African-Americans and Hispanics in a special congressional election in Los Angeles ("Race Illustrates New California," *Roll Call*, April 5, 2001):

> Welcome to the new California, a state with no racial majority, where a stunning Hispanic population spurt is redefining the roles played by minority voters and forcing every ethnic group to rethink its approach to obtaining and keeping political power.

The eventual winner of that special election, an African-American feeling the pressure of increased Hispanic influence in the community, exhorted black voters in no uncertain terms to back her candidacy:

> "No one else needs to speak for us. We can speak for ourselves . . . We've been studied and studied by people who come in here and don't have a clue as to who we are. We don't need someone from another community to come in and represent us, because they truly don't know our story. We need someone who knows our story."

Contrarily, a native of Peru said of the top candidates, all of whom are African-American: "I'm sure they're fine people. But until we can elect one of our own, I think I'm not so interested." Of course, there are hopeful, more optimistic voices. "You can't make assumptions about race anymore in Los Angeles," said a white teacher; "We've become so diverse, so racially complex, that we don't even care about race anymore. It's crazy, but I think that's a good thing."

• **Ken DeBow** and **John C. Syer**, Government Professors at California State University, Sacramento, summarize their state's political condition as one of severe challenges and uncertain outcome (*Power and Politics in California*, Sixth Edition, 2000):

> California is big and diverse. The state is huge in both population and economic terms. California is diverse ethnically, economically, and topographically. Unfortunately, the problems facing the state are also big and diverse. The once-vaunted political institutions of California may no longer be capable of resolving the issues confronting the state. (21)

CALIFORNIA GOVERNMENT

As a result of these societal and political developments, many California watchers assert that the Golden State is not addressing profound policy challenges at this crucial point in its history.

• **Ken Debow** and **John C. Syer**, for example, cite growing problems in the public sector despite economic recovery, population growth, and relatively better times heading into the new century:

> At the state level, all three branches of government—executive, legislative, and judicial—are beset by serious internal structural and political problems. Moreover, the long-term fiscal outlook for the public sector, even with the current economic upturn, remains clouded. And for local governments, despite the present economic boom, the long-term funding picture is downright grim. (*Power and Politics in California*, 2)

• Also, according to **Mark Baldassare**, popular, electoral foundations for the conventional course of state governance are deteriorating in vexing ways and in untimely manner:

> The focus group and survey responses clearly indicate that most Californians are disillusioned with their elected officials. They believe that their governments are bloated bureaucracies unable to solve problems, spend taxpayers' money efficiently, or represent the interests and policy preferences of average voters . . . The voters have signaled their disdain for political parties and elected representative in many ways . . . open primary process . . . term limits . . . initiatives . . . just at a time when California is facing increasingly complex and troublesome policy issues. (Research Brief, Public Policy Institute of California, April 2000)

• Consequently, says **David Lawrence**, the time-honored concept of common good is increasingly elusive, and the spectrum of public policy-making is a continuing free-for-all among hyperpluralized interests who cannot agree on what's best for the state:

Abortion policy is essentially a continuing struggle among diverse values and contrary views over moral authority and the meaning of personhood. Education policy is more a conglomerate of contests over how best to address enrollment growth, ethnic diversity, social change, school funding, and academic quality . . . The caseload and spending growth of California's social programs reflects a subtle rivalry between California's tax payers and tax spenders . . . California's efforts to curb the impacts of large-scale immigration reflect a growing concern over how diverse Californians are and are willing to be. (*California: The Politics of Diversity*, 2000, 283-284)

- Former California editorialist **Peter Schrag** provides additional first-hand judgment about the downward spiral of public discontent and the deteriorating state of California governance (*Paradise Lost: California's Experience, America's Future*, 1998):

> California has not just seen a sharp decline in the quality of public services— education, public parks, highways, water projects—that were once regarded as models for the nation. It has also seen the evolution of an increasingly unmanageable and incomprehensible structure of state and local government that exacerbates the same public disaffection and alienation that have brought it on, thus creating a vicious cycle of reform and frustration. (accessed online at www.amazon.com)

CALIFORNIA DEMOCRACY

In addition to their vanguard society, politics, and government, Californians have begun to reshape their political system and the Golden State's substantive public policies through a conglomeration of progressive, populist, plebiscitary mechanisms such as tax caps, term limits, initiatives, referenda, and recall. However, many analysts, speaking from a variety of perspectives, question the wisdom of these mechanisms—particularly the popular initiative—of California democracy.

- **David Lawrence**, for example, criticizes California's "Initiative Mess" as a dysfunctional part of hyperpluralism in a technological age. "The process has produced more choices and information about them than typical voters can handle, at the same time producing media-centered campaigns that insult their intelligence" (*California: The Politics of Diversity*, 2000, 73).

- **Dan Walters**, veteran political writer at the *Sacramento Bee*, disparagingly summarizes the process thusly:

> Over the last 20 years, California voters—acting at the behest of various ideological and economic interest groups—have enacted a series of ballot measures that dictate how taxes are to be levied and government revenues are to be spent . . . While each of the measures might be plausible in a vacuum, they interact with each other in ways that make it nearly impossible for

office-holders to manage public finances responsively and responsibly . . .
It's a lousy way to make public policy, whether it's managing the public's
money or its wildlife. It's the antithesis of the comprehensive, flexible
approaches that are needed to cope with California's rapidly changing
economic, social, and nature landscapes. ("Single-interest policy-making,"
The Monterey Herald, October 22, 1998)

• Journalist **Peter Schrag** maintains furthermore that popular governance by
non-deliberative plebiscite reinforces majoritarian indifference, if not hostility,
toward minority rights ("California, Here We Come"):

> To say all that, probably, is merely to say awkwardly, what the Framers of
> the Constitution said better in Philadelphia, what Hamilton, Madison, and Jay
> said in The Federalist, and what scores of delegates said in 1787-1788 at the
> various state conventions leading up to ratification, even before the Terror of
> the French Revolution: unchecked majorities are a danger to liberty almost
> as great as oligarchs and absolute monarchs. (*The Atlantic Monthly*, March,
> 1998, 30)

• Columnist **David Broder** notes that California's direct democracy ventures
often wind up in court, with unelected judges settling questions of public policy.
"On the sidelines in this whole process," he reminds us, "are the elected
representatives of the people—the very folks we thought of, in our naive days as
a nation, as the proper repository of governmental power." Broder observes that
this tension could be avoided "if California ever learns to respect the wisdom of
the Founders that a republic—with legislative power vested in elected
representatives—is   preferable   to   any   other   form   of   government"
("Californocracy in Action," *The Washington Post*, August 13, 1997).

• As might be expected, **Mark Baldassare**'s projections for the developing
course of California democracy are dramatic and apprehensive:

> California in the mid-21st century is going to be a very different state from
> the California of today . . . The proportion of Californians who are white will
> steadily decline, while Latinos become the dominant racial and ethnic group .
> . . Yet, as California enters an era when it will face some of the toughest
> challenges in its 150 years of statehood, most of its people have become
> highly cynical about their elected leaders and may have disengaged
> themselves from the political process, making public consensus on critical
> issues more difficult. (Research Brief, Public Policy Institute of California,
> April 2000)

• **Ken DeBow** and **John C. Syer** question, furthermore, whether (and how)
Golden State democracy can deal with the problems of a changing,
multicultural society:

California is becoming, at a rapid clip, a more and more diverse state. If the state is to deal successfully with this trend, it will have to do better than it has in past. California's history, unfortunately, is one of public and private exclusion, discrimination, and violence. Chances for successful diversification are also clouded by the emergence of a two-tier economy that has the potential to restrict economic opportunity for those who do not begin life in advantaged circumstances. We face the possibility of a state even more strongly stratified by economic cleavages that also correspond to racial and ethnic distinctions.

There are limits to government's power to alleviate these problems, since they are woven into the economic and social fabric of the state. But even in the sphere of government and politics, we are faced with difficult questions. Because the electorate does not resemble the population, the answers that have come out of the electoral process so far, especially in the cases of relevant ballot issues, represent predominantly Anglo responses. And these responses indicate grave reservations about multiculturalism at lease among the current voting majority. Future majorities may provide new directions. (*Power and Politics in California*, 78-79)

- California's distemperate experience thus serves stark, disconcerting notice, according to **Peter Schrag**, about the possible future of American democracy:

Given the complexity of the issues in California and the rapid way that event follows event, history's first cut may turn out to be very rough indeed. Yet the changes that have occurred—in government, in public services, in public outlook—are stark and dramatic. And the questions they raise for the nation as a whole are equally stark . . . Things had better work here, where the new American society is first coming into full view, because if it fails here, it may never work anywhere else either. California is America's most important test for that emerging society, and so far the outcome of that test remains very much in doubt. (*Paradise Lost*, 1998, accessed online at www.amazon.com.)

While California is not perfectly analogous to broader America, its size, diversity, politics, and governance are worth noting as we assess similarly developing pressures on our national democratic experiment. Nothing against California (it's a great place), but apparently the Golden State is going through inevitable systemic challenges slightly ahead of the rest of us; and Californians seem to be struggling—pretty distemperately—in that process. The analogous dynamics of the contemporary California political system thus raise particularly tricky questions and provide some useful points of guidance about important developments—the delicate, difficult, dangerous interplay among diversity, divergence, dissentience, and democracy—in future America.

....

AMERICA MAY BECOME
"THE AMERICAN FEDERATION"
BY THE MIDDLE OF THE TWENTY-FIRST CENTURY

To be summary and direct, I project that—absent a change of course—the United States of America may turn into "The American Federation" by the middle of the Twenty-First Century. More precisely for this analysis, I am projecting that our "Great Experiment" could become "a federal experiment in democratic ideals" (as distinguished from my original definition of America as a national experiment in democratic ideals).

A SYSTEMIC MODEL
OF "THE AMERICAN FEDERATION"

I have incorporated these projections into a diagrammatic model (see illustration) that allows us to define our possible future within the systemic dynamics presented in an earlier chapter.

"The American Federation" and "Subcultural Democratization". My model depicts, most fundamentally, the continuing constraints of our systemic environment (limited natural conditions and mixed support for national public authority) in "The American Federation".

Also, according to this scenario, there will be no constructive resolution of our philosophical civil war, no broad, conclusive, acceptable definition of "what America means" and "how America ought to work". Instead, the philosophical civil war will dissipate haphazardly in accord with the central strains of its two symbiotic movements—"subculturalism" and "neopopulism"—giving rise to a nation of disparate societies and aggressive democracy.

We therefore will experience a new and different version of political life—"subcultural democratization"—reflective of trending systemic, cultural, and political dynamics over the next few decades. Our country will undergo an uneven, inconsistent, unmediated onslaught of creative democratic experiments—perhaps regional pursuits of democratic ideals through subcultural perspectives and popular initiatives—that could fundamentally change America's traditional system of federal governance.

Eventually, our national experiment in democratic ideals will tend toward a federational re-ordering of American public life. Consequently, "American Federal Democracy", as depicted in this model, will represent a challenging new mixture: (a) an eclectic society with a heterogeneous majority and greater societal divergency, (b) a dissentient political process reflecting the impact of subcultural democratization, and (c) federated government to serve the changing needs of American federal democracy. The result will be "federal democratic ideals" (instead of national democratic ideals).

"THE AMERICAN FEDERATION"

Constrained Systemic
Environment

American Federal
Democracy

"Subculturalism"

"Neopopulism"

Diverse,
Divergent People

Dissentient Politics

Federated
Government

Limited
Natural Conditions

Mixed Support
for National Authority

Federal Democratic
Ideals

Altered Federal Relationships. **Within my scenario of "The American Federation," America will remain a national democratic experiment, but we may democratically redefine historic federal relationships to meet the changing demands of an increasingly diverse, divergent, dissentient America.** Subcultural democratization would be, theoretically and politically, a balancing response to two centuries of acceptable nationalization and centralization of American life. Thus "The American Federation" would represent a logical next stage in the historical development of our nation as a federal republic and pluralist democracy.

Obviously, Washington will yield or share some of its power and influence in "The American Federation". The historic nationalization of American life, the centralization of governance, and federalized redistribution of wealth will, at the least, slow down; and important issues may shift to subnational forums and policies.

These prospects should strike fear in the hearts of the Big Government Establishment; but states-righters should not get overly exuberant. The states, counties, and cities probably will suffer the same atrophy as will the national government in our new political order. These entities reflect outdated, artificial, geographic necessities and habits of by-gone society; and they likely will yield to the real-world demands of subcultural democratization.

Enhanced Flexibility. **"The American Federation" thus will address many of the philosophical problems of contemporary America by enhancing flexibility in a nationally conflicted and stagnant federalism that increasingly is unable to produce the traditional blessings of American democracy.** It also would encourage American citizens to experiment anew with their political and governmental systems. Through this more flexible arrangement, some national conflicts might be resolved subnationally—in new and different games, in new and different ways, with new and different democratic outcomes. Arguably, these developments might re-inspire and re-bond the American people to their Great Experiment.

Simple Adjustment. **Interestingly, "The American Federation" would entail simple legislative adjustment (and minimal tinkering with our constitutional foundations) since, in actuality, it represents a Twenty-First Century version of our country's original federal arrangement.** The Congress (through statutory mandates) and the President (through executive orders) already have within their constitutional jurisdiction the power to reshape American federalism. Furthermore, just as the courts historically have nationalized various aspects of American public life (through the fourteenth amendment), they can lead in other directions (perhaps by "rediscovering" the tenth amendment). Certainly legislative-executive-judicial activism, combined with administrative implementation, could redefine—just as it has done for years—the substance and process of American democracy. With popular support, the new political order could proceed without radically restructuring our fundamental law.

A Practical Transition. "**The American Federation**" **therefore represents a practical response to my original questions:** "**Can . . . ,** "**How can . . . , and** "**How far can our nation—a people of growing cultural diversity, with increasingly divergent ideals, values, and governance principles, in a constricted systemic environment—continue to sustain our collective pursuit of freedom, equality, and justice within the framework of limited, representative government?**"

The projected answer is that the "The American Federation" would continue the pursuit of democratic ideals, in a changed world, by transitionally re-arranging our federal system.

Obviously, American federal democracy will trouble many citizens and democratic theorists; but in our projected future, it likely will be the standard way of dealing with nationally contentious cultural problems such as the role of religion in civil life, affirmative action, gun control, abortion rights, and lifestyle issues. Disgruntled Americans will simply have to pursue their democratic dreams, as did earlier Americans, by going elsewhere to more acceptable environs.

A Revitalized Experiment? **In some ways,** "**The American Federation**" **could revitalize important aspects of our historic Great Experiment.** American federal democracy may also introduce new concepts that rival or eclipse or replace conventional governmental institutions and political practices. The new political order could, in some areas and under some circumstances, further the course of direct democracy or radically redefine our concept of democratic ideals; it could involve regional partnering with our various North American neighbors; it might establish transnational arrangements beyond conventional national/state/local frameworks; or it may even transcend geography altogether, bringing broad-based public interest constituencies or electronic communities into the federal relationship.

. . . .

SUMMARY COMMENT

If we mindlessly plod the path of least resistance and incrementally compromise with contemporary challenges—America may transition, by the middle of the Twenty-First Century, into "**The American Federation**"**, a practical accommodation (with perhaps questionable democratic ramifications) to the daunting realities of changing public life. Our national configuration would be more akin to the original American Confederation**

(and the Old South Confederacy) than anything within the memory of today's citizenry.

"The American Federation" therefore may be the next logical chapter in the continual drama of American history. American federal democracy would reflect the influence of systemic constraints and philosophical tensions; it would deal, practically, with many of our societal changes and the civic ills of contemporary America; and it clearly is a preferable alternative to deformation and disintegration.

But is "The American Federation" the best that we can do? Does "The American Federation" represent inspired progression of American democracy? Or is it unthinking, incremental transition to fundamental systemic and cultural transformation of the American system. Is it simply a stopover on the road to "the United State of Amerika", or "the Union of Socialist States of America", or something worse?

It seems to me that we are proceeding haphazardly—without a great deal of thought and discussion as a nation—in risky transition toward an uninspired, uninspiring future. In the next and final chapter, I will attempt to chart a more aggressive, deliberative, transformational course to "New America".

CONCLUSION

THE FUTURE
OF AMERICAN DEMOCRACY?

THE CHALLENGE OF "NEW AMERICA"

Thus it is time for me to conclude this unconventional essay on the uncertain future of American democracy. I do so by noting that invariably, early in my public lecture series, someone in the audience—impatient with the slowly unfolding logic and verbosity of the lectures—interrupts with a direct and pertinent question: "Dr. Browder, are you optimistic or pessimistic about the future of American democracy?"

While I'm sure my abbreviated answer is less than satisfactory, I usually begin by re-stating my almost mystical confidence in America. I also say somewhat deterministically that the difficult journey from traditional America to America of the future is an evolutionary, irresistible, irreversible experience in keeping with our national democratic experiment; and our contemporary democratic distemper is just part of that journey. But I usually confess that I am concerned about whether or not future America is going to be as committed to our national democratic experiment as has been the case for the past two centuries. Then, I turn the interrogation on my audience, challenging them to help redefine, redirect, and restore our Great Experiment in "New America".

I will follow the same logic in this concluding commentary, beginning with a review of my transformational thesis and moving forward with some recommendations and predictions for the transformational future of American democracy.

....

A TRANSFORMATIONAL REVIEW

The central message of this unconventional manuscript has been that America is changing in important and unsettling ways and that we have an obligation to future generations to deal constructively with these changes. I have attempted to address these transformational developments by presenting for your consideration my own unconventional analysis.

MY SUMMARY ANALYSIS

• First, I introduced my unconventional assessment of America's democratic distemper, and I posed my rhetorical question— "Is America Dying?"

• Then I defined my basic conceptions of "America" (a national experiment in democratic ideals), "American Democracy" (the magical mix of people, politics, and government whereby we pursue democratic ideals), and "Dying" (American democracy no longer works the way that it used to, and we seem to be tiring of the Great Experiment itself).

• I stated generally that fundamental patterns of American history appear to have erupted into contradictory, confounding turmoil. Two centuries of irresistible democratic nationalization now clash head-on with equally powerful forces of centrifugal democracy. I also identified some strange new developments such as "subcultural society", the "direct democracy movement", and "electronic democracy".

• I presented four propositions as the basis of my transformational analysis: (a) "The favorable systemic environment of American democracy has disappeared;" (b) "We have entrapped American democracy within a philosophical civil war;" (c) "American democracy no longer works the way it has in the past;" and (d) "We seem to be tiring of the Great Experiment itself."

• I then concluded that important changes in our systemic and philosophical environment seriously constrain the traditional functioning of American democracy; and our Great Experiment is not working the way it has in the past. Whereas my rhetorical pronouncements about lost civic virtue, broken political machinery, and malfunctioning government may have been overly dramatic, the American people are indeed evidencing symptoms of civic depression, some aspects of our parties, media, and electoral campaigns need repair or replacement, and American national government has not been working very well for several decades. I suggested furthermore that our nation is bifurcating into "Traditional America" versus "Emerging America" simultaneously and consequentially as "We the people" assume unprecedented power and control over the Great Experiment.

- I reported surprising patterns of democratic dissensus and alternative ideas about government; and I proposed that our diverse, divergent, dissentient populace appears to be reassessing the nature and future of America's Great Experiment.

- I presented several representative assessments—of both conventional and unconventional nature—by other turn-of-century commentators about the eventual destiny of our nation; and I imagined disturbing deformations (such as "Amerika" and the "USSA") and even disintegration (death) of America.

- Finally, I speculated that if we continue on our current course, America will transition into "The American Federation" by the middle of the Twenty-First Century.

AND MY CONCERNS

Beyond this summary analysis, I'm obviously concerned—on several counts—about the American national dream and our democratic destiny.

- First and importantly, I'm concerned generally that our national democratic distemper—in conjunction with the cumulative ills identified in this manuscript—may overwhelm the historic strengths of American democracy. The American people may indeed be too "tired"—as evidenced in their mixed attitudes, their low participation rates, and their alternative ideas about governance—to exercise fully the responsibilities of democratic citizenship at this critical, transformational period in American history.

- My immediate concern is the growing prospect of mass civic irrelevancy in our transformational future—in which unfortunate environment more narrow, disparate, aggressive forces radically pursue their visions of America.

- I'm most concerned substantively and for the long run about how America will deal with the changing realities of American society and democracy. Will historically majoritarian culture respond to these changes with appropriate adjustments of cherished traditions and ideals; or will it cling stubbornly, reactionarily, and dysfunctionally to an America that no longer exists. I also wonder whether our emerging culture will sufficiently embrace the essential, enduring elements of the Great Experiment. Will it continue an experiment that is as "democratically good" as we have enjoyed historically; or will it attempt to force shortsighted revisions in the American system of governance? (I will talk further about "Traditional America" versus "Emerging America" in this concluding chapter.)

- I therefore do not look forward to a nation in which we might ignore our pressing responsibilities for public discussion about American democracy. The fact is that America's contemporary systemic dynamics are so fundamentally important and unsettling that successful progression of American democracy will not occur without dramatic public deliberation of these questions and issues.

Accordingly, and within the framework of my unconventional analysis and concerns, I will attempt in these concluding pages (a) to interpret the 2000 presidential election as an important marker in the historic transformation of America, (b) to propose a national democratic renaissance for these transformational times, and (c) to predict, within reason, the transformational direction of American democracy.

....

A TRANSFORMATIONAL JUNCTURE
(ELECTION 2000)

Let me begin this discussion by reiterating, emphatically, that we stand—somewhat unsteadily because of our national democratic distemper—at a critical juncture in American history.

Generally speaking, I believe that the history of America can be viewed as an uneven but discernibly progressive journey. For over two centuries, America has redefined and redirected and restored itself—lurchingly but democratically—as a nation. Now—as I have argued extensively throughout this manuscript—important changes are stressing and straining traditional American government and democracy.

I also maintain that, at critical times—in the act of intense systemic redefinition, redirection, and restoration as a nation—America actually transforms into a qualitatively different nation. At these critical junctures, our magical mix of people, politics, and government may evidence national democratic distemper; but these critical elements eventually "re-mix" in order to continue, under different conditions, the traditional pursuit of democratic ideals through limited, representative governance.

TURN-OF-CENTURY DISTEMPER

Critical junctures in American history usually are defined by political events, technological breakthroughs, and societal developments—such as the Constitutional Convention of 1787, the Civil War, the Industrial Revolution, the Great Depression, World Wars I and II, the Cold War, and the Civil Rights Movement. But in addition to wars, depressions, and social traumas, America also experiences transformational distemper at centennial turnings of the calendar.

Of course, transformational and turn-of-century talk can quickly degenerate into gibberish about manifest destiny, theological predestination, and astrological prophecy. The fact is that America is always arguing and changing. But it seems to be true that, as Americans enter a new century, they tend in unusually distemperate directions, reflecting anxiously and noisily about where the country has been and where it is heading. These times encourage vigorous, sometimes irrational, almost violent public debate; and our national elections consequently can produce new leadership and political realignment. Most importantly during these historic periods, the American democratic system sometimes transforms itself to meet the needs of a changing America. While such turn-of-century elections may not resolve—clearly and absolutely—national disarray and distemper, they seem to energize the redefinition, redirection, and restoration of American democracy.

Considered from a transformational perspective, Election 2000 is more than a passing curiosity. George W. Bush's assumption of presidential power through the Electoral College despite Al Gore's popular vote majority (the first such occurrence in well over a century) serves as a primetime showcase for fundamentally reordering dynamics at this critical point in American history. In many ways, Election 2000 resembles previous turn-of-century elections—specifically the Jefferson-Adams contest (1800) and the McKinley-Bryan showdown (1896)—as redefining and redirecting events in American history (and time will tell if our current experience includes a restorational component).

As the following electoral accounts demonstrate, the closing decades of the Eighteenth and Nineteenth Centuries were indeed times of pronounced societal division and political anxiety—akin in many ways to the distemperate tone of contemporary America. The 1800 and 1896 national elections proved to be critical junctures in American history, with strong leaders, opportune circumstances, and a responsive nation working together to strengthen American democracy in the new century.

Election 1800. **The national election of 1800 proves very illustrative as an early critical juncture for the United States of America.** Then, just as now, competing social, economic, and geographic sectors of American society clashed and questioned their common destiny as a nation. Throughout those early years (our constitutional republic had existed for only a decade) and within a tumultuous environment (of partisan factionalism, charges of seditious intent, and actual war on the high seas), infant America experienced theoretical and political torment.

As historian **James West Davidson** and his colleagues tell us (*Nation of Nations: A Narrative History of the American Republic*, 1994), we too easily forget how turbulent and violent was American politics of the 1790s:

> Some of the violence was physical. Irate crowds roughed up federal marshals who tried to enforce the whiskey tax; the leading Republican newspaper editor in Philadelphia plunged into a street brawl with his Federalist rival; Representative Matthew Lyon of Vermont spit in the eye of Representative Roger Griswold of Connecticut, the two of them wrestling on the floor of Congress . . . President John Adams actually smuggled guns into

his home for protection . . . Republicans accused patriots like Washington and Hamilton of being British agents, tyrants, and monarchists; Federalists portrayed Jefferson as an irreligious Jacobin, and the Republicans as "blood-drinking cannibals." Washington complained that he was abused "in such exaggerated and indecent terms as could scarcely be applied . . . to a common pickpocket." (Vol. I, p.295)

The entire American political system, according to the British minister, was "tottering to its foundations;" and many were convinced that the American experiment had failed (297).

The 1800 election itself was a squeaker, with Thomas Jefferson (strongly supported in the farming south) besting John Adams (who carried the commercial north) in the Electoral college by a vote of 73-65; but he had to go thirty-six ballots in the House of Representatives before overtaking vice-presidential running mate Aaron Burr who also had received 73 electoral college votes and therefore had a shot at the presidency. (The Twelfth Amendment corrected that electoral untidiness four years later.) To his good political fortune, Jefferson's Democratic-Republican Party captured both the House of Representatives and the Senate.

Despite the uncertainty and turbulence of those times, America charged forward with startling triumphs for the Great Experiment.   President Thomas Jefferson, pleading for unity, entered the White House with a disputed mandate for a "wise and frugal" government that would respect states rights and agriculture. Once in office, and through the course of two terms, he pursued executive power and scored unprecedented achievements—stable representative governance, the two-party system, and western expansion. Just as importantly, these early decades launched an impressive era of American nationalism and influence during the Nineteenth Century.

Election 1896. As the Twentieth Century beckoned, Americans again were foundering in a sea of uncertain and uneasy national identity.
According to **Peter Levine**, research scholar at the University of Maryland's Institute for Philosophy and Public Policy, the problems of that period severely challenged American democratic government (*The New Progressive Era*, 2000):

As the nineteenth century came to a close, Americans confronted powerful forces that transformed almost everyone's life and that seemed beyond the capacity of government to shape or control. The frontier was closed; cities had grown to unprecedented size. There were terrible slums and factories that perpetually darkened the sky. Corporations had accumulated astounding wealth but seemed insensible to the needs of workers and consumers. Social classes had become more distinct, self-conscious, and mutually hostile than ever before in American history. An elaborate system of discrimination was being erected to oppress former slaves. Diesel engines, electric dynamos, assembly lines, and skyscrapers promised a golden age, but in the short term they produced wrenching changes. The whole world was now a single marketplace, so that a crisis in one continent was quickly felt in all the others.

Finally, at least according to some, deep moral corruption had permitted saloons and brothels to pollute the nation's cities. (Excerpt reprinted in *Kettering Review*, Spring 2001)

According to **John M. Murrin** and his fellow historians (*Liberty, Equality, Power: A History of the American People*, Second Edition, 1999), America was deeply divided socially and economically as our country continued its painful movement toward a commercial-industrial world:

> Most important of all, the social and political upheavals of the 1890s shocked many people into recognition that the liberty and equality they had taken for granted as part of the American dream was in danger of disappearing before the onslaught of wrenching economic changes that had widened and rigidified the gulf between classes. (656-657)

The 1896 election was impassioned and exciting. " Many Americans believed that the fate of the nation hinged on the outcome as surely as it had in 1860" (656). William McKinley (the Republican backed by business interests) rarely campaigned, supposedly considering such self-promotion beneath the dignity of the office; William Jennings Bryan (the Democrat-Populist) conducted nationwide speechifying, mainly about free coinage of silver.

McKinley won with 51% of the popular vote, scoring well in the northeast, industrial midwest, and west coast; Bryan carried the south and inland west (a pattern of substantive and regional division inversely comparable to the Bush-Gore landscape). Like Jefferson a century earlier, he enjoyed the benefits of a partisanly-allied legislative branch; and this favorable alignment, coupled with a growing economy, enhanced his political power and influence. He repeated his electoral victory by a wider margin in 1900.

William McKinley is not known as one of our great presidents (and most are unaware that he died from an assassin's bullet in 1901); but most historians acknowledge that he presided effectively during a fitful time in American history. More specifically, he pulled together diverse elements—business interests, populist followings, and progressive reformers—of American society into a coalition of national identity; and that national coalition charted an aggressive new course of economic prosperity, progressive government, and international expansion in "The American Century".

Election 2000. **Obviously, our most recent presidential election conveyed a mixed and arguable mandate; but Election 2000 presented conditions similar and comparable to those of a century ago. As we prepared for a new century without the structuring dominance of world wars and cold war ideology, America seemed to be searching for a different framework of self-perception and national destiny.**

According to Columnist **Donald F. Kettl** in "Is the Past Prologue?" *Governing*, December 2000):

The 1896 election framed the transition to the 20th century. The election of 2000 is likely to do the same for the generation to come. Both elections provided a path for each party to escape its traditional constituencies and to define new roles for government and federalism . . .

In the early 20th century, the major transformation was strengthening government to balance private power. In the early 21st century, the historic change could well prove to be the melting of policy boundaries—among federal, state and local government; and between government and its private and nonprofit partners. As in the election of 1896, the political future could well lie with the party that figures out, first and best, how to make the switch. (accessed online at www.governing.com)

As the following discussion will show, similarly important cultural and political dynamics of our recent election suggest opportune foundation for the redefinition, redirection, and restoration of American democracy in the new century.

THE TRANSFORMATIONAL DYNAMICS OF ELECTION 2000

In essence, the 2000 presidential election reflected requisite ingredients—cultural tension, political turmoil, and new leadership—for transformation of American democracy. Even before the American people cast their votes on election day, astute media analysts were identifying the fundamental dynamics of our electoral distemper.

A Striking Cultural Divide. The most prominent national phenomenon of Election 2000 clearly was a cultural bifurcation of American society that confounded political prognosticators, precipitated a mini-crisis of presidential succession, and promised intense, partisan discomfort for the eventual next President of the United States.

• **Laura Ingraham**, an author and columnist, accurately assessed our cultural split personality—and the potential for political mischief—in whimsical, biting, prescient terms ("Who's Your Candidate?" *The Los Angeles Times*, November 6, 2000) the day before the election:

If you look closely at the electoral map, it is increasingly clear that this election represents a cultural battle between the two great camps in American life: the sophisticates of the large cities and the boring, middle-class Americans of the heartland.

Look at the way the states are breaking: Democrat Al Gore has all the cool parts of the country: New York, Los Angeles, San Francisco, Boston, Washington (and he's very close in Florida).

Republican George W. Bush's stronghold lies in the most boring, out-of-the-way parts of middle America: Oklahoma, Mississippi, Wyoming, Indiana (and he's very close in West Virginia) . . .

If Gore loses—and especially if it's close and he carries both New York and California—we will hear screaming from liberals unlike almost anything we have ever heard. After all, Middle America types are used to losing to New York and L.A.; those places have the money, and they usually get their money's worth . . . But New York and L.A. are not used to losing to the likes of Norman, Okla., and Clemson, S.C.

• Two days after the presidential election, Journalist **Jill Lawrence** of *USA Today* documented and color-coded the striking divide—attitudinally, behaviorally, and geographically—between "Bush Country" and "Gore Country". Long before we would learn the outcome of seemingly endless counts, recounts, and legal maneuvers, she and her fellow researchers mapped the United States with red counties for Bush and blue counties for Gore ("Country vs. City, Spelled in Red, Blue," *USA Today*, November 9, 2000); and they produced a grabbing, graphic portrait of bifurcated America:

The map tells the story. Vast stretches of red across the rural heartland, all Republican George W. Bush country. A coastal perimeter and urban patches of blue, where Democrat Al Gore prevailed.
Geography is perhaps the most striking yardstick by which to measure the gulf between those who voted for Bush and those who voted for Gore. The election results might be inconclusive as to who won the presidency, but they are clear when it comes to who was won over by the presidential candidates . . .

According to Lawrence's statistics, Bush Country was the home of small town and rural Americans, covering 2,424,039 square miles of our approximately three-million-square-mile nation; Gore country, on the other hand, was restricted to a relatively small geographic portion (580,134 square miles) inhabited by an equally populous and more urbane populace.

Furthermore, the two competing electorates differed greatly in opinions and lifestyles:

The cultural differences between Gore's voters and Bush's, as illuminated by exit polls, were striking. Bush attracted people who go to church more than once a week, who think it's more important that the president be a moral leader than a good government manager, who oppose stricter gun laws and who believe that if a school is failing, the government should pay for private school. Honesty is the quality they value most in a leader, followed by leadership and likability.

Gore drew heavy majorities of gay and Jewish voters, those who rarely or never attend church, who support stricter gun laws and who say a school should be fixed if it is failing. Their paramount value is experience, followed by competence to handle complex issues and caring about "people like me."

• Gannett News Service columnist **Chuck Raasch** performed similarly sharp analysis in identifying a continuing pattern of demographic, geographic, and political division over the past decade ("Divided We Stand, And Have Stood For A While," *USA Today*, November 20, 2000):

> Let's get this straight . . . The election last week, besides producing a disputed presidency, showed how deep the divide remains. If you took a cleaver to the nation's demography and geography, you couldn't split it better.

> Democrats overwhelmingly won the coasts and big cities. Republicans handily won the heartland, small towns and rural areas. It was the Coasts vs. Flyover Country . . . Women voted decisively for Gore, men for Bush. Gun Owners went 2-1 for Bush, union members 2-1 for Gore . . . Blacks voted for Gore in even bigger margins than they voted for Clinton, a man who had such black support he once was described as America's first black president . . . Married people voted decisively for Bush, singles just as decisively for Gore.

> Since 1994, Republicans have controlled Congress, but by ever-narrowing margins. Clinton won a game of shut-down-the-government chicken with Republicans in Congress in 1995 and 1996. That was followed by a series of bitter investigations—of Democratic fund raising in the 1996 campaign, of Clinton in the Lewinsky scandal.

> The dividing lines in the Florida controversy, then, are familiar. And they are driven by more than concern for laws or democracy. There are deep and abiding political beliefs on both sides of the dispute that do not bode well for a happy ending.

Political Volatility. **The national deans of political journalism duly noted their concerns about the destructive turmoil of Election 2000—with particular discomfort over widespread public ambivalence, the electoral college controversy, and the bitter, partisan, protracted aftermath of Election 2000.** **George Will** lamented the undermining of "the very thing that elections are supposed to confer—legitimacy" ("Had 'Em All the Way," *Newsweek*, November 27, 2000); and **David Broder** proclaimed that "it is not a president but the presidency that may have been lost" ("A Cloud Over Thanksgiving," *The Washington Post*, November 21, 2000). **David Gergen** called for a "healing president" to appeal to the better angels in our nature ("Legitimizing Victory," *U.S. News & World Report*, November 27, 2000).

• **Chris Matthews,** savvy ex politico and host of TV's "Hardball", quickly focused on the foreboding ramifications of our contentious election for democratic leadership of the American nation ("U.S. Political Geography: One Nation, Divisible," *The San Francisco Examiner*, November 11, 2000):

> The new U.S. electoral map looks like the old Yugoslavia. Whoever takes the presidential oath next January will have to deal with this stark, disturbing fact of American politics: The country is divided as much by geography as by party.

Matthews lamented an electorate divided into "the bi-coastal nation of pro-choice, somewhat hip, ethnically diverse Democrats and the inland nation of culturally conservative Republicans"; and he worried that candidates Bush and Gore might carry our societal tensions unabated into the future. "The danger is that both winner and loser will proceed in the direction he took in carving out his half of the electorate on election day."

• Washington Journalist **John Harris**, who talked extensively with national political leaders in the early aftermath of the corrosive 2000 election, speculated about the practical consequences for American governance ("Roadblocks Ahead For Governing," *The Washington Post,* November 9, 2000):

> For years, the surveys have shown what Americans want most of all from their national government is less argument, fewer personality wars, more willingness to compromise and solve problems. What they sent Washington on Tuesday, according to many prominent voices in both parties, was the potential for a crisis of governance—a tightening of gridlock beyond even the acrimony and stalemate of the Clinton years . . .

• Campaign consultant **Dick Morris** predicted that the electoral divide might extend beyond politics to our democratic national faith ("Florida: The More We See, The Sicker We Get," *VOTE.com*, November 22, 2000):

> As the grievances pile up, it becomes increasingly clear that we are a nation at risk of deep division as our foundation and bedrock—the reliability of the electoral process—is split down the middle like a boulder on the San Andreas fault. What is at issue here is not an election, it is fast becoming a question of faith in our democratic system on which we all depend and rely.

• Finally, popular author **Hunter S. Thompson** provided this over-the-edge warning of national political anarchy in the form of an internet letter supposedly written from his fortified compound in Colorado ("Hey Rube," *Page 2 ESPN*, November 21, 2000):

> We have seen Weird Times in this country before, but the year 2000 is beginning to look super weird. This time, there really is nobody flying the plane . . .

There is an eerie sense of Panic in the air, a silent Fear and Uncertainty that comes with once-reliable faiths and truths and solid institutions that are no longer safe to believe . . . There is a Presidential Election, right on schedule, but somehow there is no President. A new Congress is elected, like always, but somehow there is no real Congress at all—not as we knew it, anyway, and whatever passes for Congress will be as helpless and weak as Whoever has to pass for the "New President."

If this were the world of sports, it would be like playing a Super Bowl that goes into 19 scoreless Overtimes and never actually Ends . . . or four L.A. Lakers stars being murdered in different places on the same day. Guaranteed Fear and Loathing. Abandon all hope. Prepare for the Weirdness. Get familiar with Cannibalism.

Good luck, Doc.

New Leadership. **Thus came President George Walker Bush into the volatile arena of American politics with considerable resources for transformational leadership.**

Our first President of the New Millennium inherited more than a famous name, a decent economy, and international peace. Most notably, he entered office with a fairly clean personal slate; and, as was the case with Jefferson and McKinley, he possessed narrow but allegiant control of both the House and Senate. Finally, there was public support for his promise to be "a unifying leader" who would help us deal with our cultural and political anxieties. These resources positioned George W. Bush for effective governance—and perhaps more fundamental change in the American political system.

Without question in my mind, Bush's predecessor, William Jefferson Clinton, could have been America's transformational leader for the new century; but, also in my opinion, his tenure can be viewed as the "Clinterim Presidency". He presided over a nation ripe for turn-of-century redefinition and redirection—the end of the Cold War, unprecedented economic prosperity, and federal budget surpluses—and he possessed impressive political skills for democratic restoration. Just as importantly, he understood and ambitiously pursued his transformational opportunity. However, critical conditions changed early in his tenure (due in great part to his own over-reaching ambition and personal problems), and his masterful skills were diverted toward political survival. As a political scientist who has studied "the Man from Hope" since before his Washington tenure and as a politician who served in Congress during the Clinton administrations, I've been awed both positively and negatively by his performance as President. But I suspect that historians will consider Bill Clinton a bold, talented, interim political leader rather than a transformational "bridge" to the Twenty-First Century.

Certainly President Bush operates in a different and difficult environment. In the first place, the conditions of leadership have changed adversely. Most significantly, economic and international problems have complicated the American agenda. Politically, a single Republican defection tilted the Senate in

Democratic directions at the outset; and he still labors under the burden of strong partisan opposition on Capitol Hill. Resentment and distrust linger especially among African-American citizens, as reflected in the post-election comment by the head of the Congressional Black Caucus: "The wounds on Lady Liberty . . . may be deeper than some think and are dangerously close to becoming infected" ("CBC Lashes Out at Bush," *Roll Call,* December 18, 2000.

Thus far, even after considerable time in the White House, George W. Bush is a man of uncertain historical substance and significance. As *The New York Times* editorialized following his State of the Union speech against the forces of terrorism, "the test of his leadership will come when he better defines the difficult choices lying ahead" (January 30, 2002). It is not likely that President Bush (or any future administration) can succeed along the lines of conventional politics. Certainly, Bush can govern effectively through bipartisan coalitions; more importantly, for the long run, it is conceivable that a two-term President Bush—mindful of our cultural divide and political anxiety—might (as Kettl recommends) escape traditional constituencies, melt policy boundaries, and define new roles for American government.

I'll not attempt to specify the policy platform or political alchemy for such an initiative; but, arguably, our turn-of-century national environment presents real transformational opportunity for bold, forceful, Twenty-First Century presidential leadership.

"EMERGING AMERICA"

The Election of 2000, similar in many ways to previous turn-of-century elections, showcased the general theme and specific elements of my unconventional analysis of American democracy. The electoral debate generally demonstrated that America is undergoing important, unsettling change; and, more specifically, the electoral vote documented broad, balanced, volatile tension between two national cultures—simultaneously competitive, commingled, and interdependent—that have very different ideas about what America means and how America ought to work.

Two Societies. While the American people are not universally, rigidly, or violently polarized, we divide evenly in our partisan attachments; we split fairly consistently on a wide variety of political issues; and we differ deeply on a handful of moral concerns. Our nation is indeed bifurcating into two distinct cultural societies and political personalities—"Traditional America" and "Emerging America"—each with legitimate but starkly different visions of our national destiny.

On one hand is "Traditional America"—an historically-dominant white society, rooted in rural, small town, middle regions, which subscribes to religious convictions, community values, and conservative government. On the other hand is "Emerging America"—a growing, eclectic society of relatively progressive, minority, and historically-disadvantaged citizens in urban and coastal areas who are inclined toward social diversity, moral tolerance, and liberal government.

"Traditional America" vehemently asserts its right of national political control as the historic, vital, majoritarian democratic culture and, in the recent case of choosing our presidential leadership, by constitutional virtue of the Electoral College. Just as vehemently, "Emerging America" boldly defines itself as the energetic political core of our nation, not only in demographic terms but also as the recently demonstrated electoral majority of American democracy.

Continuing Political Tensions. **Apparently, this is not a fixed, static standoff between traditional and emerging societies.** The competing cultures subscribe to peculiarly convenient and inconsistent visions of public authority and the democratic process, supporting or opposing "big government" and "direct democracy" as suits their philosophical propensities of the moment. Furthermore, it is apparent from ongoing analysis of demographic and political data that we are trending towards greater bifurcation (and the underlying dynamics seem to favor "Emerging America" over "Traditional America").

In a way, too, our recent presidential election can be viewed as a legitimately arguable, very narrow, perhaps transient triumph—through an obtuse constitutional mechanism—of a relatively traditional and dominant constituency over an emerging popular majority. The Electoral College worked as it was originally intended; but its invocation in the 2000 election served to emphasize serious division and anxiety in American society. Our cultural and political tensions will continue to dominate American government for years to come.

Presidential Opportunity. **Finally, the contemporary mix of culture and politics presents significant opportunity for President Bush (and successive national leaders).** Just as in previous critical junctures, the American president has been entrusted by the American people to chart an acceptable course for American democracy.

To put it in transformational terms, Election 2000, more so than any other election in memory, noisily and clearly reflected a divided, volatile nation. We now embody competing cultural movements anxiously pushing distempered America toward an uncertain "New America".

....

A TRANSFORMATIONAL CHALLENGE
FOR TWENTY-FIRST CENTURY AMERICA
("NATIONAL DEMOCRATIC RENAISSANCE")

Election 2000 can be viewed, then—within the broad systemic and philosophical developments of my transformational thesis—as a noteworthy event in the history of American democracy; and it provides a prime

vantage point for normative reflection and recommendation. Therefore, as we proceed in this critical period, I want to issue a transformational challenge for Twenty-First Century America.

In preceding discussions, I maintained that America is not likely to travel the course of radical deformation ("Amerika" / "USSA") or disintegration ("death"). But I also projected that, if we continue on our current course, America may transition into "The American Federation" by the middle of the Twenty-First Century. It seems to me that we can do better than any of these options.

My challenge for "New America" is rediscovering the essence of our national democratic experiment and reworking that experiment for the Twenty-First Century. My challenge is politically non-partisan (neither Democratic nor Republican) and philosophically neutral (neither liberal nor conservative); nor is it an endorsement of more or less nationalization, centralization, and government. My challenge simply calls for serious deliberation about progressive democracy as defined over the course of American history. Or, to put it in question form, "How can we continue our traditional Great Experiment in keeping with a changing America?"

While I cannot define the specifics of transformational democracy, it is clear that my challenge requires innovative thinking about our national democratic experiment. Philosophically, for example, we must balance new dynamics of national community, social diversity, economic globalism, technological progress—and the vagaries of democratic ideals in "New America".

Clearly, too, our people, politics, and government will have to restore themselves in some different manner before they can work anew the magic of their historic civic mix. To be specific, we first must revive democratic spirit among a people who no longer believe, to the extent that they did in the past, in the goodness of their political leaders (or even the national democratic system itself); in particular, we need to figure out how to reconnect young people personally with their rights and responsibilities in the national community. Secondly, our political machinery requires extensive repair; political parties, the news media, and the electoral system will have to reorient and reconstruct themselves if they are to continue as serious players in the democratic arena. Finally, our governmental institutions will have to be re-invented; entrenched elements of today's outmoded federal establishment must adjust—and in some instances devolve or dissolve—in accord with the realities of a more intense, empowered, and pluralistic society.

Undoubtedly, the road from historic America to "New America" is a journey of comprehensive, fundamental, systemic change that accommodates the dynamics of the past few decades without weakening our Great Experiment. To return to my three-part question at the beginning of this discussion:

> "Can . . . "How can . . . and "How far can our nation—a people of growing cultural diversity, with increasingly divergent ideals, values, and principles of governance, in a constrained systemic environment—continue our collective

pursuit of freedom, equality, and justice within the traditional framework of limited, representative government?"

Or, to put it more urgently: "Can we deal with the powerful dynamics of systemic constraint, philosophical turmoil, subculturalism, neopopulism, and electronic democracy without going too far, without succumbing to the inherent, destructive tendencies of democracy?"

"NATIONAL DEMOCRATIC RENAISSANCE"

My conclusion, after three decades of public service, is that successfully addressing our systemic, philosophical, and political distemper will be possible only through a transformational effort whereby we recommit our historic experiment to a new course of democracy. I propose, then, that we launch a "National Democratic Renaissance". While we cannot specify in advance the substantive nature and outcome of this transformational experience, we can at least begin redefining, redirecting, and restoring American democracy in line with the essential concepts of our historic Great Experiment.

National Democratic Renaissance
Clearly Requires Presidential Leadership
(and an American Democracy Commission).

Restoring the American system to its historic health is no small assignment (particularly during a period of relative contentment), and it certainly is not a job for government alone. Redefining, redirecting, and restoring American democracy clearly are public responsibilities requiring participation by the totality of people and institutions that make up America's public life. We all must engage in an open, far-ranging, freewheeling search for our democratic destiny in the new century.

However, after placing responsibility upon all of us for the future of American democracy, I now put the primary, immediate burden of democratic renaissance squarely upon the shoulders of America's leadership. To be more specific, an American democratic renaissance requires formal and active leadership by the President of the United States. Despite my earlier comments about the democratization movement, initiating and guiding such a public effort will depend inevitably upon the actions of the American political elite simply because that is the way things get done in the real world of organized society. There are those of us who (by virtue of our democratically-vested power, personal resources, or societal standing) occupy positions of authority and accountability for exercising positive, small-r republican influences upon small-d democratic inclinations. It therefore is in the interest of continued representative democracy that responsible leaders exercise their "r" – "d" responsibilities in such manner as to guide public policy and inspire public confidence. In sum, "We the people" are all in this together, but "we the leaders"—particularly politicians, educators, and private-sector leaders—must jump-start national democratic renaissance.

American democratic renaissance also clearly requires the development of a super civic institution—the American Democracy Commission— something like but much bigger than the Commission on the Bicentennial of the U.S. Constitution. This organization would sponsor and coordinate educational programs, conferences, debates, contests, and other activities. Democratic renewal would necessitate a broad, focused, aggressive campaign— a public/private partnership involving government of all levels and forms, political parties, interest groups, the business community, unions, schools, churches, foundations, the news media, the entertainment world, influential leaders, and celebrities from across the American spectrum.

Actually, the creation of a democracy commission is not such a far-fetched idea. Numerous initiatives already are engaged in civic renewal—consider, for example, the efforts of the Nunn-Bennett National Commission on Civic Renewal, Colin Powell's America's Promise, The Leon and Sylvia Panetta Institute, The Pew Charitable Trusts, The Kettering Foundation, The Century Foundation, The Center for Civic Education, The Center for Civic Networking, The Institute for the Study of Civic Values, The Close-Up Foundation, C-SPAN, The Center for Democracy and Citizenship, and Democracy Forum USA. I currently am in the process of beginning a pilot project on democratic citizenship with my local public school system in Alabama. Perhaps the American President could merge these initiatives into a comprehensive national movement for rediscovering America and reworking our democratic experiment.

We Must Rediscover
the Essence of Our American Nation
(Theoretically, Politically, and Personally).

Initially, it is critical for America to rediscover itself—theoretically, politically, and personally—by putting ourselves through a democratic rebirthing similar to the civic ordeal of our Founders.

Our rediscovery might focus, theoretically, on the original essential concepts of American democracy. In the beginning, a hodge-podge of diverse, divergent peoples committed themselves to inspired nationhood—the sense that we are all in this together; and they based their aspirations primarily on the pursuit of democratic ideals instead of royalty, religion, or rigid class distinctions; then they entrusted public power to a limited, representative system of government. We would do well to revisit the simple genius of our national origins.

I suggest furthermore that, politically, we need to emphasize and accept America for what it is—an inspired, uncertain experiment that has served us well. Our exercise in popular self-governance is sometimes awkward, faulty, and painful; but it has allowed us to pursue practical democratic ideals and the American dream, within the framework of limited, representative governance, fairly successfully, for over two centuries.

My idea of rediscovery also requires that we come to terms politically with what America is not—perfection. Our historic experiment searches for "a more perfect union"—not "a perfect union"; and America provides an opportunity for—not a guarantee of—the American dream.

• **Robert Samuelson** rightly observes, in *The Good Life and Its Discontents* (1997), that America's current distemper derives in great part from our unrealistic expectations of American democracy. Americans, as a nation, have made more public commitments to ourselves than we can keep; and, unfortunately we have become a prisoner of our expectations:

> We feel like the country hasn't lived up to its promises, and we are right. But the fault lies as much with the promise as with the performance. Our present pessimism is a direct reaction to the excessive optimism of the early postwar decades. It stems from the confusion of progress with perfection. Having first convinced ourselves that we were going to create the final American utopia—an extravagant act of optimism—we are now dismayed that we haven't—a burst of unwarranted pessimism. (XV)

Critical to rediscovery, too, is the simple idea that "we the people" must, personally, re-ordain and re-establish our commitment to the fundamental principles of our national experiment in democratic ideals.

• **Alan Ehrenhalt** advises, in *Democracy in the Mirror* (1998), that we take a close look at ourselves as responsible citizens of a new democratic order:

> So if we wish to remedy the failures of our public life, or even understand it well enough to talk intelligently about changing it, the first step is not to conduct hearings or appoint commissions or hire special prosecutors. The first step is much simpler than that. It is to look in the mirror. (4)

Looking in the mirror may be the most challenging and difficult aspect of American democratic renaissance; but proper theoretical, political, and personal reflection of the origins, possibilities, and limitations of America would put us well on the course of national recovery.

We Then Can Rework
Our Great Experiment
for Today's World.

Having rediscovered—theoretically, politically, and personally—the essence of our American nation, we then must proceed to rethink, transformationally, how we run American democracy. We need to address the practical requirements of a changing national environment while respecting the basic theoretical parameters of our Great Experiment.

It is clear, for example, that progression of democratic ideals will have to proceed with renewed appreciation for the realities of our Great Experiment. This experiment is a contentious, messy, meandering journey toward an elusive destiny. We must now chart our course within a relatively bounded systemic environment; and we will have to acknowledge the risky dynamics of philosophical turmoil. We also must adjust our historical magical mix to accommodate the challenges of a more diverse populace, the coming of electronic democracy, and the restructuring of our governmental system.

We have available for our use in this transformational assignment the experiences and insights of the original founders; and there is evidence of clear rethinking among contemporary American theorists and practitioners.

• For example, in the area of governance, **C. Eugene Steuerle** and co-authors from The Urban Institute have provided a start with *The Government We Deserve: Responsive Democracy and Changing Expectations* (1998). This talented group has attempted to chart a theoretic vision for future government by acknowledging where we are today:

> The resulting picture is one of misleading expectations intertwined with legitimate public concerns. Yes, we have come to expect government to finance more than it can, but at the same time prior fiscal restraints of our own making are preventing government from meeting new needs it should and otherwise could afford to finance. Yes, there has been economic growth, but many are not sharing enough in that growth to have reasonable prospects for either opportunity or security. Yes, exaggerated government promises have fueled public expectations, but public expectations are also being deliberately manipulated in our increasingly open and distrusted democratic system. (125)

The authors ignore the question of whether government is too big or too little and avoid projecting cultural concerns upon government; instead, they focus our attention on three basic rules of common-sense pragmatism: (a) Rethinking our commitments, (b) Rethinking our responsibilities, and (c) Rethinking our decision-making process. Then they proceed with their rational checklist of practical "to do" assignments: "Freeing Up the Fiscal Future", "Giving Social Insurance a Modern Face", "Making a Government for All Ages", "Increasing Everyone's Chances To Build Financial Security", "Investing in Learning Over a Lifetime", "Engaging the Nation's Youth", and "Fostering a New Democratic Citizenship".

• **B. Guy Peters**, in *The Future of Governing* (1996), offers an equally useful typology of alternative governance models (market, participative, flexible, and deregulated government) for re-organizing the public sector. He further suggests that we consider matching specific problems with specific solutions, in other words accomplishing particular governmental tasks with different forms of organizing and managing:

> It may well be that for the provision of certain marketable services, the market model is adequate and desirable, but that same model would be totally inappropriate for many social services, for example, education. Likewise, the participatory model would be well suited for urban planning or environmental issues but would produce difficulties for many criminal justice programs . . . My purpose is not so much to force choices among the alternative models of governance but to make the implications of the choices that now face governments more evident . . . the benefits and sacrifices should be clear in making judgments about governance. (133)

Peters asserts furthermore that, while we cannot restore the "status quo ante", basic, functional elements of America's traditional governmental system can and should be salvaged. In response to his own question ("Can we go home again?"), he says:

> Perhaps most fundamentally, analysts and citizens alike should ask which components of the old system, once abandoned, are worth saving. Clearly some critics would say absolutely nothing should be salvaged and would be quite willing to throw it all out and start anew. It should be obvious by now that I am less sure of the vices of the old system or confident in the virtues of alternative replacements. The old system did place a high value on accountability and on service to the public as a whole, if not always to each individual client or customer. Those values are crucial for any public organization and should not be dismissed without adequate reflection. (133)

Step-by-Step to "New America"

There is no such thing, of course, as a simple, straightforward "how to" manual—something like a *New America For Dummies*—with a short list of procedures and instructions for rediscovering America and reworking American democracy. However, my analysis suggests five steps or mile posts on the transformational road to "New America"; and fortunately, there already are in place numerous initiatives which might be organized around these guidelines into a national movement of democratic renaissance.

Step 1. Revitalizing the systemic environment of American democracy. We cannot replicate our original natural frontier or endlessly expand national public authority, but we can revitalize our environment in the process of rediscovering ourselves, as a nation, and recommitting ourselves to America and American democracy. At the least, if we recognize the reality of our current predicament, we should be able to accommodate and mitigate some systemic constraints on our Great Experiment.

Step 2. Resolving the philosophical civil war. Complementary to revitalizing our systemic environment is the requisite resolution of our philosophical civil war. We have to decide collectively that America is worth saving and that the philosophical civil war is crippling America. Then we can institute forums and procedures for debating—civilly—democratic ideals, cultural values, and principles of governance.

Step 3. Reviving our civic culture. Citizenship—in all its facets—must be revived among our general population and leadership. This does not mean that every single American becomes a revolutionary democrat; however, it is imperative that we achieve a sufficient civic mixture for popular self-governance.

Step 4. Repairing our political machinery. Perhaps no aspect of American democracy has been scrutinized so thoroughly as have been America's parties, media, and electoral system. We cannot return to earlier conditions and institutions of by-gone America, so our parties, media, and elections must adjust—or be replaced—for a different democratic experiment.

Step 5. Re-inventing our government. The term "re-invention" sounds like a superficial, bumper sticker idea, but we understand theoretically what has to be done and we know from experience that governance at all levels can be redesigned to work more efficiently and effectively. We simply must be ready to conduct ourselves as a national community in ways that may be far different from what we have known for most of our lives.

This five-step plan, somewhat like the gimmicky, "no-sweat" pitch of infomercial television, obviously ignores the hard, tedious, heavy lifting of democratic bodybuilding. As has been noted before, there are no simple solutions or secret formulas or hidden agendas for our mission of democratic renaissance. However, the challenge outlined here—rediscovering America and reworking our democratic experiment—(along with my five-step roadmap to "New America") provides a beginning framework for national discussion. More speculatively, this challenge and roadmap suggest the evolving direction of American democracy in the Twenty-First Century.

....

AND SOME TRANSFORMATIONAL PREDICTIONS
ABOUT THE EVOLVING DIRECTION
OF AMERICAN DEMOCRACY

The original objective of this unconventional manuscript was to examine American democracy in order, as Tocqueville said, "to learn what we have to fear or to hope from its progress" at the beginning of the Twenty-First

Century. Thus far in these concluding pages I have attempted to show that we live in transformational times with transformational opportunity. We'll have to wait to see whether America experiences a democratic renaissance in "New America" or becomes "The American Federation" (or assumes another, less attractive identity) in the long run. But I feel comfortable presenting a general observation about what's happening in contemporary America and some specific predictions about how American democracy might evolve in the next few decades.

A GENERAL OBSERVATION

To generalize broadly, America is indeed experiencing national democratic distemper. While we cannot affirm my provocative propositions, this analysis has suggested some seriously troubling tendencies and vulnerabilities of contemporary American democracy. Relative to historic America, our systemic environment is somewhat constrained; we're tangled in philosophical dissension; our people, politics, and government no longer work their collective magic as well as they used to; and we evidence mixed, uncertain attitudes toward the national democratic experiment. Furthermore, after two centuries of popular centralization and nationalization, equally powerful forces of centrifugal democracy now pressure American governance in contradictory directions.

These developments naturally raise some important questions about America's future. For example, despite the historic progression of American democracy, are there limits to our national democratic endeavor? How far can we push our experiment without pushing too far? To repeat more comprehensively my underlying concern, "How far can a diverse, divergent people pursue theoretical democratic ideals through limited representative governance without succumbing to the inherent, destructive tendencies of democracy?" In summary, is our historic magical mix really losing its magic; and is America, as we have known it, dying? Will the United States of America become "The American Federation"? Or, on the other hand, is America transforming into something bigger and better in "New America"?

SOME SPECIFIC PREDICTIONS

Here, finally, are my specific predictions (actually a mixture of predictions, expectations, and personal observations) about the evolving, transformational direction of American democracy:

(1) America is not going to die! Nor or we likely to morph into "Amerika" or the "USSA" or any other deformed version of democratic decline. My rhetorical inquiry about our possible national demise serves simply as the heuristic mechanism for an unconventional analysis of American democracy in the Twenty-First Century. Our national democratic distemper should subside as

we acknowledge and deal effectively with the challenges and opportunities of transformational life. Who knows—we may even transform into "New America"!

(2)   Systemically, America of the future will operate in a fundamentally different, less propitious, and more challenging setting than has been the case in the past two centuries. A constrained environment and philosophical tension will limit and exacerbate our troubled national experiment in democratic ideals; and American democracy will have to achieve effective balance between historic popular nationalization and irresistible forces of democratic decentralization in the coming century. Thus systemic realities will both force and complicate our transformational future.

(3)   Culturally, "Traditional America" will yield to "Emerging America" in the next few decades. America inevitably is going to become a more expansive, inclusive, pluralistic society, with intensified cultural dissension over democratic ideals, values, and governance; and traditional, majoritarian, homogeneous, advantaged society will yield its dominant status to emerging, minoritarian, heterogeneous, disadvantaged society. It is likely that traditional society will maintain political control—as a plurality force—for some time; and emerging society will be an eclectic numerical majority, thereby further segmenting the American electorate. Transforming a nation of such pronounced social diversity and philosophical tension obviously will pose unprecedented challenges to American democracy.

(4)   Politically, American democracy will never again work the way it has worked in the past. Simply by historic definition of our Great Experiment, democratic destiny, and demographic reality, American democracy probably will continue to move in progressive directions; meanwhile, transformational dynamics dictate that the entire process (particularly our parties, media, and elections) will have to accommodate the demands of several simultaneous developments—defined in this manuscript as "uncivil society", "democratic dissensus", "subcultural democratization", and "electronic democracy"—of systemic importance.

I anticipate, as a result of these developments, that basic national public authority will continue and that fundamental freedoms will survive in some form and manner; and those responsibilities that are consensually broad, general, and beyond provincial capabilities (such as national defense, foreign policy, and economic/monetary policy) will still be handled by the central government. But other responsibilities (or at least certain aspects of important policy areas) such as social security, health care, education, and public safety will have to be redefined more rationally among varying jurisdictions of the federalist system. Finally, the representational process must become more direct, open, and practical in Twenty-First Century America.

Consequently, over the next several decades, Washington and our national political institutions will recede somewhat (but the states will not necessarily rise again) as non-governmental interests, regional authorities, and the individual citizen assume increasing control over our national democratic experiment. Transformation will be a tricky endeavor, but America should be able to make these adjustments without radical revolution; and the American democratic system should work sufficiently well—albeit differently—in the Twenty-First Century.

(5) President George W. Bush has an opportunity to be a transformational leader at this critical juncture in American history; and if Mr. Bush, for some reason, fails to provide appropriate leadership, I'm confident that his successor will inherit similar challenge and similar opportunity. My contention is that systemic constraints, cultural tension, and political anxiety are challenging America to address shifting, dissensual notions of democratic ideals, values, and governance. The struggle between "Traditional America" and "Emerging America" will have to be mediated; and, eventually, we must deal with nagging, fundamental questions about "what America means" and "how America ought to work." Such transformational dynamics will create challenging circumstances and will demand forceful action; and bold presidential leadership will be necessary if we are to proceed successfully toward "New America". Those who dismiss our President's potential role in the redefinition, redirection, and restoration of our political system are ignoring important lessons of history, the power of presidential leadership, and the responsive spirit of an anxious, challenged America.

(6)   Speaking more personally, those of us in academia and politics will have to assume special responsibilities during these transformational times. Political scientists (and other scholars) will need to analyze—in expeditious manner—the changing systemic, philosophical, and political dynamics of American democracy; and elected public officials (and the broader community of political operatives) must facilitate our collective journey in the new century.

I will not attempt to predict or recommend our national fate beyond these fanciful, heuristic observations about the future of American democracy. I anticipate—drawing from my almost mystical confidence in America—that, under the best of circumstances, we will enjoy "National Democratic Renaissance", a fundamental renewal of American democracy, and a new golden age for our historic Great Experiment in the Twenty-First Century. On the other hand—if we unthinkingly continue our current course of distemperate drift—future generations could experience a diminished experiment in democratic ideals.

....

AN EVEN GREATER DEMOCRATIC EXPERIMENT?

America indeed has been an historically glorious, albeit imperfect, national experiment in democratic ideals. However, the future of our Great Experiment will be determined by the manner in which we manage systemic, cultural, and political transformations in the next few years. Whether or not our President can provide the requisite leadership—and whether or not we will respond with appropriate citizenship—is a central issue at this critical juncture in American history.

Thus it would be in our national interest to begin exploring—now, rationally, together—the future of American democracy. While I doubt that America will be transformed by ideological arguments from the likes of writer-activist **Patrick Buchanan** and scholar-activist **Cornel West**, I suspect that most of us (and both of them) can agree with their judgments about the common interest of our national destiny. Buchanan, for example, says that "America is still a country worth fighting for and the last best hope of earth" (*The Death of the West: How Mass Immigration, Depopulation, and a Dying Faith Are Killing Our Culture and Country*, 2002; 268); and West maintains that "We must admit that the most valuable sources for help, hope, and power consist of ourselves and our common history" (*Race Matters* 2001; 11-13).

MYSTICAL CONFIDENCE

I am admittedly biased (as a former congressman, political science professor, and "American dreamer"); therefore, as I have said previously, I'm mystically confident about America and the future of American democracy.

For example, I subscribe unapologetically to the gushy sentiment of English Historian **Paul Johnson** in his panoramic *History of the American People* (1997):

> The great American republican experiment is still the cynosure of the world's eyes. It is still the first, best hope for the human race. Looking back on its past, and forward to its future, the auguries are that it will not disappoint an expectant humanity. (976)

I find equally inspiring the personal testimony of my friend, congressional colleague, and civil-rights legend **John Lewis** (*Walking with the Wind: A Memoir of the Movement*, written with **Michael D'Orso**, 1998):

> I believe in America. I love this country. That's why I've tried so hard over the years to make it better. This is unquestionably the greatest nation on earth, a land of limitless opportunity and possibility, not just in material terms but in moral, ethical and spiritual terms. (487)

Finally, I take cautious comfort in the remarks of Pulitzer Prize winner **Arthur M. Schlesinger, Jr.**, who acknowledged realistic vulnerabilities and hopeful prospects of our democratic experiment in addressing the keynote question of a special presentation at the Institute of United States Studies in London (*Has Democracy A Future?* 1997):

> Has democracy a future? Sure it does, but not the glorious, irresistible, inevitable future predicted in the triumphalist moment. Democracy has survived the 20th century by the skin of its teeth. It will not enjoy a free ride throughout the century to come . . .Still, with the failures of democracy in the 20th century at the back of their minds, men and women of the century to come may do a better job than we have done in making the world really safe for democracy. (15-18)

POSITIVE DEVELOPMENTS

Obviously, America is much stronger and more durable than suggested in my original, rhetorical "dying" inquiry; and I am encouraged by recent, positive developments and upbeat messages about America's democratic endeavor.

In the first place, our national mood seems to have stabilized. Or, to put it another way, subjective observation and statistical measures indicate that we're not getting any more distempered. I even detect a sense of reborn spirit, an almost indignant positiveness about American democracy in audiences at my public lectures. I'm also impressed with the attitudes expressed by students in my seminars about the state of American democracy.

Additionally, most recent data from the American Freshman Survey show "reversal in a long slide toward political apathy on college campuses" ("College Freshmen More Liberal, Less Apathetic, Poll Finds, *Los Angeles Times*, January 28, 2002). My former congressional colleague and White House Chief of Staff **Leon Panetta** (now at the Leon and Sylvia Panetta Institute for Public Policy at California State University Monterey Bay) reports that today's young people are interested in the national policy debate and hold a far more optimistic view of the country's direction than do other adults:

> What we find here tends to reinforce the results of our survey last November, which showed that students have little interest in voting or in careers in politics or government, yet tend to be interested in the issues and to volunteer at a very high rate for community service. They're turned off by politics, but turned on by issues and by service to others. ("Though Few Students Vote, Poll Shows Them Still Interested in Issues and Upbeat About the Country," Panetta Institute, April 25, 2000)

I'm encouraged further in this respect by the positive counsel of distinguished scholar **Everett Carll Ladd** in *The Ladd Report* (1999):

My own conclusion, from two years of rummaging through the assembled findings, is that we have allowed our persistent anxieties about the quality of our citizenship to blind us to the many positive trends that have been occurring . . . when it comes to civic engagement it's just not true that the sky is falling. The stars are in their place, and the sky is pretty bright. (5)

TRAUMATIC NATIONAL CHALLENGE

Finally, I am more confident because of national response to the traumatic challenge of the September 11, 2001 "Attack on America". It would be easy, here in the emotion of the moment, to get deliriously patriotic and overstate the lasting effect of the terrorist killing of thousands of innocent American citizens. However, as has been noted, this assault apparently has rattled and rallied the American people just as did Pearl Harbor (1941) for what has been called perhaps the "greatest generation" in American history. At the least, this infamous experience will cause us to pause and reflect on the nature and future of American democracy. Already, the American people are evidencing greater solidarity and patriotic fervor; and according to news reports, they have dramatically altered their attitudes toward the federal government:

> The terrorist attacks of Sept. 11 have caused a stunning reversal in public attitudes about government and the people who work for it, new surveys show.
>
> A Washington Post-ABC News poll conducted late last week showed that 64 percent of Americans said they trusted "the government in Washington to do what is right" just about always or most of the time. That's up from only 30 percent in April, the last time the news organizations asked the question . . .
>
> "These figures are sort of pre-Vietnam, pre-Watergate-era levels," said Paul Light, director of governmental studies at the Brookings Institution . . . This is probably the greatest 'Rally 'round the flag' effect since Pearl harbor." ("Trust in Government up Dramatically, Polls Show," GovExec.com, October 1, 2001, accessed at www.govexec.com)

Indicative too, is the fact that this reaction stretches across common social divides:

> "The signs of this upsurge are everywhere. The grass-roots response of the American people has been phenomenal," reacts Walter Berns, resident scholar at Washington's American Enterprise Institute.
>
> In his opinion, the display of bottom-up public patriotism has been "unseen in this nation in at least half a century, slicing across boundaries of race, class, age, and gender" . . .
>
> "Not since Pearl Harbor, and perhaps not even then, has there been anything like it," says Mr. Berns. "There surely was nothing like it during

the years of Korea, Vietnam, or even the Gulf War. Not then did crowds of people gather in the streets, shouting 'USA, USA, USA!" ("Inside the Beltway," *The Washington Times*, October 16, 2001)

Finally, our post-terror environment is an opportune challenge, as Harvard Professor Robert Putnam says, for America to rebuild its social capital:

> America at this moment has an incredible opportunity, the kind that comes along only once every half century, to become better connected with one another . . . But if all our leaders ask of us is that we go shopping, nothing will happen. (quoted by **Nancy Benac**, in "The Altered State of the Union: Anxious, Optimistic, Civil," Associated Press, January 27, 2002)

I witnessed such "connecting" reaction in my hometown as our community packed the First Baptist Church to commemorate the life of Major Dwayne Williams, a native son who perished at The Pentagon. I'm not an overly emotional person, but I was moved—not simply because Jacksonville is a small, deep south community and Major Williams was of African-American descent, not simply because of the spiritual renditions of "I'll Fly Away" and "Battle Hymn of the Republic" by Jacksonville State University's Gospel Choir, not simply because of friends sharing their grief and remembrances. What was moving was the special democratic chemistry (Alexis de Tocqueville might have called it an "associational" experience) as the entire cross-section of our community came together—as Americans dealing positively with personal and national challenge—in a celebration of family, god, and country. I confess to patriotic bias, but I can say detachedly that Tocqueville would have been duly impressed had he been there with us; and I feel with certainty that—on that day, in the First Baptist Church of Jacksonville, Alabama, and probably at similar events throughout the country—America was alive and well and getting better.

DETERMINATION AND FAITH

I hope that my readers derive from this unconventional analysis a healthy, renewed appreciation for the strengths, limitations, and fragilities of our Great Experiment. We all should accept the responsibilities of democratic citizenship articulated by former American Political Science Association president and Pulitzer Prize-winner **James MacGregor Burns** and his colleagues in *Government by the People* (2002):

> The future of democracy in America will be shaped by those citizens who care about preserving and extending our political rights and freedoms. Our individual liberties will never be assured unless there are people willing to take responsibility for the progress of the whole community, people willing to exercise their determination and democratic faith. Carved in granite on one of the long corridors in a building on the Harvard University campus are these words of American poet Archibald MacLeish: "How shall freedom be defended? By arms when it is attacked by arms, by truth when it is attacked

by lies, by democratic faith when it is attacked by authoritarian dogma. Always, in the final act, by determination and faith." (433)

If we collectively embrace our transformational responsibilities with determination and faith at this critical historical juncture, then perhaps we will achieve inspired, inspiring renewal of American democracy in "New America".

....

"QUELLE GRAND EXPÉRIENCE!"

I wonder what our young friend, Monsieur Tocqueville, would say if he were to travel with us on the road to "New America"? Would he smile, and exclaim "Oh, quel spectacle! Quelle grand expérience!" Or would he mutter something to the effect that "Frankly, it's not what I had hoped!"

I seriously doubt that "The American Federation", as I have projected it, is what Tocqueville had in mind for America; nor am I convinced that any other similarly diminished experiment in democratic ideals is our pre-destined future. I believe that our ultimate destiny will be an even greater democratic experiment in "New America". Of course, we must consider the sober realities of contemporary American life; and we must acknowledge the possibility that our democratic destiny could be less spectacular than that of the past two centuries. But perhaps—blessed anew with George Washington's "sacred fire of liberty," Abraham Lincoln's "new birth of freedom," and Martin Luther King's "dream" of equality—we will devise an even more spectacular Great Experiment in the New Millennium.

As we conclude our unconventional discussion, it may be worthwhile to take note of Tocqueville's final words in *Democracy in America* (1835):

> The nations of our time cannot prevent the conditions of men from becoming equal; but it depends upon themselves whether the principle of equality is to lead them to servitude or freedom, to knowledge or barbarism, to prosperity or wretchedness. (Vol. II, p. 334)

America is not dying. But we clearly are undergoing a democratic metamorphosis that, for better or worse, is transforming our nation and world history. In our hands, in our hearts, in our minds, lie prosperity, and knowledge, and freedom—or wretchedness, and barbarism, and servitude. The future of American democracy demands our attention.

REFERENCES

Adams, James Truslow. 1931. *The Epic of America.* Little, Brown.

Albanesius, Chloe. October 11, 2001. "A Lesson in Democracy." *Roll Call.*

Almond, Gabriel, and Sidney Verba. 1963. *Civic Culture: Political Attitudes and Democracy in Five Nations.* Little, Brown.

Almond, Gabriel A., and Sidney Verba. 1980. *The Civic Culture Revisited.* Sage.

Anderson, Caitlin E. June 3, 2000. "Harvard Goes to Washington? Not Anymore". *Harvard Crimson.*

Baldassare, Mark. 2000. *California in the New Millennium: The Changing Social and Political Landscape.* University of California Press.

Barber, Benjamin R. 2000. *A Passion for Democracy: American Essays.* Princeton University Press.

Barlett, Donald L., and James B. Steele. 1992. *America: What Went Wrong?* Andrews and McMeel.

Barlett, Donald L., and James B. Steele. 1996. *America. Who Stole the Dream?* Andrews and McMeel.

Barone, Michael. 2001. *The New Americans.* Regnery.

Barzun, Jacques. 2000. *From Dawn to Decadence: 500 Years of Western Cultural Life, 1500 to Present.* Harper Trade.

Beard, Charles Austin. 1925. *An Economic Interpretation of the Constitution of the United States.* Transaction.

Beck, Paul Allen, and Marjorie Randon Hershey. 2001. *Party Politics in America.* Ninth Edition. Longman.

Becker, Theodore Lewis, and Christa Daryl Slaton. 2000. *The Future of Teledemocracy: Visions and Theories—Action Experiments—Global Practices.* Greenwood.

Bell, Art. 1998. *Quickening: Today's Trends, Tomorrow's World.* Paper Chase Press.

Ben, Lui. June 20, 1999. "Bubble Economy and Bubble Culture". *China Youth Daily.*

Benac, Nancy. January 27, 2002. "The Altered State of the Union: Anxious, Optimistic, Civil". *Associated Press.*

Benjamin, Caren. June 27, 2000. "Survey: Students Fail History Test". *Associated Press.*

Bennett, Stephen Earl, and Linda L. M. Bennett. June, 2001. "What Political Scientists Should Know about the Survey of First-Year Students in 2000". *PS: Political Science and Politics.*

Bennett, W. Lance. 1996. *News - The Politics of Illusion.* Longman.

Berns, Walter. 1998. "Constitutionalism and Multiculturalism". In Arthur, M. Melzer, Jerry Weinberger, and M. Richard Zinman, *Multiculturalism and American Democracy.* University Press of Kansas.

Bernstein, Aaron. August, 2001. "The Human Factor". *Business Week Magazine.*

Blakey, Edward J., and Mary Gail Snyder. 1997. *Fortress America: Gated Communities in the United States.* Brookings.

Bloom, Allan. 1988. *The Closing of the American Mind: How Higher Education Has Failed Democracy and Impoverished the Souls of Today's Students.* Simon and Schuster.

Bok, Derek. 1997. *The State of the Nation.* Harvard University Press.

Bok, Derek. 2001. *The Trouble With Government.* Harvard University Press.

Borrus, Amy. August 27, 2001. "Land of Shrinking Opportunity". *Business Week Magazine.*

Bovard, James. 1999. *Freedom in Chains: The Rise of the State and the Demise of the Citizen.* St. Martin's.

Bovard, James. 1995. *Lost Rights: The Destruction of American Liberty.* St. Martin's.

Box, Richard C. 1998. *Citizen Governance: Leading American Communities into the 21st Century.* Sage.

Brecke, Ronald F. 1999. *A Republic, If You Can Keep It.* Lexington.

Broder, David. August 13, 1997. "Californocracy in Action". *The Washington Post.*

Broder, David S. November 21, 2000. "A Cloud Over Thanksgiving". *The Washington Post*.

Broder, David S. 2000. *Democracy Derailed: Initiative Campaigns and the Power of Money*. Harcourt.

Brookings Review. Winter, 2000. *The State of Governance in America*.

Bryce, James. 1888. *The American Commonwealth*. Liberty Fund.

Buchanan, Patrick J. 2002. *The Death of the West: How Mass Immigration, Depopulation, and A Dying Faith Are Killing Our Culture*. Dunne.

Burns, James MacGregor, et al. 2002. *Government by the People*. Prentice Hall.

Bush, George. January 20, 1989. "Inaugural Address".

Bush, George W. January 20, 2001. "Inaugural Address".

Business Week Magazine. August 27, 2001. *America's Future: The Boom, the Bust, Now What?*

Carter, Stephen L. 1998. Civility: *Manners, Morals, and the Etiquette of Democracy*. HarperCollins.

Cash, W. J. 1941. *Mind of the South*. Knopf.

Ceaser, James. 1998. "Multiculturalism and American Liberal Democracy". In Arthur M. Melzer, Jerry Weinberger, and Richard Zinman, *Multiculturalism and American Democracy*. University Press of Kansas.

Chancellor, John. 1990. *Peril and Promise: A Commentary on America*. Harper.

Chittum, Thomas W. 1997. *Civil War II: The Coming Breakup of America*. American Eagle.

Clinton, William Jefferson. January 23, 1996. State of the Union Message.

Cohen, Richard E. June 18, 1994. "When There's Too Much Of A Good Thing". *National Journal*.

Coy, Peter. August 27, 2001. "The New Economy: How Real Is It?" *Business Week Magazine*.

Crevecoeur, Hector St. John de. 1997. *Letters from an American Farmer*. Oxford University Press.

Crozier, Michel, Joji Watanuki, and Samuel P. Huntington. 1975. *The Crisis of Democracy*. New York University Press.

Dahl, Robert. 1963, 1990. *A Preface to Democratic Theory*. University of Chicago Press.

Dahl, Robert. 1994. *The New American Political (Dis)order*. University of California Institute of Government Studies.

Dahl, Robert. 1999. *On Democracy*. Yale University Press.

Dahl, Robert. 2001. "Political Equality in the Coming Century". In Keith Dowding, James Hughes, and Helen Margetts (ed.), *Challenges to Democracy: Ideas, Involvement and Institutions*. Palgrove.

Davidson, James West, William E. Gienapp, Christine Leigh Heyrman, Mark H. Lytle, Michael A. Stoff. 1994. *Nation of Nations: A Narrative History of the American Republic*. McGraw-Hill.

DeBow, Ken, and John C. Syer. 2000. *Power and Politics in California*. Longman.

Diamond, Jared. 1997. *Guns, Germs and Steele: The Fates of Human Societies*. Norton.

Dietze, Gottfried. 1968. *America's Political Dilemma*. University Press of America.

Dionne, E.J., Jr. 1991. *Why Americans Hate Politics*. Simon and Shuster.

Dionne, E. J., Jr. 1996. *They Only Look Dead: Why Progressives Will Dominate the Next Political Era*. Touchstone.

Dionne, E. J. Jr. 1998. *Community Works: The Revival of Civil Society in America*. Brookings.

Dionne, E .J. Jr. November 30, 1999. "The Civics Deficit". *The Washington Post*.

Donahue, John D. 1997. *Disunited States*. Basic Books.

Dowding, Keith, James Hughes, and Helen Martetts. 2002. *Challenges to Democracy: Ideas, Involvement and Institutions*. Palgrave.

Drew, Elizabeth. 1999. *The Corruption of American Politics: What Went Wrong and Why*. Overlook.

Dunham, Richard, and Ann Therese Palmer. August 27, 2001. "Governing a Nation Divided". *Business Week Magazine*.

Dye, Thomas R., and Harmon Ziegler, 2000, *The Irony of Democracy: An Uncommon Introduction to American Politics*. Harcourt Brace.

Dyer, Joel. 1997. *Harvest of Rage: Why Oklahoma City Is Only the Beginning*. Westview.

Easton, David. 1965. *A Systems Analysis of Political Life*. John Wiley and Sons.

Eberly, Don E. 1999. *America's Promise: Civil Society and the Renewal of American Culture*. Rowman and Littlefield.

Eberly, Don E. 2000. *The Essential Civil Society Reader*. Rowman and Littlefield.

Economist, The. April 16, 1998. "America's Bubble Economy".

Edsall, Thomas Byrne, and Mary D. Edsall. 1991. *Chain Reaction: The Impact of Race, Rights, and Taxes on American Politics*. Norton.

Ehrenhalt, Alan. 1991. *The United States of Ambition: Politicians, Power, and the Pursuit of Office*. Times Books.

Ehrenhalt, Alan. 1996. *The Lost City: The Forgotten Virtues of Community in America*. Basic Books.

Ehrenhalt, Alan. 1998. *Democracy in the Mirror: Politics, Reform, and Reality in Grassroots America*. Congressional Quarterly.

Eisenstadt, S.N. 1999. *Paradoxes of Democracy: Fragility, Continuity, and Change*. Johns Hopkins University Press.

Elshtain, Jean Bethke. 1995. *Democracy on Trial*. Basic Books.

Elshtain, Jean Bethke. 1998. *Democratic Authority at Century's End*. The Institute of United States Studies.

Erikson, Robert S., and Kent L. Tedin. 1995. *American Public Opinion*. Fifth Edition. Allyn and Bacon.

Esman, Milton J. 2000. *Government Works: Why Americans Need the Feds*. Cornell University Press.

Fallows, James. 1996. *Breaking the News: How the Media Undermine American Democracy*. Random House.

Flynt, J. Wayne. 1979. *Dixie's Forgotten People*. Indiana University Press.

Foner, Eric. 1999. *The Story of American Freedom*. Norton.

Frey, William. 1998. *New Demographic Divide in the U.S.* The Public Perspective.

Frey, William H., and Ross C. DeVol. 2000. *America's Demography in the New Century*. Milken Institute.

Friel, Brian. 1997. *Why People Don't Trust Government*. Harvard University Press.

Fukuyama, Francis. 1992. *The End of History and the Last Man*. Free Press.

Fuller, Graham. 1991. *The Democracy Trap: Perils of the Post-Cold War World.* Dutton/Plume.

Fullinwilder, Robert K. 1999. *Civil Society, Democracy, and Civic Renewal.* Rowman and Littlefield.

Galbraith, John Kenneth. 1992. *The Culture of Contentment.* Houghton Mifflin.

Gans, Curtis. July-August 2000. "Table for One Please: America's Disintegrating Democracy". *The Washington Monthly.*

Gardner, James. 1997. *The Age of Extremism: The Enemies of Compromise in American Politics, Culture, and Race Relations.* Carol.

Gergen, David. November 27, 2000. "Legitimizing Victory". *U.S. News & World Report.*

Geyer, Georgia Anne. 1996. *Americans No More: The Death of Citizenship.* Grove/Atlantic, Inc.

Gitlin, Todd. 1995. *The Twilight of Common Dreams.* Henry Holt.

Goad, Jim. 1998. *The Redneck Manifesto: How Hillbillies, Hicks, and Whitae Trash Became America's Scapegoats.* Touchstone.

Gore, Al. 1993. *The Gore Report On Reinventing Government.* Times Books.

Gottschalk, Peter (Contributor), Sheldon H. Danziger. 1997. *America Unequal.* Harvard University Press.

Gray, John. January 22, 1995. *Does Democracy Have a Future?* The New York Times Book Review.

Guehenno, Jean-Marie, and Victoria Pesce Elliott. 2000. *The End of the Nation-State.* University of Minnesota Press.

Hague, Barry N., and Brian D. Loader. 1999. *Digital Democracy: Discourse and Decision Making in the Information Age.* Routledge.

Hall, John A., and Charles Lindholm. 1999. *Is America Breaking Apart?* Princeton University Press.

Halstead, Ted, and Michael Lind. 2001. *The Radical Center: The Future of American Politics.* Doubleday.

Harris, John. November 9, 2000. "Roadblocks Ahead for Governing". *The Washington Post.*

Harrison, Lawrence E., and Samuel P. Huntington. 2000. *Culture Matters: How Values Shape Human Progress.* Basic Books.

Heclo, Hugh. Winter, 1999. "Hyperdemocracy". *The Wilson Quarterly.*

Henley, Wallace. 1993. *Escape from America.* Lithocolor.

Himmelfarb, Gertrude. 1999. *One Nation, Two Cultures.* Knopf.

Hodge, Carl Cavanagh. 1998. *All of the People, All of the Time: American Government at the End of the Century.* Peter Lang.

Hollinger, David A. 1995. *Postethnic America: Beyond Multiculturalism.* Basic Books.

Howard, Philip K. 1996. *The Death of Common Sense: How Law Is Suffocating America.* Warner Books.

Hudson, William E. 1997. *American Democracy in Peril: Seven Challenges to America's Future.* Seven Bridges.

Hughes, Robert. 1993. *Culture of Complaint: The Fraying of America.* Oxford University Press.

Hunter, James Davison. 1991. *Culture Wars: The Struggle To Define America.* Basic Books.

Hunter, James Davison. 1994. *Before the Shooting Begins: Searching for Democracy in America's Culture War.* Free Press.

Huntington, Samuel. 1981. *American Politics.* Belknap.

Inglehart, Ronald. 2000. "Culture and Democracy". In Lawrence E. Harrison and Samual P. Huntington, *Culture Matters: How Values Shape Human Progress.* Basic Books.

Ingraham, Laura. November 6, 2000. "Who's Your Candidate?" *The Los Angeles Times.*

Jacoby, Russell. 2000. *The End of Utopia: Politics and Culture in an Age of Apathy.* Basic Books.

Jackson, Jesse L., Jr. 2001. *A More Perfect Union : Advancing New American Rights.* Welcome Rain.

Jamieson, Kathleen Hall. 1993. *Dirty Politics: Deception, Distraction, and Democracy.* Oxford University Press.

Jefferson, Thomas, Adrienne Koch (ed.), and William Peden (ed.). 1998. *The Life and Selected Writings of Thomas Jefferson.* Random House.

Johnson, Haynes, and David S. Broder. 1996. *The System: The American Way of Politics at the Breaking Point.* Little, Brown.

Johnson, Paul. 1998. *A History of the American People.* HarperCollins.

Journal of Democracy. January, 2000. Democracy in the World: Tocqueville Reconsidered.

Judis, John B. 2000. *Paradox of American Democracy: Elites, Special Interests, and the Betrayal of Public Trust.* Pantheon.

Kamber, Victor. 1997. *Poison Politics: Are Negative Campaigns Destroying Democracy?* Perseus Books.

Kaplan, Robert. December, 1997. "Was Democracy Just a Moment?" *The Atlantic Monthly.*

Kaplan, Robert. 1998. *An Empire Wilderness: Travels into America's Future.* Random House.

Kaplan, Robert. June, 2000. "The Return of Ancient Times". *The Alantic Monthly.*

Kaplan, Robert. 2000. *The Coming Anarchy: Shattering the Dreams of the Post Cold War.* Random House.

Karatnycky, Adrian (Ed.). July 25, 2000. *Freedom in the World: The Annual Survey of Political Rights and Civil Liberties, 2000-2001).* Freedom House.

Katz, Jon. April, 1997. "Birth of a Digital Nation". *Wired Magazine.*

Kennan, George F. 1993. *Around the Cragged Hill: A Personal and Political Philosophy.* Norton.

Keenan, George F. 1996. *At a Century's Ending: Reflections, 1982-1995.* Norton.

Kennon, Patrick. 1995. *The Twilight of Democracy.* Doubleday.

Kettl, Donald F. December, 2000. "Is the Past Prologue?" *Governing.*

Key, V.O., Jr. 1949. *Southern Politics in State and Nation.* University of Tennessee Press.

Key, V.O., Jr. 1961. "Public Opinion and the Decay of Democracy". *Virginia Quarterly Review.*

King, Martin Luther, Jr. August 28, 1993. "I Have A Dream".

Kingdon, John W. 1999. *America the Unusual.* Bedford.

Klinkner, Philip A., and Rogers M. Smith. 1999. *The Unsteady March: The Rise and Decline of Racial Equality in America.* University of Chicago Press.

Kosterlitz, Julie. November 20, 1999. "Sovereignty's Struggle". *National Journal.*

Kressley, Konrad M. 1998. *Living in the Third Millennium: Forecasts To Master Your Future.* Factor Press.

Ladd, Everett Carll. 1999. *The Ladd Report.* Simon and Schuster.

Lasch, Christopher. 1995. *Revolt of the Elites: And the Betrayal of Democracy.* Norton.

Lawrence, David. 1998. *America: The Politics of Diversity.* Wadsworth

Lawrence, David. 2000. *California: The Politics of Diversity.* Second Edition. Wadsworth.

Lawrence, Jill. November 9, 2000. "Country vs. City, Spelled in Red, Blue". *USA Today.*

Lazare, Daniel. 1996. *The Frozen Republic: How the Constitution Is Paralyzing Democracy.* Harcourt Brace.

Lester, Will. February 10, 1999. "Survey: Young Voters Uninterested". *Associated Press.*

Levine, Peter. 2000. *The New Progressive Era: Toward a Fair and Deliberative Democracy.* Rowman and Littlefield.

Levine, Peter. Spring, 2001. "A New Progressive Era". *Kettering Review,*

Lewis, John, with Michael D'Orso. 1998. Walking with the Wind: A Memoir of the Movement. Harvest.

Lewis, Michael. 2001. *Next: The Future Just Happened.* W.W. Norton.

Lincoln, Abraham. November 19, 1863. "The Gettysburg Address".

Lind, Michael. 1995. *The Next American Nation: The New Nationalism and the Fourth American Revolution.* Free Press.

Lukacs, John. 1984. *Outgrowing Democracy: A History of the United States in the Twentieth Century.* Doubleday.

MacDonald, Andrew/William L. Pierce. 1978. *The Turner Diaries.* Barricade Books.

Mann, Thomas. Winter, 2000. "Governance in America 2000". *Brookings Review.*

Marshall, Will, and Martin Schram. (editors). 1993. *Mandate For Change.* Progressive Policy Institute.

Matthews, Chris. November 11, 2000. "U.S. Political Geography: One Nation, Divisible". *The San Francisco Examiner.*

McElroy, John Harmon. 1999. *American Beliefs: What Keeps a Big Country and a Diverse People United.* Ivan R. Dees.

Melzer, Arthur M., Jerry Weinberger, and M. Richard Zinman. 1998. *Multiculturalism and American Democracy.* University Press of Kansas.

Mercurio, John. April 5, 2001. "Race Illustrates New California". *Roll Call.*

Mills, Nicholas. 1997. *The Triumph of Meanness: America's War Against Its Better Self.* Houghton Mifflin.

Morin, Richard. January 14-20, 2002. "A Record Low—and No One's Cheering: A Census Survey Shows that Fewer Young Voters Are Going to the Polls". *The Washington Post National Weekly Edition.*

Morris, Dick. November 22, 2000. "Florida: The More We See, The Sicker We Get". *VOTE.com.*

Morris, Dick. March 2, 2001. "Textbook Triangulation". *The New York Post.*

Morrow, William Lockhart. 1999. *A Republic, If You Can Keep It.* Prentice Hall.

Muncy, Mitchell. 1999. *The End of Democracy? II: A Crisis of Legitimacy.* Spence.

Murrin, John M., James M. McPherson, Paul E. Johnson, Gary Gerstle, Emily S. Rosenburg, and Norman L. Rosenburg. 1999. *Liberty, Equality, Power: A History of the American People.* Second Edition. Harcourt.

Naisbitt John. 1982. *Megatrends: Ten Directions Transforming Our Lives.* Mass Market Paperback.

Naisbitt., John, and Patricia Aburdene. 2000. *Megatrends 2000: Ten New Directions for the 1990s.* Mass Market Paperback.

National Academy of Public Administration. June, 1999. *A Government to Trust and Respect: Rebuilding Citizen-Government Relations for the 21st Century.*

National Commission on Civic Renewal. June, 1998. *A Nation of Spectators.*

Neuhaus, Richard John. 1992. *America Against Itself: Moral Vision and the Public Order.* University of Notre Dame Press.

Neuhaus, Richard John. 1997. *The End of Democracy? The Celebrated First Things Debate with Arguments Pro and Con on 'the Anatomy of a Controversy.* Spence.

Ohmae, Kenichi. 1996. *The End of the Nation State: The Rise of Regional Economies.* Simon and Schuster.

Olson, Mancur. 1982. *The Rise and Decline of Nations.* Yale University Press.

O'Neill, Michael J. 1993. *The Roar of the Crowd: How Television and People Power Are Challenging the World.* Times Books.

Osborne, David, and Ted Gaebler. 1992. *Reinventing Government: How the Entrepreneurial Spirit Is Transforming the Public Sector*. Dutton/Plume.

Osborne, David. 1993. "A New Federal Compact: Sorting Out Washington's Proper Role". In Will Marshall and Martin Schram, *Mandate For Change*. Progressive Policy Institute.

Panetta Institute. April 25, 2000. "Though Few Students Vote, Poll Shows Them Still Interested in Issues and Upbeat About the Country".

Peters, B. Guy. 1996. *The Future of Governing*. University Press of Kansas.

Pharr, Susan J., and Robert D. Putnam. 2000. *Disaffected Democracies: What's Troubling the Trilateral Countries?* Princeton University Press.

Pierson, George Wilson. 1938. *Tocqueville in America*. Johns Hopkins University Press.

Pink, Daniel H. December-January, 1998. "Free Agent Nation". *Fast Company*.

Plattner,Marc.1998. "Liberal Democracy, Universalism, and Multiculturalism". In Arthur M. Melzer, Jerry Weinberger, and M. Richard Zinman, *Multiculturalism and American Democracy*. University of Kansas Press.

Price, Angel. 1997. "Working Class Whites". http://xroads.virginia.edu.

Putnam, Robert D. January, 1995. "Bowling Alone: America's Declining Social Capital". *Journal of Democracy*.

Putnam, Robert D. 2000. *Bowling Alone: The Collapse and Revival of* American *Community*. Simon and Schuster.

Raasch, Chuck. November 20, 2000. "Divided We Stand, And Have Stood For A While". *USA Today*.

Rauch, Jonathan. 1994. *Demosclerosis: The Silent Killer of American Government*. Times Books.

Rauch, Jonathan. 1999. *Government's End: Why Washington Stopped Working*. Public Affairs.

Reagan, Ronald. January 20, 1981. "Inaugural Address".

Reed, Ishmael. 1996. *Multi-America: Essays on Cultural Wars and Cultural Peace*. Viking Penguin.

Reich, Robert. July 17, 2000. "The Era of Great Social Rest". *The American Prospect Online*.

Richardson, Elliot. 1996. *Reflections of a Radical Moderate*. Random House.

Robertson, Wilmot. 1993. *The Ethnostate*. Howard Allen Enterprises.

Robinson, Randall. 2000. *The Debt: What America Owes To Blacks*. Dutton/Plume.

Rollins, Ed. 1996. *Bare Knuckles and Back Rooms: My Life in American Politics*. Broadway.

Rosenthal, Alan. 1997. *The Decline of Representative Democracy*. Congressional Quarterly.

Rosenthal, Alan. December, 1997. "Too Much Democracy". *State Legislatures*.

Rossiter, Clinton. 1962. *Conservatism in America*. Knopf.

Rowan, Carl T. 1996. *The Coming Race War in America: A Wakeup Call*. Little, Brown.

Sabato, Larry J. 1991. *Feeding Frenzy: How Attack Journalism Has Transformed American Politics*. Free Press.

Sachs, Jeffrey. 2000. "Notes on a New Sociology of Economic Development". In Lawrence E. Harrison and Samuel P. Huntington, *Culture Matters: How Values Shape Human Progress*. Basic Books.

Samuelson, Robert. 1997. *The Good Life and Its Discontents: The American Dream in the Age of Entitlement*. Vintage Books.

Sandel, Michael J. 1996. *Democracy's Discontent: America in Search of a Public Philosophy*. Harvard University Press.

Sanchez, Rene. January 12, 1998. "College Freshmen Have the Blahs, Survey Indicates". *The Washington Post*.

Sassen, Saskia. 1996. *Losing Control? Sovereignty in an Age of Globalization*. Columbia University Press.

Schlesinger, Arthur M., Jr. 1992. *The Disuniting of America: Reflections on Multicultural Society*. Norton.

Schlesinger, Arthur M., Jr. 1997. *Has Democracy A Future?* The Institute of United States Studies.

Schmelser, Neil J., and Jeffrey C. Alexander (Editors). 1999. *Diversity and Its Discontents: Cultural Conflict and Common Ground in Contemporary American Society*. Princeton University Press.

Schrag, Peter. 1973. *The End of the American Future*. Simon and Schuster.

Schrag, Peter. March, 1988. "California, Here We Come". *The Atlantic Monthly*.

Schrag, Peter. 1998. *Paradise Lost: California's Experience, America's Future.* New Press.

Schumer, Charles E. December 11, 2001. "Big Government Looks Better Now". *The Washington Post.*

Shaefer, Byron, Joel H. Silbey, Michael Barone, Charles O. Jones, Alan Ehrenhalt, and Ed Carmines. 1997. *Present Discontents.* Seven Bridges.

Skocpol, Theda, and Morris P. Fiorina (Editors). 1999. *Civic Engagement in American Democracy.* Brookings.

Staeheli, Lynn A., Janet E. Kodras, and Colin Flint. 1997. *State Devolution in America: Implications for a Diverse Society.* Sage.

Steuerle, Eugene C., Hugh Heclo, Edward M. Gramlich, Demetra Smith Nightingale. 1998. *The Government We Deserve: Responsive Democracy and Changing Expectations.* Urban Institute.

Steuerle, Eugene C., Edward M. Gramlich, Hugh Heclo, Demetra Smith Nightingale. 1998. *The Bills for Rights: How Can the U. S. Political System Keep the Promises Americans Have Made to Themselves.* Urban Institute.

Strauss, William, and Neil Howe. 1998. *The Fourth Turning: An American Prophecy.* Broadway Books.

Streisand, Betsy. December 7, 1998. "Where America is Heading: Why California Represents the Shape of Politics to Come". *U. S. News and World Report.*

Taylor, George Rogers. 1972. *The Turner Thesis: Concerning the Role of the Frontier in American History.* Houghton Mifflin.

Teepen, Tom. October 10, 1998. "Cultural Battle Rages in House over Clinton and United States". *The Monterey Herald.*

Thompson, Hunter S. November 21, 2000. "Hey Rube". *Page 2 ESPN.*

Time Magazine. October 28, 1989. *"Is Government Dead ?"*

Tocqueville, Alexis de. 1951. *Democracy in America.* Alfred A. Knopf.

Tocqueville, Alexis de. 2000. *Democracy in America* (Translated, edited, and with an introduction by Harvey C. Mansfield and Delba Winthrop). University of Chicago Press.

Toffler, Alvin, and Heidi Toffler. 1995. *Creating A New Civilization: The Politics of the Third Wave.* Turner.

Tolchin, Susan. 1996. *The Angry American: How Voter Rage Is Changing the Nation.* Westview.

Turner, Frederick J. 1893, 1920. *The Significance of the Frontier in American History.* Frederick Unger.

Turner, Frederick. J., and John Mack Faragher. 1999. *Re-reading Frederick Jackson Turner: The Significance of the Frontier in American History and Other Essays.* Yale University Press.

Vazsonyi, Balint. 1998. *America's Thirty Years War: Who Is Winning?* Regnery.

Walters, Dan. October 22, 1998, "Single-Interest Policy-Making". *The Monterey Herald.*

Walczak, Lee, Alexandra Starr, Richard S. Dunham, and Ann Therese Palmer. August 27, 2001. "America's Future - The Mood Now". *Business Week Magazine.*

Washington, George. April 30, 1789. "Inaugural Address".

Wattenberg, Ben J. 1996. *Values Matter Most.* Regnery.

Webb. Walter Prescott. October, 1951. "Ended: 400 Year Boom: Reflections on the Age of the Frontier," *Harper's Magazine.*

Webb, Walter Prescott. 1986. *The Great Frontier.* University of Nebraska Press.

West, Cornel. 2001. *Race Matters.* Beacon.

Whitman, David, and Christopher Jencks. 1998. *The Optimism Gap: The I'm OK—They're Not Syndrome and the Myth of American Decline.* Walker.

Will, George F. June 17, 1999. "Footnote to 'The End of History'". *Washington Post.*

Will, George F. November 27, 2000. "Had 'Em All the Way". *Newsweek.*

Wilson, James Q. 1997. *Two Nations.* American Enterprise Institute for Public Policy Research.

Wilson, James Q. 1999. *The History and Future of Democracy.* Pepperdine University School of Public Policy.

Wolfe, Alan. 1998. *One Nation, After All.* Penguin USA.

Woodward, C. Vann. 1998. "Meanings for Multiculturalism". In Arthur M. Melzer, Jerry Weinberger, and M. Richard Zinman, *Multiculturalism and American Democracy.* University Press of Kansas.

Wuthnow, Robert. 1998. *Loose Connections: Joining Together in America's Fragmented Communities.* Harvard University Press.

Wuthnow, Robert. 1999. "The Culture of Discontent". In Neil J. Schmelser and Jeffrey C. Alexander, *Diversity and its Discontents.* Princeton University Press.

INDEX

ABOUT THE AUTHOR

Glen Browder has bridged the gap between classroom civics and real-world government during a diverse career as public official, political activist, and professional educator. Browder's extensive public service (as United States Congressman, Alabama Secretary of State, and Alabama State Legislator), political experience (as party official and campaign consultant), and academic background (as political science professor) have focused on political reform and adjustment to a changing world. Now, as Eminent Scholar in American Democracy at Jacksonville State University (in Alabama) and Distinguished Visiting Professor of National Security Affairs at Naval Postgraduate School (in California), Browder is using his broad experience and expertise to promote democracy here and abroad. Dr. Browder and his wife Becky (parents of grown daughter Jenny) spend their time mainly in Alabama and California.